Lecture Notes in Computer Science 13710

Founding Editors

Gerhard Goos
Juris Hartmanis

The series Lecture Notes in Computer Science (LNCS), including its subseries Lecture Notes in Artificial Intelligence (LNAI) and Lecture Notes in Bioinformatics (LNBI), has established itself as a medium for the publication of new developments in computer science and information technology research, teaching, and education.

LNCS enjoys close cooperation with the computer science R & D community, the series counts many renowned academics among its volume editors and paper authors, and collaborates with prestigious societies. Its mission is to serve this international community by providing an invaluable service, mainly focused on the publication of conference and workshop proceedings and postproceedings. LNCS commenced publication in 1973.

Alexandre Madeira · Manuel A. Martins
Editors

Recent Trends in Algebraic Development Techniques

26th IFIP WG 1.3 International Workshop, WADT 2022
Aveiro, Portugal, June 28–30, 2022
Revised Selected Papers

 Springer

Editors
Alexandre Madeira (iD)
University of Aveiro and CIDMA
Aveiro, Portugal

Manuel A. Martins (iD)
University of Aveiro and CIDMA
Aveiro, Portugal

ISSN 0302-9743   ISSN 1611-3349 (electronic)
Lecture Notes in Computer Science
ISBN 978-3-031-43344-3   ISBN 978-3-031-43345-0 (eBook)
https://doi.org/10.1007/978-3-031-43345-0

This Springer imprint is published by the registered company Springer Nature Switzerland AG
The registered company address is: Gewerbestrasse 11, 6330 Cham, Switzerland

Preface

The 26th International Workshop on Algebraic Development Techniques (WADT 2022) happened in Aveiro, Portugal, during June 28–30, 2022. The workshop took place under the auspices of IFIP WG 1.3 and was organized by the Department of Mathematics of the University if Aveiro with the support of CIDMA - *Center for Research and Developments in Mathematics and Applications* (UIDB/04106/2020) and of the project *IBEX - Quantitative methods for cyber-physical programming* (PTDC/CCI-COM/4280/2021).

Having their origins as formal methods for reasoning about abstract data types, algebraic approaches to systems specification evolved into several new specification frameworks, programming paradigms, and a wide range of application areas. Topics raised in the call for papers of WADT22 included:

- Foundations of algebraic specification
- Other approaches to formal specification, including process calculi and models of concurrent, distributed, and mobile computing
- Specification languages, methods, and environments
- Semantics of conceptual modelling methods and techniques
- Model-driven development
- Graph transformations, term rewriting, and proof systems
- Integration of formal specification techniques
- Formal testing, quality assurance, validation, and verification

Following the trend of recent editions, beyond its main track, the event included two special tracks: one on *Algebra for timed and hybrid systems*, chaired by Renato Neves, and another one on *Algebraic approaches to quantum computation*, chaired by Rui S. Barbosa.

The program of the workshop was constituted by 29 contributed talks, distributed on the three tracks, which were presented by people that travelled from Canada, France, Germany, Ireland, Italy, The Netherlands, Norway, Portugal, Romania, Singapore, Spain, Sweden, USA, and UK. Moreover, there were also the following invited talks

- Radu Mardare, with *On Phenomenology of Computation*
- José Meseguer, with *Building Correct-by-Construction Systems with Formal Patterns*
- José Nuno Oliveira, with *Why Adjunctions Matter*, and
- Peter Selinger, with *Number-theoretic methods in quantum computing*

As usual in the previous WADT events, all the authors were invited to extend and submit their works to these post-proceedings. Each submission was reviewed by three referees. This volume contains the eight accepted papers, which includes two papers from the invited speakers José Meseguer and José Nuno Oliveira.

WADT represents a core reference in the area of algebraic specification. This workshop series was launched in 1982 in Sorpesee, and was followed in Passau (1983), Bremen (1984), Braunschweig (1986), Gullane (1987), Berlin (1988), Wusterhausen (1990),

Dourdan (1991), Caldes de Malavella (1992), S. Margherita (1994), Oslo (1995), Tarquinia (1997), Lisbon (1998), Chateau de Bonas (1999), Genoa (2001), Frauenchiemsee (2002), Barcelona (2004), La Roche en Ardenne (2006), Pisa (2008), Etelsen (2010), Salamanca (2012), Sinaia (2014), Gregynog (2016), Egham (2018), and the edition in 2020, which, due to COVID-19 restrictions, was realized on-line.

July 2023   Alexandre Madeira
                                                            Manuel A. Martins

Organization

General Chairs

Alexandre Madeira   Aveiro University, Portugal
Manuel A. Martins   Aveiro University, Portugal

Special Track Chairs

Rui S. Barbosa   INL, Portugal
Renato Neves   Minho University, Portugal

Steering Committee

Andrea Corradini   University of Pisa, Italy
José Fiadeiro   University of Dundee, UK
Rolf Hennicker   LMU Munich, Germany
Alexander Knapp   University of Augsburg, Germany
Hans-Jörg Kreowski   University of Bremen, Germany
Till Mossakowski   University of Magdeburg, Germany
Fernando Orejas   Universitat Politècnica de Catalunya, Spain
Leila Ribeiro   UFRGS, Brazil
Markus Roggenbach   University of Swansea, UK
Grigore Roşu   University of Illinois at Urbana-Champaign, USA

Program Committee

Erika Abraham   RWTH Aachen, Germany
Luís S. Barbosa   University of Minho, Portugal
Rui S. Barbosa   INL, Portugal
Carlos Caleiro   University of Lisbon, Portugal
Andrea Corradini   University of Pisa, Italy
José Luiz Fiadeiro   University of Dundee, UK
Ichiro Hasuo   NII, Japan
Rolf Hennicker   LMU Munich, Germany
Marieke Huisman   University of Twente, The Netherlands

Martti Karvonen	University of Ottawa, Canada
Aleks Kissinger	University of Oxford, UK
Alexander Knapp	University of Augsburg, Germany
Alexandre Madeira	University of Aveiro, Portugal
Manuel A. Martins	University of Aveiro, Portugal
Narciso Martí-Oliet	Universidad Complutense de Madrid, Spain
Dominique Mery	LORIA, France
Till Mossakowski	University of Magdeburg, Germany
Renato Neves	University of Minho, Portugal
Peter Ölveczky	University of Oslo, Norway
Fernando Orejas	Universitat Politècnica de Catalunya, Spain
Markus Roggenbach	Swansea University, UK
Georg Struth	University of Sheffield, UK
Ionuţ Ţuţu	Simion Stoilow Institute of Mathematics, Romania
Benoît Valiron	Université Paris-Saclay, France
Vladimir Zamdzhiev	Inria, France

Additional Reviewer

Matthias Volk	University of Twente, The Netherlands

Contents

Content.

Invited Talks

Building Correct-by-Construction Systems with Formal Patterns

José Meseguer[(✉)]

Department of Computer Science, University of Illinois at Urbana-Champaign, Urbana, USA
meseguer@illinois.edu

Abstract. Formal patterns are formally specified generic solutions to commonly occurring computational problems. A formal pattern applies to a typically infinite class of systems that satisfy specified semantic requirements. Application of a formal pattern to a system satisfying the formal pattern's input requirements results in a new system with new functionality that is correct by construction and enjoys specific formal properties. This paper explains the semantics of formal patterns and illustrates their usefulness from the software engineering, programming methodology, and formal methods perspectives by means of specific formal patterns in several application areas.

1 Introduction

Patterns in software engineering are generic solutions to common computational problems, so that the same pattern can be applied to solve many instances of a problem. This paper explains and summarizes work on *formal patterns* that I have carried out with various colleagues over the last fourteen years. A previous snapshot of this body of work appeared in 2014 [58]. Since then, formal patterns have been applied to new areas, so that a second snapshot seems appropriate.

The main difference between "informal" patterns and the formal patterns presented here is that informal patterns are illustrated by means of code in some imperative language, whereas formal patterns are *formal executable specifications*, that is, *declarative programs* that provide a mathematical model for the pattern, have formally specified *semantic requirements* for the *contexts* in which they can be correctly applied, and come with precise *assume-guarantee* formal properties. That is, if the formal pattern is applied in a context enjoying the assumed semantic requirements, then the declarative program obtained by applying the formal pattern is guaranteed to enjoy specific formal properties.

By their very nature formal patterns are related to software engineering, programming methodology, and formal methods. From the programming methodology standpoint, as I further explain in Sect. 2.3 and Sect. 4.1, they endow a declarative programming language supporting them with powerful *meta-programming* capabilities that greatly increase software modularity and reuse and that extend, yet go far beyond, those of parameterized modules and generic

© Springer Nature Switzerland AG 2023
A. Madeira and M. A. Martins (Eds.): WADT 2022, LNCS 13710, pp. 3–24, 2023.
https://doi.org/10.1007/978-3-031-43345-0_1

programming. From the software engineering and formal methods perspective they support new ways of making software *design* much more efficient and cost-effective and of greatly increasing the *predictive power* of designs before systems are built. They also support the construction and verification of high-quality *correct* software in a much more scalable way than with current methods. This is because formal patterns can be incorporated into the early software design stages to design and verify new systems by means of highly reusable and already verified patterns, and allow formal verification efforts to become much more scalable, because the cost of the formal verification of a pattern is amortized over a potentially infinite set of pattern instantiations. Furthermore, some formal patterns such as PALS [61,65] and Multi-Rate PALS [12–14] can achieve state space reductions so drastic as to render the formerly unfeasible model checking verification of distributed real-time systems scalable up to sophisticated designs such as the one reported in [12]. Finally, since formal patterns generate declarative code and come with formal guarantees, they support the *correct-by-construction* generation of code from formally specified software designs.

The paper is organized as follows. In Sect. 2 a precise, yet concise, explanation of what formal patterns are, their relationship to parameterized theories, and a summary of the areas where they have been applied so far is given. Then, in Sect. 3 I give a high-level overview of some formal patterns in new areas not covered in the previous 2014 snapshot [58]. Related work is discussed in Sect. 4.1, and some concluding remarks are given in Sect. 4.2.

2   Formal Patterns in a Nutshell

Formal patterns are formally specified *generic solutions to commonly occurring computational problems*. Being generic, a formal pattern applies, not just to a single system, but to a typically infinite class of systems that satisfy specified *semantic requirements*. Application of a formal pattern to a system satisfying the formal pattern's input requirements results in a new system with new functionality that is *correct by construction*. Such correctness takes the form of an *assume-guarantee formal assurance*: assuming that the original system meets the formal pattern's semantic requirements, then the application of the formal pattern to such a system is guaranteed to enjoy specific correctness properties.

2.1   Formal Patterns in Declarative Programming Languages

The application of a formal pattern to the code of a system meeting its requirements results in a *program*. But how is this reconciled with a formal pattern being a *formal specification*? The distinction between a program and a formal (executable) specification evaporates using a *declarative programming language*, where a program is a *theory* T in a *computational logic* $\mathcal{L}$.

Mathematically, a formal pattern is a *theory transformation* P that maps any theory T in the class $\mathcal{C}$ of theories satisfying the pattern's input requirements, perhaps with some *additional parameters* $\vec{p}$, into a new theory $P(T, \vec{p})$ specifying the new correct-by-construction system generated by P, i.e., we can describe P as a (possibly partial) function,[1]

$$P : \mathcal{C} \times \mathit{Params} \ni (T, \vec{p}) \mapsto P(T, \vec{p}) \in \mathit{Th}_{\mathcal{L}}$$

where $\mathit{Th}_{\mathcal{L}}$ denotes the category of theories in the language's computational logic $\mathcal{L}$. We can therefore view P as a *meta-program*, that is, as a program that transforms a declarative program T into another declarative program $P(T, \vec{p})$.

In general, the formal pattern P may transform not just one theory T, but a vector $\vec{T} = T_1, \ldots, T_n$ of theories, that is, it may be of the general form $P(T_1, \ldots, T_n, \vec{p})$. Since we can see the vector of theories $T_2, \ldots, T_n$ as part of the vector of additional parameters $\vec{p}$, I will focus in what follows on the case when P transforms a single theory $T \in \mathcal{C}$.

In general, for a theory T in a computational logic $\mathcal{L}$ to be *executable* as a declarative *program*, some additional *executability requirements* must be met. For example, when $\mathcal{L}$ is equational logic, the minimum executability requirement for T to be an *equational program* is that its equations, when oriented as left-to-right rewrite rules, should be *confluent*. In some applications (see, e.g., [59]) the class of theories $\mathcal{C}$ transformed by P may not necessarily consist of already executable theories, because the main point of P may be to transform a theory $T \in \mathcal{C}$ into an executable declarative program $P(T, \vec{p})$. In some rare cases the opposite can be the case, that is, $T \in \mathcal{C}$ may be an executable declarative program, but $P(T, \vec{p})$ may not be executable. This actually happens, for example, for the P transformation defined in [47] and described in §3.1, although further transformations make P's result executable. However, in most applications $\mathcal{C}$ will already be a class of declarative programs in $\mathcal{L}$, i.e., a class of theories that already enjoy the needed executability conditions, and $P(T, \vec{p})$ will likewise be a declarative program.

Although in some applications (e.g., [8]) the purpose of a formal pattern P may be one of *optimization and/or specialization* of a declarative program $T \in \mathcal{C}$, in $\mathcal{L}$, in many other applications $P(T, \vec{p})$ may instead be a *substantial extension* of T with completely new features and capabilities; that is, $P(T, \vec{p})$ is often *a more sophisticated system*, enjoying new features and properties not available in T. Nevertheless, the assume-guarantee properties of P often include the fact that P will in some appropriate sense be *semantics-preserving*. But in general this should not be understood in the sense that T and $P(T, \vec{p})$ have the same semantics. Instead, the semantics of $P(T, \vec{p})$ will often *extend* that of T while respecting T itself, which may remain intact as a *subcomponent* of $P(T, \vec{p})$. This is in fact the case for many formal patterns (see, e.g., [10, 19, 34, 43, 60, 79–81]). From the point of view of code reusability this means that the *code* of T is *not changed at all* by P. That is, T is kept intact and *encapsulated* as a subcomponent. This gives

---

[1] In general, the domain of P may be a *subset* of the Cartesian product $\mathcal{C} \times \mathit{Params}$. This is because for each $T \in \mathcal{C}$ the choice of adequate parameters in Params may not be arbitrary, since it may depend on T itself. See Sect. 2.3 for an example.

formal patterns powerful modularity, code understandability and reusability, and verification scalability properties.

In yet other kinds of examples of formal pattern (e.g., [13, 47, 49, 50, 61]), the input theory T may not be kept as a subcomponent of $P(T, \vec{p})$. Instead, the assume-guarantee properties relating T and $P(T, \vec{p})$ may include considerably more general semantics-preserving properties such as the existence of a *simulation* or *bisimulation* (including the case of a *stuttering* simulation or bisimulation), between $P(T, \vec{p})$ and T.

For a somewhat dated, yet informative, taxonomy of formal patterns that can help the reader gain further insights about this notion and some of its possible uses, sometimes as *compositions* of previously defined patterns, see [58].

2.2 Requirements on the Computational Logic $\mathcal{L}$

Declarative languages based on expressive computational logics will support a richer variety of formal patterns than less expressive ones. In my own experience, for a computational logic $\mathcal{L}$ to be an expressive *semantic framework* for formal patterns it is highly desirable that $\mathcal{L}$ supports features such as the following:

1. logical reflection
2. concurrency
3. concurrent object reflection and adaptation
4. support for real-time and probabilistic computations, and
5. advanced formal verification methods and tools.

I will use Maude's [21] computational logic, namely, *rewriting logic* [16, 55], as a semantic framework satisfying requirements (1)–(5) (for how requirements (1)–(5) are met, see [57] and references there). I will illustrate in Sect. 3 Maude's practical adequacy to specify and verify a rich variety of formal patterns by summarizing some of those patterns, and will give references in Sect. 2.5 to pubications where full details can be found for those and other formal patterns.

2.3 Relationship to Parameterized Theories

Parameterized theories, that is, theory inclusions $P \overset{J}{\hookrightarrow} B$, usually denoted $B[P]$, from a *parameter theory* P to a *body theory* B support very high levels of code *and* proof reusability, and a so-called *generic programming* style. For example, P may be the theory of totally ordered sets, and B may define a sorting algorithm on lists whose elements belong to a totally ordered set. Then, this generic sorting algorithm can be instantiated to sort lists whose elements belong to *any* computable totally ordered set $(A, <)$ of elements. Likewise, its proof of correctness can be carried out *once and forall* at the parametric level, so that any of the, potentially infinite, instantiations of the algorithm to a given totally ordered set of elements will be *correct by construction*. Parameterized theories are obvious and easy examples of formal patterns. Since parameterized theories should *protect* their parameter instantiations, they belong to the broader class of formal patterns $P(T, \vec{p})$, already discussed in Sect. 2.1, that extend their input theory T while keeping it unchanged as a subcomponent. In fact, the notion of a formal pattern can be seen as a *vast generalization* of parameterized theories.

Let me explain the precise sense in which the instantiation of a parameterized theory is a special case of the formal pattern notion. First of all, recall that the class of theories $Th_\mathcal{L}$ of a computational logic $\mathcal{L}$ is not just a set-theoretic class but is actually a *category*, where theories are the objects and the arrows are *theory interpretations* (called *views* in OBJ [41] and Maude [21]). Furthermore, under mild conditions on $\mathcal{L}$, the category $Th_\mathcal{L}$ has *pushouts*. Then, the *instantiation* of a parameterized theory $B[P]$ by a theory interpretation $P \xrightarrow{H} T$ is defined by the pushout diagram:

$$
\begin{array}{ccc}
B[P] & \xrightarrow{\ H'\ } & B[H] \\
{\scriptstyle J}\big\uparrow & & \big\uparrow{\scriptstyle J'} \\
P & \xrightarrow[\ H\ ]{} & T
\end{array}
$$

This is an obvious example of a formal pattern, namely, a function:

$$B : (T, H) \mapsto B[H]$$

where the class $\mathcal{C}$ of theories over which T ranges is:

$$\mathcal{C} =_{def} \{T \in Th_\mathcal{L} \mid \exists\, (H : P \to T) \in Arrow_{Th_\mathcal{L}}\}$$

and where the parameter vector $\vec{p}$ is just a theory interpretation $H : P \to T$. That is, the domain of B is:

$$\{(T, H) \in \mathcal{C} \times Arrow_{Th_\mathcal{L}} \mid H : P \to T\}.$$

The reason why formal patterns are a vast generalization of parameterized theories is that the pushout construction $B[H]$, while very useful, is quite a simple way of "gluing B and T together" as a quotient of the disjoint union of theories $B \uplus T$, so that its axioms (i.e., its code) are a slight renaming of the axioms in $B \backslash P$ and those in T. In general, however, the theory $P(T, \vec{p})$, generated by a formal pattern P for an input theory T and parameters $\vec{p}$, may depend on T and $\vec{p}$ in much more sophisticated ways. For example, both its *type structure*, such as its sorts and subsorts, and its *axioms* (i.e., its code) may depend in fairly complex ways on both T and $\vec{p}$. Also, T may, but need not remain as a subcomponent of $P(T, \vec{p})$.

From the programming methodology point of view, what this all means is that formal patterns are *meta-programs* which provide a vast generalization of what is possible within current generic programming methodologies, because the kinds of genericity that now become possible are both unlimited and user-definable. Mathematically, what makes all this possible is *logical reflection* (for logical reflection in equational and rewriting logic see [22]). In fact, formal patterns are a further development of the idea of endowing a declarative programming language with an extensible and user-definable *module algebra* by means of logical reflection proposed in [28,32].

2.4   The Importance of Logical Reflection

Let me explain why logical reflection supports meta-programming and, in particular, why formal patterns are *meta-programs*. A theory T in a logic is a *meta-level* entity. We can think *inside T* at the so-called *object level*, for example by proving theorems *in T*. But how can we reason *across* different theories inside a logic, for example to manipulate or transform T itself? In particular, how can we formalize a theory transformation $P : (T, \vec{p}) \mapsto P(T, \vec{p})$ by axioms *inside* the logic? Such axioms should belong to a theory, but *which* theory, when even T itself is not fixed but is a parameter ranging over a typically infinite class of theories?

Logical reflection [22] is the answer to all these questions. As already mentioned, both equational and rewriting logic are reflective [22]. For rewriting logic this means that it can faithfully represent its own theories and their deductions, because it has a finitely presented rewrite theory $\mathcal{U}$ that is *universal*, in the sense that for any finitely presented rewrite theory $\mathcal{R}$ (including $\mathcal{U}$ itself) we have the following equivalence:

$$\mathcal{R} \vdash t \rightarrow^* t' \;\Leftrightarrow\; \mathcal{U} \vdash \langle \overline{\mathcal{R}}, \overline{t} \rangle \rightarrow^* \langle \overline{\mathcal{R}}, \overline{t'} \rangle,$$

where $\overline{\mathcal{R}}$ and $\overline{t}$ are terms representing $\mathcal{R}$ and t as data elements of $\mathcal{U}$, and $\langle \_, \_ \rangle$ is a pairing operator also in $\mathcal{U}$. In particular, the universal theory $\mathcal{U}$ has a type, called *Theory*, whose terms meta-represent rewrite theories. That is, a theory T is meta-represented by the term $\overline{T}$ of type *Theory*.

It is now easy to explain why a theory transformation $P : (T, \vec{p}) \mapsto P(T, \vec{p})$ is a meta-program, that is, a program in a theory that extends the universal theory $\mathcal{U}$. We can meta-represent such a theory transformation as a function $\overline{P} : Theory \times Params \longrightarrow Theory : (\overline{T}, \vec{p}) \mapsto \overline{P}(\overline{T}, \vec{p})$, where *Params* is the data type for the additional parameters of the transformation. Of course, the domain of $\overline{P}$ is typically a subset of the cartesian product *Theory* × *Params*; but we can give an error value for pairs $(\overline{T}, \vec{p})$ outside the domain of $\overline{P}$. A meta-theorem of Bergstra and Tucker [15] ensures that if the theory transformation $\overline{P}$ is effective —that is, is computable— we can always axiomatize $\overline{P}$ by means of a *finite* set of confluent and terminating equations. Since rewriting logic contains equational logic as a sublogic, this means that any effective formal pattern $\overline{P}$ transforming rewrite theories can be meta-programmed with a finite set of confluent and terminating equations in a finitary extension of the universal theory $\mathcal{U}$.

In Maude, reflection and reflection-based meta-programming are efficiently supported by its META-LEVEL module [21]. For example, although instantiation of parameterized modules by theory interpretations is currently supported by Maude itself at the C++ level, in earlier versions of Maude this was supported by meta-programming, precisely as the formal pattern described in Sect. 2.3, using the META-LEVEL module (see [28,32]).

2.5 Application Areas

Formal patterns specified as Maude *meta-programs* have been defined and proved correct in various application areas, including:

1. **Cyber-physical systems**
   - Formal Patterns for Safe Operation of Medical Devices [79–81]
   - PALS [61,65] and Multi-Rate PALS [12–14]
2. **Security: DDoS protection**
   - Cookies [19]
   - Adaptive Selective Verification (ASV) [10]
   - Server Replicator (SR) and ASV+SR [34]
3. **Distributed systems' implementation and model checking**
   - The D Transformation [50]
   - The P, *Sim* and M transformations for statistical model checking (SMC) analysis [47]
   - The M Transformation for automatically verifying consistency properties of Distributed Transaction Systems [49]
4. **Theorem proving and executability transformations**
   - The $\mathcal{E} \mapsto \mathcal{E}^=$ [43] and $\vec{\mathcal{E}} \mapsto \vec{\mathcal{E}}$: [60] Transformations
   - The $\mathcal{R} \mapsto \overline{\mathcal{R}}_l$ and $\mathcal{R} \mapsto \overline{\mathcal{R}}_{\Sigma_1,l,r}^{\Omega}$, Transformations [59]
   - The $\mathcal{R} \mapsto \mathcal{R}_U$ Transformation [31]
   - Partial Evaluation Transformations [8].

3   High-Level Overview of Some Formal Patterns

Since a high-level overview of formal patterns in the areas of *cyber-physical systems* and *DDoS protection* can be found in [58], here I will summarize some formal patterns in the areas of *distributed systems* and of *theorem proving and executability transformations*. This overview will, by choice, be incomplete, since: (i) the areas covered in [58] will be excluded; and (ii) even in the selected areas I will not cover all the examples. Therefore, to gain a more complete overview of formal patterns this paper should be read in conjunction with the earlier paper

[58], as well as the papers describing those patterns in the two selected areas which are not covered in what follows, namely, [8, 31, 49, 59, 60].

As already mentioned, from the software engineering point of view —and just as it holds true for *informal* patterns described by code in some imperative language— formal patterns are *generic solutions to commonly occurring computational problems*. Therefore, to better describe each concrete formal pattern I will explain: (i) the *problem* that the pattern solves; (ii) its *context* of applicability, i.e., the input requirements of the formal pattern as a transformation; (iii) the *solution* to the given problem provided by the pattern; (iv) the formal *guarantees* that, assuming the pattern is instantiated to inputs in the rightful context, the instantiation of the pattern provides; and (v) the *applications* of the pattern to solve specific problems.

3.1 Distributed Systems and Their Analysis

The D Transformation

Problem. Since rewrite theories formally specify concurrent systems, Maude, as a rewriting-logic-based declarative language, is naturally well-suited to *design* new distributed systems and is routinely used for this purpose. Furthermore, Maude itself and its environment of formal tools support various forms of both model checking and theorem proving *formal verification*. In addition Maude is also a *concurrent programming language*, since Maude's declarative programs can be executed in a distributed manner across different machines. Indeed, Maude supports concurrent objects that can communicate with each other across machines (or within a given machine), as well as with other objects outside Maude through so-called *external objects* [29], such as socket I/O objects and file I/O objects. Of course for design and verification purposes the mathematical model of a concurrent system provided by a rewrite theory, executed in a Maude interpreter, and verified and analyzed by various formal tools provides an ideal setting for simulation and formal verification; and also for performance estimation (see the P transformation below). Once a new system design has been prototyped, analyzed and verified this way, its distributed implementation is "only" a matter of explicitly mapping different objects of the thus designed system into different machines and of supporting their communication by means of I/O sockets. But, since this implementation of the design has up to now been done manually, there is still a *formality gap* between the verified design given by a rewrite theory and its distributed implementation with the help of I/O sockets. Bridging this gap is the purpose of the D-transformation [50].

Context. Since actors [3], that is, concurrent objects that communicate with each other through asynchronous message passing are arguably the most natural way to specify and program concurrent algorithms and systems, and they can be specified in Maude as rewrite theories in a completely natural way, the input to the D transformation is a rewrite theory $\mathcal{A}$ (a so-called Maude *system module*) that specifies an actor system (see [47,50,56] for detailed descriptions of how actor systems, and generalizations of them, determine classes of rewrite theories).

Solution. The D transformation automatically transforms a Maude actor-based system module (i.e., an actor-based rewrite theory $\mathcal{A}$) into a distributed implementation by: (i) mapping the various actors into different machines; and (ii) providing the required *middleware* (also written in Maude as so-called *mediator* objects) for communication between objects across different machines. Pictorially, if we represent actors by circles and messages by envelopes traveling between actors, we can visualize the D transformation by means of the following figure:

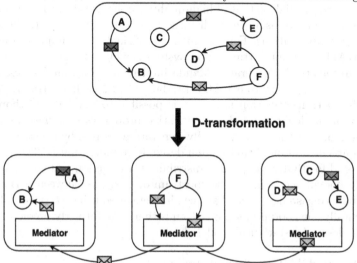

The D transformation has the form:

$$D : (\mathcal{A}, \mathit{init}, \mathit{di}) \mapsto D(\mathcal{A}, \mathit{init}, \mathit{di})$$

where:

- $\mathcal{A}$ is a *Maude system module* defining an actor system
- init is an *initial state* of $\mathcal{A}$
- di is a *distribution information function* $\mathit{di} : \mathit{id}_{obj} \mapsto (\mathit{ip}, \mathit{session\#})$, and
- $D(\mathcal{A}, \mathit{init}, \mathit{di})$ is the Maude program distributing $\mathcal{A}$ according to di with initial state $\mathit{init}_{D_{di}}(\mathit{ip}, i)$.

Guarantees. The main guarantee is provided by the following (see [50]):

Theorem 1. $\mathcal{A}$ *and* $D(\mathcal{A}, \mathit{init}, \mathit{di})$ *are* stuttering bisimilar.

Therefore, for any formula $\varphi \in \mathit{CTL}^* \backslash \bigcirc$ we have:

$$(\mathcal{A}, \mathit{init}) \models \varphi \quad \Leftrightarrow \quad (D(\mathcal{A}, \mathit{init}, \mathit{di}), \mathit{init}_{D_{di}}(\mathit{ip}, i)) \models \varphi.$$

That is, all $CTL^*\backslash\bigcirc$ properties already verified about the mathematical model $\mathcal{A}$ from the initial state $init$ are also satisfied by the implementation $D(\mathcal{A}, init, di)$ [51]. The trusted code base includes the Maude implementation itself and the correct behavior of the TCP-IP implementation used by the socket I/O objects.

Applications. The D transformation has been automated and prototyped in Maude, and has been experimentally validated through some case studies [50]. The D prototype is a proof of concept that should be optimized in a mature tool. However, the experience gained so far suggests two encouraging advantages: (1) Although the efficiency of the automatically generated distributed Maude implementation is not as high as that of high-quality implementations in conventional languages, its code size is much smaller and its performance may still be acceptable for some applications. For example, an efficient C++ implementation of the NO_WAIT distributed transaction system in [44] is roughly 6 times faster than the automatically generated Maude implementation, but has about 12K LOC in C++, as opposed to 600 LOC in Maude. (2) Another attractive advantage of the D transformation is that it is possible to develop and thoroughly analyze both the logical and the quantitative properties of a *new* distributed system design, and then automatically generate a correct-by-construction distributed implementation of that system design in Maude using D. This has been demonstrated for ROLA [48], a new distributed transaction system occupying a previously unexplored point in the spectrum of tradeoffs between performance and database consistency, which has been implemented using D, thus confirming experimentally the good performance trends that were formerly predicted about its Maude design by statistical model checking.

The P, Sim and M Transformations

Problem. For distributed systems, both logical correctness and competitive performance are key requirements. The problem is that, at present, the formal verification of logical properties such as safety and liveness properties —done by model checking and theorem proving—, and the quantitative performance estimation of a system design —done by simulation and by probabilistic or statistical model checking— use very different mathematical models, so that there is currently a *model schizophrenia*, since there is often no clear way to semantically relate these different models and it is actually quite challenging to do so. For model-checking-based performance estimation, finite-automata-based models enriched with probabilities and time are analyzed in tools such as UPPAAL SMC [24] and PRISM [46,70]. The problem is that object-based distributed system features such as: (i) unbounded data structures in object attributes; (ii) unbounded increase in the number of both asynchronous messages and dynamicaly created objects; and (iii) the need for *parametric* families of *user-specified* distributions whose parameter values may change *dynamically* so as to faithfully model their behavior, are quite hard or impossible to represent in such automata-based models. For quantitative analysis of performance properties based on *statistical model checking* (SMC) [5], a further challenge is the need to use models of a distributed system that are *purely probabilistic*, i.e., at any time t, the state s_t reached at time t can perform *at most one* probabilistic transition; this is also called the *absence of nondeterminism* (AND) property.

Context. As already mentioned for the D transformation, *actors* [3] that communicate with each other through asynchronous message passing are a very natural way to specify and program concurrent systems. The actor model can be made more expressive by allowing *generalized actor systems*, which extend the already very large class of Agha's message-passing *actor systems* by allowing "active actors" that can change their state without receiving a message. They can be naturally specified in Maude as *generalized actor rewrite theories* [47].

Solution. The model schizophrenia problem is solved by deriving all models necessary for quantitative analysis of a distributed system from the rewriting logic specification of that system as a generalized actor rewrite theory $\mathcal{A}$ through three semantics-preserving model transformations. The first transformation, called the *P-transformation*, has the form:

$$P : (\mathcal{A}, \Pi) \mapsto \mathcal{A}_\Pi$$

where $\mathcal{A}_\Pi$ is a *timed probabilistic rewrite theory* [6] suitable for quantitative SMC analysis, and Π is a user-specified family of *parametric probability distributions* that model quantitatively the *message communication delays*. Since the probabilistic rewrite theory $\mathcal{A}_\Pi$ is a *non-executable* mathematical model, a second theory transformation, called the *Sim* transformation,

$$Sim : \mathcal{A}_\Pi \mapsto Sim(\mathcal{A}_\Pi)$$

associates to the non-executable probabilistic model $\mathcal{A}_\Pi$ an executable rewrite theory $Sim(\mathcal{A}_\Pi)$ that simulates $\mathcal{A}_\Pi$'s behaviors by sampling its distributions using the Inverse Transform Method [42,73]. But —in a way analogous as how to model check qualitative, temporal logic properties of the original concurrent system model $\mathcal{A}$ the specification $\mathcal{A}$ has to be extended with the relevant state predicates—, a similar extension, specifying the relevant events to be observed, is likewise needed for quantitative properties. That is, it is not always possible to directly express desired quantitative properties on either $\mathcal{A}$ or $Sim(\mathcal{A}_\Pi)$. To support the specification and SMC analysis of quantitative properties, a third theory transformation, called the M *transformation*,

$$M : (Sim(\mathcal{A}_\Pi), m) \mapsto M(Sim(\mathcal{A}_\Pi), m)$$

adds to $Sim(\mathcal{A}_\Pi)$ a monitor that "records" the *events* needed to measure quantitative properties during a run, as specified by the partial function m.

Except for the *user specification* of the probability distributions Π and the events map m, the composition of the P, Sim and M transformations *fully automates* the derivation from the original generalized actor rewrite theory $\mathcal{A}$ of an executable rewrite theory $M(Sim(\mathcal{A}_\Pi), m)$ in Maude which, together with the desired quantitative property φ to be analyzed (expressed in the QUATEX quantitative temporal logic [6]), can be directly entered into the PVESTA [9] statistical model checker. All these transformations have been integrated with the PVESTA tool in the ACTORS2PMAUDE tool [47], which supports automatic SMC analysis of the quantitative system properties of a concurrent system design $\mathcal{A}$ when the relevant probability distributions Π and events to be observed m as well as the QUATEX property φ are specified by the user. The architecture of the ACTORS2PMAUDE tool is summarized in the following diagram:

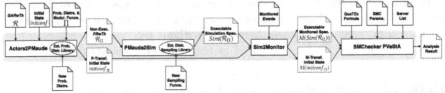

Guarantees include the following (see [47]): (1) For any generalized actor rewrite theory $\mathcal{A}$ and any initial state satisfying natural requirements, all behaviors of $\mathcal{A}_\Pi$ are *purely probabilistic*, i.e., $\mathcal{A}_\Pi$ enjoys the AND property and is therefore a suitable model for SMC analysis. (2) $\mathcal{A}_\Pi$ is semantically related to $\mathcal{A}$ by means of a *stuttering simulation*. (3) $Sim(\mathcal{A}_\Pi)$ correctly simulates $\mathcal{A}_\Pi$. (4) $Sim(\mathcal{A}_\Pi)$ and $M(Sim(\mathcal{A}_\Pi), m)$, with respective initial states $init(initconf)$ and $M(init(initconf))$, are *bisimilar* rewrite theories.

Applications. In combination, the P, Sim and M transformations solve several hard problems in the quantitative analysis of distributed system, namely: (i) the need to develop special-purpose models for such analysis, usually quite different from the models used for formal verification of logical properties (the model schizophrenia problem); (ii) the serious barrier to perform statistical model checking quantitative analysis of distributed systems by non-experts due to the need for ensuring absence of non-determinism (the AND property), which may be hard to check; (iii) furthermore, non-experts are typically unfamiliar with probabilistic simulation techniques for analyzing probabilistic systems; and (iv) when model checking quantitative system properties expressed as probabilistic temporal logic formulas, such formulas often refer to basic system properties that are *not* part of the distributed system's specification, so the model must be extended by hand to define such basic properties, which can be both tedious and error-prone. Problems (i)–(ii) are solved by the P transformation; problem (iii) is solved by the Sim transformation; and problem (iv) is solved by the M transformation. Thanks to the ACTORS2PMAUDE tool, the P, Sim and M transformations are *automated*, making automated quantitative analysis of distributed systems by non-experts both much easier and much more reliable. The paper [47] discusses a wide variety of distributed systems that have been automatically analyzed using ACTORS2PMAUDE.

3.2   Theorem Proving and Executability Transformations

The $\mathcal{E} \mapsto \mathcal{E}^=$ Transformation

Problem. Equational inductive theorem proving is the most common formal method used to verify the correcteness properties of equational programs. This exactly means proving inductive theorems about the *initial algebra* defined by the equational program. To scale up inductive proofs there is a need to *automate* as much as possible the inductive proof process by means of *formula simplification methods* that *build in* as much knowledge as possible about the initial algebra we are reasoning on. Since the atomic predicates on which formulas are built are equalities $u = v$ between terms, it can be very useful to build in a sound and complete axiomatization of the given initial algebra's equality predicate as an equationally defined Boolean-valued predicate $\_ \equiv \_$ such that $u = v$ (resp. $u \neq v$) is an inductive theorem iff $u \equiv v = \textit{true}$ (resp. $u \equiv v = \textit{false}$) is an inductive theorem in the initial algebra obtained by adding $\_ \equiv \_$ and its defining equations to the original specification. This is precisely what the $\mathcal{E} \mapsto \mathcal{E}^=$ transformation [43] does, so that the equations of $\mathcal{E}^=$ become powerful simplification rules to simplify formulas in $\mathcal{E}$. For example, for 0 and s the constructors for natural numbers, and $\_, \_$ an associative-commutative multiset union constructor, the equations $s(x + s(y)) = s(s(x) + y)$, $0 = s(y + z)$, and $U, V = U, W$ are automatically simplified to, respectively, $x + s(y) = s(x) + y$, $\bot$, and $V = W$.

Context. In expressive equational languages such as OBJ [41] and (the functional sublanguages of) CafeOBJ [38] and Maude [21], an equational program is specified by an order-sorted equational theory $\mathcal{E} = (\Sigma, E \cup B)$ such that B is a combination of associativity, commutativity and unit element axioms for some binary operators, and the (possibly conditional) equations E, when oriented as rewrite rules $\vec{E}$ are *ground convergent* modulo the axioms B. Furthermore, it is possible to specify a subsignature $\Omega \subseteq \Sigma$ of constructor symbols and show that the equations defining symbols in $\Sigma \backslash \Omega$ are *sufficiently complete*, meaning that the $\vec{E}/B$-canonical form $t!_{\vec{E}/B}$ of any ground term is a ground Ω-term. The constructors Ω in $\mathcal{E}$ are called *free modulo B* iff we have an Ω-algebra isomorphism $\mathbb{T}_{\Sigma/E \cup B}|_\Omega \cong \mathbb{T}_{\Omega/B}$, where $\mathbb{T}_{\Sigma/E \cup B}|_\Omega$ denotes the Ω-reduct of the initial algebra $\mathbb{T}_{\Sigma/E \cup B}$ of $\mathcal{E}$, which can be abbreviated to $\mathbb{T}_\mathcal{E}$. The input to the $\mathcal{E} \mapsto \mathcal{E}^=$ transformation is given by order-sorted equational theories $\mathcal{E}$ that are ground convergent modulo axioms B consisting of combinations of associativity and/or commutativity axioms and such that its constructors Ω are free modulo B. The absence of unit axioms is not a serious restriction, since the already mentioned formal pattern $\mathcal{R} \mapsto \mathcal{R}_U$, defined in [31], turns unit axioms into rules and yields an equational theory equivalent to $\mathcal{E}$ and enjoying the same executability conditions.

Solution. For absolutely free constructors, defining equality predicates is quite easy and well-known. But for constructors that only are free *modulo* axioms B such as associativity or associativity-commutativity, the problem is considerably harder and, to the best of my knowledge, had not been solved until the $\mathcal{E} \mapsto \mathcal{E}^=$ transformation was proposed. The theory $\mathcal{E}^=$ adds equality predicates for both (absolutely) free constructors and for free constructors modulo B.

Guarantees include the following (see [43]): (i) $\mathcal{E}^{\equiv}$ is ground convergent modulo axioms $B^{\equiv}$ extending B, and sufficiently complete modulo $\Omega \uplus \{true, false\}$; (ii) $\mathcal{E}^{\equiv}$ *protects* the original theory $\mathcal{E}$, i.e., $\mathbb{T}_{\mathcal{E}^{\equiv}}|_{\Sigma} \cong \mathbb{T}_{\mathcal{E}}$; and (iii) for any Σ-equation $u = v$ we have the equivalence,

$$\mathbb{T}_{\mathcal{E}} \models u = v \;\;\Leftrightarrow\;\; \mathbb{T}_{\mathcal{E}^{\equiv}} \models u \equiv v = true$$

which shows that $\mathcal{E}^{\equiv}$ is a sound and complete equational axiomatization of the equality predicate in $\mathbb{T}_{\mathcal{E}}$.

Applications. A first application area is *inductionless induction* theorem proving, where various authors, e.g., [23,40,68], have used an equationally-defined equality predicate to prove or disprove inductive conjectures automatically. In inductionless induction work, such equality predicates have been defined for *free constructors*. What the $\mathcal{E} \mapsto \mathcal{E}^{\equiv}$ transformation makes possible it to reason the same way about order-sorted initial algebras whose constructors obey associativity and/or commutativity axioms. The $\mathcal{E} \mapsto \mathcal{E}^{\equiv}$ transformation has been used as an effective simplification technique in Maude's *Invariant Analyzer* tool [71,72], and also in Maude's *Constructor-Based Reachability Logic Prover* [77], where, in conjunction with other inductive simplification techniques, was instrumental in automating large parts of the security verification of the IBOS browser [76]. The $\mathcal{E} \mapsto \mathcal{E}^{\equiv}$ transformation plays also a key role in the inductive simplification techniques of Maude's new inductive theorem prover (NuITP) under construction, where it is used in two of its formula simplification rules [52].

The $\mathcal{R} \mapsto \overline{\mathcal{R}}_l$ Transformation

Problem. A *rewrite theory* [55] is a triple $\mathcal{R} = (\Sigma, E \cup B, R)$, where $(\Sigma, E \cup B)$ is an equational theory, which I will assume order-sorted, and R is a collection of Σ-rewrite rules. The intended meaning of $\mathcal{R}$ is that it is the formal specification of a concurrent system whose states are elements of the initial algebra $\mathbb{T}_{\Sigma/E \cup B}$, and whose concurrent transitions between such states are axiomatized by the rules R. This exactly means that, conceptually, the application of the rules R takes place *modulo* the equations $E \cup B$; that is, by means of the rewrite relation $\rightarrow_{R/(E \cup B)}$. The problem, however, is that rewriting modulo $E \cup B$ is in general undecidable. Therefore, further executability conditions are needed to compute efficiently with $\mathcal{R}$. For the equational part they are the obvious ones, namely, ground convergence of $\vec{E}$ modulo B. For R, the needed condition is the so-called *ground coherence* of the rules R with the oriented equations $\vec{E}$ modulo B [33,84]. This exactly means that for each ground Σ-term t and one-step rewrite modulo B, $t \rightarrow_{R/B} v$, there exists a one-step rewrite modulo B, $t!_{\vec{E}/B} \rightarrow_{R/B} w$, such that $v!_{\vec{E}/B} =_B w!_{\vec{E}/B}$. What this accomplishes is to eliminate the need for rewriting modulo $E \cup B$: only rewriting modulo axioms B is needed for both $\vec{E}$ and R. The problem addressed by the formal pattern $\mathcal{R} \mapsto \overline{\mathcal{R}}_l$ is how to *automatically complete* a rewrite theory $\mathcal{R}$ into a semantically equivalent one (i.e., having the same initial model), that has all the required executability conditions.

Context. The rewrite theories $\mathcal{R}$ admissible as inputs to the $\mathcal{R} \mapsto \overline{\mathcal{R}}_l$ transformation are so-called *topmost* rewrite theories $\mathcal{R} = (\Sigma, E \cup B, R)$, i.e., theories whose rules R can only be applied *at the top* of a term t, never at a proper subterm of a term. Many theories that are not topmost such as, for example, actor system rewrite theories, can be easily transformed into topmost ones. The additional requirements are that: (i) the equational theory $(\Sigma, E \cup B)$ is ground convergent modulo B, and (ii) is sufficiently complete with respect to a constructor signature Ω and is such that $\mathbb{T}_{\Sigma/E \cup B}|_\Omega \cong \mathbb{T}_{\Omega/E_\Omega \cup B_\Omega}$, where $E_\Omega \cup B_\Omega \subseteq E \cup B$, and $E_\Omega \cup B_\Omega$ is ground convergent and enjoys the *finite variant property* (FVP) [37]; and (iii) the lefthand sides of rules in R are all Ω-terms. Requirement (iii) is very natural and is satisfied in virtually all examples, since giving a transition rule for a state with unevaluated defined functions goes against basic programmer intuitions. The requirement that $E_\Omega \cup B_\Omega$ is FVP is not overly restrictive in practice, since equations between constructors are rare and tend to be quite simple. However, equations $E_\Omega \cup B_\Omega$, besides appearing in well-know examples such as sets (where E_Ω is the idempotency of set union and B_Ω is its associativity-commutativity) are also very useful to model check a (possibly infinite-state) rewrite theory by means of an *equational abstraction* [62], a state space reduction technique based on the addition of new constructor equations $E_\Omega \cup B_\Omega$ to collapse many states of a rewrite theory into a single equivalence class in its quotient under $E_\Omega \cup B_\Omega$. In general, such a quotient rewrite theory may not be executable, but it may become so by applying the $\mathcal{R} \mapsto \overline{\mathcal{R}}_l$ transformation.

Solution. The solution is provided by the theory $\overline{\mathcal{R}}_l$. The lefthand sides of the rules in $\overline{\mathcal{R}}_l$ are precisely the E_Ω, B_Ω-*variants* of the lefthand sides for the rules in $\mathcal{R}$.

Guarantees include the following (see [59]): If $\mathcal{R}$ satisfies the above-mentioned context requirements, then: (i) $\mathcal{R}$ and $\overline{\mathcal{R}}_l$ are semantically equivalent in the sense of having the same initial model; (ii) if the rules in $\overline{\mathcal{R}}_l$ do not have extra variables in their righthand sides, then $\overline{\mathcal{R}}_l$ is indeed executable; in particular, the rules in $\overline{\mathcal{R}}_l$ are coherent with the equations E modulo B. If extra variables appear in some righthand sides of rules, the theory $\overline{\mathcal{R}}_l$ is only executable symbolically by *narrowing* [30,54]. However, further inductive reasoning may succeed in eliminating the extra variables in the righthand sides of the rules in $\overline{\mathcal{R}}_l$.

Applications. The $\mathcal{R} \mapsto \overline{\mathcal{R}}_l$ transformation has two important, yet related, applications. First, since ground coherence is an essential requirement for the executability of a rewrite theory, it can complete the rules of a non-executable topmost rewrite theory to make it ground coherent. Second, ground coherence completion is frequently needed in model checking applications when an infinite-state system is made finite-state by means of an *equational abstraction* [62], because the originally ground coherent rewrite rules of the given topmost rewrite theory frequently cease to be ground coherent when the abstraction equations are added. This problem has been previously managed by hand (see, e.g., [21]), but can now be semi-automated thanks to the $\mathcal{R} \mapsto \overline{\mathcal{R}}_l$ transformation.

4   Related Work and Concluding Remarks

4.1   Related Work

The most obviously related work is that on what might be called "informal" *patterns* in software engineering, e.g., [18,39,75], and on various formalizations of such patterns, e.g., [2,7,27,35,64,74,78,82], which are further discussed in [58].

The assume-guarantee properties of a formal pattern are clearly related to the notion of a *contract* [63] that will be kept if a pattern is instantiated in a way that respects its semantic requirements, and to the extensive literature on *assume-guarantee reasoning* for concurrent systems, e.g., [1,20,66,85].

Formal patterns for distributed systems are closely related to work on *distributed object reflection* [4,26,53,83].

As pointed out in Sect. 2.3, formal patterns are a vast generalization of *parameterized* theories à la Clear [17], supported by declarative languages such as OBJ [41], CafeOBJ [38] and Maude [21], and by various algebraic specification languages, e.g., [36,67]. Likewise, they generalize ideas in *generic programming*, e.g., [25,69]. Also, they further develop the notion of an *extensible module algebra* for Maude proposed in [28,32].

There are also clear relationships to *meta-programming, program transformations* and software *reflection*. These areas are too vast to represent by giving a few references. Just note that some of these ideas go back to LISP, were further expanded in Smalltalk, have been widely used in both functional and logic programming, and that there are regular conferences on declarative program synthesis and transformation such as LOPSTR. For example, the formal pattern on partial evaluation transformations [8] mentioned in Sect. 2.5 is part of a large body of work in this area. The work on *aspect-oriented programming* (AOP) [45] is also a style of meta-programming related to formal patterns, in the sense that the automated enrichment of a software system with new capabilities and features provided by AOP is likewise provided by patterns that automatically extend a distributed system with new features, capabilities and properties.

4.2   Concluding Remarks

The formal patterns listed in Sect. 2.5 can be grouped in two main categories:

1. *Design and correct-by-construction implementation patterns*: [8,10,12–14,19, 34,49,50,61,65,79–81].
2. *Patterns for analysis and verification, or for transforming a program to ensure specific program properties*: [31,43,47,49,59,60].

In Sect. 2 I have emphasized the meaning of type-(1) formal patterns, while in Sect. 3, the P, Sim and M transformations, the $\mathcal{E} \mapsto \mathcal{E}^{\equiv}$ transformation, and the $\mathcal{R} \mapsto \overline{\mathcal{R}}_l$ transformation have illustrated type-(2) formal patterns. What this means is that type-(1) and type-(2) formal patterns can be used *in combination* both for system design and correct-by-construction code generation, and as helpful aids in the analysis and verification process. For example, the combined availability of the D transformation and the P, Sim and M transformations (plus the possibility of performing both explicit-state [21] and symbolic model checking [11,30] verification within Maude) means that there is a seamless path within rewriting logic supporting both the design and verification of qualitative and quantitative properties of a concurrent system, and its correct-by-construction distributed implementation, all within Maude.

The formal pattern examples in Sect. 2.5 and Sect. 3 show that Maude and its underlying rewriting logic provide an expressive *semantic framework* for defining and reasoning about formal patterns. However, the idea of a formal pattern is *parametric* on the computational logic $\mathcal{L}$ chosen as semantic framework and could be equally useful in other declarative languages, particularly in declarative languages whose computational logic supports logical reflection, or that have a rich enough type structure to describe formal patterns as type transformations.

Acknowledgements. The development of formal patterns is a collective effort with various colleagues. The references given in Sect. 2.5 provide a list of authors who have contributed to advance the entire area. My collaborations with Kyungmin Bae, Peter Csaba Ölveczky, Lui Sha, and Mu Sun in developing various formal patterns for cyber-physical systems and for the safety of medical devices were an important early stimulus that has inspired the development of formal patterns in other areas. Focusing just on the formal patterns presented in Sect. 3, I would like to thank David Basin, Raúl Gutiérrez, Si Liu, Peter Csaba Ölveczky, Camilo Rocha, Atul Sandur, Qi Wang and Min Zhang for their contributions in developing some of them. I thank the WADT 2022 organizers for giving me the opportunity to present these ideas in an invited talk, and the WADT 2022 participants for their insightful comments and questions. I also presented these ideas in seminar talks at King's College London, University College London, and the University of Leicester during the Summer of 2022. I thank the participants in those seminars for their insightful comments and questions, and the Leverhulme Trust for funding my visiting professorship at King's College London, during the Summer of 2022, which made those seminar presentations possible. Last but not least, I wish to thank the anonymous reviewers for their excellent suggestions, which have helped me improve the exposition and further explain these ideas. The present text has benefited from the comments received in all these ways. This research has been partially supported by NRL Contract N0017323C2002.

References

1. Abadi, M., Lamport, L.: Composing specifications. ACM Trans. Program. Lang. Syst. **15**(1), 73–132 (1993)
2. Abrial, J.R., Hoang, T.S.: Using Design Patterns in Formal Methods: An Event-B Approach. In: Fitzgerald, J.S., Haxthausen, A.E., Yenigün, H. (eds.) ICTAC. LNCS, vol. 5160, pp. 1–2. Springer (2008)

3. Agha, G.: Actors. MIT Press (1986)
4. Agha, G., Frolund, S., Panwar, R., Sturman, D.: A linguistic framework for dynamic composition of dependability protocols. IEEE Parall. Distrib. Technol.: Syst. Appl. **1**, 3–14 (1993)
5. Agha, G., Palmskog, K.: A survey of statistical model checking. ACM Trans. Model. Comput. Simul. **28**(1), 6:1–6:39 (2018)
6. Agha, G.A., Meseguer, J., Sen, K.: PMaude: Rewrite-based specification language for probabilistic object systems. Electr. Notes Theor. Comput. Sci. **153**(2) (2006)
7. Alencar, P.S.C., Cowan, D.D., Lucena, C.J.P.: A formal approach to architectural design patterns. In: Gaudel, M.-C., Woodcock, J. (eds.) FME 1996. LNCS, vol. 1051, pp. 576–594. Springer, Heidelberg (1996). https://doi.org/10.1007/3-540-60973-3_108
8. Alpuente, M., Cuenca-Ortega, A., Escobar, S., Meseguer, J.: A partial evaluation framework for order-sorted equational programs modulo axioms. J. Log. Algebraic Methods Program. **110**, 100501 (2020)
9. AlTurki, M., Meseguer, J.: PVeStA: a parallel statistical model checking and quantitative analysis tool. In: Corradini, A., Klin, B., Cîrstea, C. (eds.) CALCO 2011. LNCS, vol. 6859, pp. 386–392. Springer, Heidelberg (2011). https://doi.org/10.1007/978-3-642-22944-2_28
10. AlTurki, M., Meseguer, J., Gunter, C.: Probabilistic modeling and analysis of DoS protection for the ASV protocol. Electr. Notes Theor. Comput. Sci. **234**, 3–18 (2009)
11. Bae, K., Escobar, S., Meseguer, J.: Abstract Logical Model Checking of Infinite-State Systems Using Narrowing. In: Rewriting Techniques and Applications (RTA'13). LIPIcs, vol. 21, pp. 81–96. Schloss Dagstuhl-Leibniz-Zentrum fuer Informatik (2013)
12. Bae, K., Krisiloff, J., Meseguer, J., Ölveczky, P.C.: Designing and verifying distributed cyber-physical systems using multirate PALS: an airplane turning control system case study. Sci. Comput. Program. **103**, 13–50 (2015)
13. Bae, K., Meseguer, J., Ölveczky, P.C.: Formal patterns for multirate distributed real-time systems. Sci. Comput. Program. **91**, 3–44 (2014)
14. Bae, K., Ölveczky, P.C., Meseguer, J.: Definition, semantics, and analysis of multirate synchronous AADL. In: Jones, C., Pihlajasaari, P., Sun, J. (eds.) FM 2014. LNCS, vol. 8442, pp. 94–109. Springer, Cham (2014). https://doi.org/10.1007/978-3-319-06410-9_7
15. Bergstra, J.A., Tucker, J.V.: A characterisation of computable data types by means of a finite equational specification method. In: de Bakker, J., van Leeuwen, J. (eds.) ICALP 1980. LNCS, vol. 85, pp. 76–90. Springer, Heidelberg (1980). https://doi.org/10.1007/3-540-10003-2_61
16. Bruni, R., Meseguer, J.: Semantic foundations for generalized rewrite theories. Theor. Comput. Sci. **360**(1–3), 386–414 (2006)
17. Burstall, R.M., Goguen, J.A.: The semantics of clear, a specification language. In: Bjørner, D. (ed.) Abstract Software Specifications. LNCS, vol. 86, pp. 292–332. Springer, Heidelberg (1980). https://doi.org/10.1007/3-540-10007-5_41
18. Buschmann, F., Meunier, R., Rohnert, H., Sommerlad, P.: Pattern-Oriented Software Architecture, Volume 1: A System of Patterns. Addison-Wesley (1996)
19. Chadha, R., Gunter, C.A., Meseguer, J., Shankesi, R., Viswanathan, M.: Modular preservation of safety properties by cookie-based DoS-protection wrappers. In: Barthe, G., de Boer, F.S. (eds.) FMOODS 2008. LNCS, vol. 5051, pp. 39–58. Springer, Heidelberg (2008). https://doi.org/10.1007/978-3-540-68863-1_4

20. Chandy, K.M., Misra, J.: Parallel Program Design: A Foundation. Addison-Wesley (1988)
21. Clavel, M., et al.: All About Maude - A High-Performance Logical Framework. LNCS, vol. 4350. Springer, Heidelberg (2007). https://doi.org/10.1007/978-3-540-71999-1
22. Clavel, M., Meseguer, J., Palomino, M.: Reflection in membership equational logic, many-sorted equational logic, Horn logic with equality, and rewriting logic. Theoret. Comput. Sci. **373**, 70–91 (2007)
23. Comon, H., Nieuwenhuis, R.: Induction=i-axiomatization+first-order consistency. Inf. Comput. **159**(1–2), 151–186 (2000)
24. David, A., Larsen, K.G., Legay, A., Mikucionis, M., Poulsen, D.B.: Uppaal SMC tutorial. Int. J. Softw. Tools Technol. Transf. **17**(4), 397–415 (2015)
25. Dehnert, J.C., Stepanov, A.: Fundamentals of generic programming. In: Jazayeri, M., Loos, R.G.K., Musser, D.R. (eds.) Generic Programming. LNCS, vol. 1766, pp. 1–11. Springer, Heidelberg (2000). https://doi.org/10.1007/3-540-39953-4_1
26. Denker, G., Meseguer, J., Talcott, C.: Rewriting semantics of meta-objects and composable distributed services. ENTCS 36, Elsevier (2000). In: Proceedings of the 3rd International Workshop on Rewriting Logic and its Applications (2000)
27. Dong, J., Alencar, P.S.C., Cowan, D.D., Yang, S.: Composing pattern-based components and verifying correctness. J. Syst. Softw. **80**(11), 1755–1769 (2007)
28. Durán, F.: A reflective module algebra with applications to the Maude language (1999), Ph.D. Thesis, University of Málaga
29. Durán, F., et al.: Programming and symbolic computation in Maude. J. Log. Algebraic Methods Program. **110**, 100497 (2020)
30. Durán, F., Eker, S., Escobar, S., Martí-Oliet, N., Meseguer, J., Rubio, R., Talcott, C.L.: Equational unification and matching, and symbolic reachability analysis in maude 3.2 (system description). In: Automated Reasoning - 11th International Joint Conference, IJCAR 2022. Lecture Notes in Computer Science, vol. 13385, pp. 529–540. Springer (2022). https://doi.org/10.1007/978-3-031-10769-6_31
31. Durán, F., Lucas, S., Meseguer, J.: Termination modulo combinations of equational theories. In: Ghilardi, S., Sebastiani, R. (eds.) FroCoS 2009. LNCS (LNAI), vol. 5749, pp. 246–262. Springer, Heidelberg (2009). https://doi.org/10.1007/978-3-642-04222-5_15
32. Durán, F., Meseguer, J.: Maude's module algebra. Sci. Comput. Program. **66**(2), 125–153 (2007)
33. Durán, F., Meseguer, J.: On the Church-Rosser and coherence properties of conditional order-sorted rewrite theories. J. Algebraic Logic Programm. **81**, 816–850 (2012)
34. Eckhardt, J., Mühlbauer, T., AlTurki, M., Meseguer, J., Wirsing, M.: Stable availability under denial of service attacks through formal patterns. In: de Lara, J., Zisman, A. (eds.) FASE 2012. LNCS, vol. 7212, pp. 78–93. Springer, Heidelberg (2012). https://doi.org/10.1007/978-3-642-28872-2_6
35. Eden, A.H., Hirshfeld, Y.: Principles in formal specification of object oriented design and architecture. In: Stewart, D.A., Johnson, J.H. (eds.) CASCON. p. 3. IBM (2001)
36. Ehrig, H., Claßen, I.: Overview of algebraic specification languages, environments and tools, and algebraic specification of software systems. Bull. Europ. Assoc. Theor. Comput. Sci. **39**, 103–111 (1989)
37. Escobar, S., Sasse, R., Meseguer, J.: Folding variant narrowing and optimal variant termination. J. Algebraic Logic Program. **81**, 898–928 (2012)

38. Futatsugi, K., Diaconescu, R.: CafeOBJ Report. World Scientific (1998)
39. Gamma, E., Helm, R., Johnson, R., Vlissides, J.: Design Patterns. Elements of Reusable Object-Oriented Software. John Wiley & Sons (1994)
40. Goguen, J.A.: How to prove algebraic inductive hypotheses without induction. In: Bibel, W., Kowalski, R. (eds.) CADE 1980. LNCS, vol. 87, pp. 356–373. Springer, Heidelberg (1980). https://doi.org/10.1007/3-540-10009-1_27
41. Goguen, J., Winkler, T., Meseguer, J., Futatsugi, K., Jouannaud, J.P.: Introducing OBJ. In: Software Engineering with OBJ: Algebraic Specification in Action, pp. 3–167. Kluwer (2000)
42. Grimmett, G., Stirzaker, D.: Probability and Random Processes (3rd, Ed.). Oxford University Press (2001)
43. Gutiérrez, R., Meseguer, J., Rocha, C.: Order-sorted equality enrichments modulo axioms. Sci. Comput. Program. **99**, 235–261 (2015)
44. Harding, R., Aken, D.V., Pavlo, A., Stonebraker, M.: An evaluation of distributed concurrency control. Proc. VLDB Endow. **10**(5), 553–564 (2017)
45. Kiczales, G., Mezini, M.: Aspect-oriented programming and modular reasoning. In: 27th International Conference on Software Engineering ICSE 2005, pp. 49–58. ACM (2005)
46. Kwiatkowska, M., Norman, G., Parker, D.: PRISM 4.0: verification of probabilistic real-time systems. In: Gopalakrishnan, G., Qadeer, S. (eds.) CAV 2011. LNCS, vol. 6806, pp. 585–591. Springer, Heidelberg (2011). https://doi.org/10.1007/978-3-642-22110-1_47
47. Liu, S., Meseguer, J., Ölveczky, P.C., Zhang, M., Basin, D.: Bridging the semantic gap between qualitative and quantitative models of distributed systems 6(OOPSLA2) (2022). https://doi.org/10.1145/3563299
48. Liu, S., Ölveczky, P.C., Wang, Q., Gupta, I., Meseguer, J.: Read atomic transactions with prevention of lost updates: ROLA and its formal analysis. Formal Aspects Comput. **31**(5), 503–540 (2019)
49. Liu, S., Ölveczky, P.C., Zhang, M., Wang, Q., Meseguer, J.: Automatic analysis of consistency properties of distributed transaction systems in Maude. In: Vojnar, T., Zhang, L. (eds.) TACAS 2019. LNCS, vol. 11428, pp. 40–57. Springer, Cham (2019). https://doi.org/10.1007/978-3-030-17465-1_3
50. Liu, S., Sandur, A., Meseguer, J., Ölveczky, P.C., Wang, Q.: Generating Correct-by-Construction Distributed Implementations from Formal Maude Designs. In: Lee, R., Jha, S., Mavridou, A., Giannakopoulou, D. (eds.) NFM 2020. LNCS, vol. 12229, pp. 22–40. Springer, Cham (2020). https://doi.org/10.1007/978-3-030-55754-6_2
51. Meseguer, J., Palomino, M., Martí-Oliet, N.: Algebraic simulations. J. Log. Algebr. Program **79**(2), 103–143 (2010)
52. Meseguer, J., Skeirik, S.: Inductive reasoning with equality predicates, contextual rewriting and variant-based simplification. In: Escobar, S., Martí-Oliet, N. (eds.) WRLA 2020. LNCS, vol. 12328, pp. 114–135. Springer, Cham (2020). https://doi.org/10.1007/978-3-030-63595-4_7
53. Meseguer, J., Talcott, C.: Semantic models for distributed object reflection. In: Magnusson, B. (ed.) ECOOP 2002. LNCS, vol. 2374, pp. 1–36. Springer, Heidelberg (2002). https://doi.org/10.1007/3-540-47993-7_1
54. Meseguer, J., Thati, P.: Symbolic reachability analysis using narrowing and its application to the verification of cryptographic protocols. J. Higher-Order Symbol. Comput. **20**(1–2), 123–160 (2007)
55. Meseguer, J.: Conditional rewriting logic as a unified model of concurrency. Theoret. Comput. Sci. **96**(1), 73–155 (1992)

56. Meseguer, J.: A logical theory of concurrent objects and its realization in the Maude language. In: Agha, G., Wegner, P., Yonezawa, A. (eds.) Research Directions in Concurrent Object-Oriented Programming, pp. 314–390. MIT Press (1993)
57. Meseguer, J.: Twenty years of rewriting logic. J. Algebraic Logic Programm. **81**, 721–781 (2012)
58. Meseguer, J.: Taming distributed system complexity through formal patterns. Sci. Comput. Program. **83**, 3–34 (2014)
59. Meseguer, J.: Generalized rewrite theories, coherence completion, and symbolic methods. J. Log. Algebraic Methods Program. **110**, 100483 (2020)
60. Meseguer, J.: Checking sufficient completeness by inductive theorem proving. In: Rewriting Logic and Its Applications - 14th International Workshop, WRLA@ETAPS 2022. Lecture Notes in Computer Science, vol. 13252, pp. 171–190. Springer (2022). https://doi.org/10.1007/978-3-031-12441-9_9
61. Meseguer, J., Ölveczky, P.C.: Formalization and correctness of the PALS architectural pattern for distributed real-time systems. Theor. Comput. Sci. **451**, 1–37 (2012)
62. Meseguer, J., Palomino, M., Martí-Oliet, N.: Equational abstractions. Theoret. Comput. Sci. **403**(2–3), 239–264 (2008)
63. Meyer, B.: Object-Oriented Software Construction. Prentice Hall (1997)
64. Mikkonen, T.: Formalizing design patterns. In: ICSE, pp. 115–124 (1998)
65. Miller, S., Cofer, D., Sha, L., Meseguer, J., Al-Nayeem, A.: Implementing logical synchrony in integrated modular avionics. In: Proceedings of the 28th Digital Avionics Systems Conference. IEEE (2009)
66. Misra, J.: A Discipline of Multiprogramming. Springer-Verlag (2001)
67. Mosses, P.D. (ed.): CASL Reference Manual. LNCS, vol. 2960. Springer, Heidelberg (2004). https://doi.org/10.1007/b96103
68. Musser, D.: On proving inductive properties of abstract data types. In: Proceedings, 7th Symposium on Principles of Programming Languages. Association for Computing Machinery (1980)
69. Gianni, P. (ed.): ISSAC 1988. LNCS, vol. 358. Springer, Heidelberg (1989). https://doi.org/10.1007/3-540-51084-2
70. PRISM: PRISM-SMC (Accessed April 2022). https://www.prismmodelchecker.org/manual/RunningPRISM/StatisticalModelChecking
71. Rocha, C., Meseguer, J.: Proving safety properties of rewrite theories. In: Corradini, A., Klin, B., Cîrstea, C. (eds.) CALCO 2011. LNCS, vol. 6859, pp. 314–328. Springer, Heidelberg (2011). https://doi.org/10.1007/978-3-642-22944-2_22
72. Rocha, C., Meseguer, J.: Mechanical analysis of reliable communication in the alternating bit protocol using the Maude invariant analyzer tool. In: Iida, S., Meseguer, J., Ogata, K. (eds.) Specification, Algebra, and Software. LNCS, vol. 8373, pp. 603–629. Springer, Heidelberg (2014). https://doi.org/10.1007/978-3-642-54624-2_30
73. Rubinstein, R., Kroese, D.: Simulation and the Monte Carlo Method (3rd, Ed.). J. Wiley & Sons (2017)
74. Saeki, M.: Behavioral specification of GOF design patterns with LOTOS. In: APSEC. pp. 408–415. IEEE Computer Society (2000)
75. Schmidt, D., Stal, M., Rohnert, H., Buschmann, F.: Pattern-Oriented Software Architecture, Volume 2: Patterns for Concurrent and Networked Objects. John Wiley & Sons (2000)

76. Skeirik, S., Meseguer, J., Rocha, C.: Verification of the IBOS browser security properties in reachability logic. In: Escobar, S., Martí-Oliet, N. (eds.) WRLA 2020. LNCS, vol. 12328, pp. 176–196. Springer, Cham (2020). https://doi.org/10.1007/978-3-030-63595-4_10

77. Skeirik, S., Stefanescu, A., Meseguer, J.: A constructor-based reachability logic for rewrite theories. Fundam. Inform. **173**(4), 315–382 (2020)

78. Soundarajan, N., Hallstrom, J.O.: Responsibilities and rewards: Specifying design patterns. In: ICSE, pp. 666–675. IEEE Computer Society (2004)

79. Sun, M., Meseguer, J.: Distributed real-time emulation of formally-defined patterns for safe medical device control. In: Ölveczky, P.C. (ed.) Proceedings of the 1st International Workshop on Rewriting Techniques for Real-Time Systems, RTRTS 2010. Electronic Proceedings in Theoretical Computer Science, vol. 36, pp. 158–177 (2010)

80. Sun, M., Meseguer, J.: Formal specification of button-related fault-tolerance micropatterns. In: Escobar, S. (ed.) WRLA 2014. LNCS, vol. 8663, pp. 263–279. Springer, Cham (2014). https://doi.org/10.1007/978-3-319-12904-4_15

81. Sun, M., Meseguer, J., Sha, L.: A formal pattern architecture for safe medical systems. In: Ölveczky, P.C. (ed.) WRLA 2010. LNCS, vol. 6381, pp. 157–173. Springer, Heidelberg (2010). https://doi.org/10.1007/978-3-642-16310-4_11

82. Taibi, T., Ling, D.N.C.: Formal specification of design patterns - a balanced approach. J. Object Technol. **2**(4), 127–140 (2003)

83. Venkatasubramanian, N., Talcott, C.L., Agha, G.: A formal model for reasoning about adaptive QoS-enabled middleware. ACM Trans. Softw. Eng. Methodol. **13**(1), 86–147 (2004)

84. Viry, P.: Equational rules for rewriting logic. Theoret. Comput. Sci. **285**, 487–517 (2002)

85. Viswanathan, M., Viswanathan, R.: Foundations for circular compositional reasoning. In: Orejas, F., Spirakis, P.G., van Leeuwen, J. (eds.) ICALP 2001. LNCS, vol. 2076, pp. 835–847. Springer, Heidelberg (2001). https://doi.org/10.1007/3-540-48224-5_68

Why Adjunctions Matter—A Functional Programmer Perspective

José Nuno Oliveira[(✉)] [ID]

High Assurance Software Laboratory, INESC TEC and University of Minho,
Braga, Portugal
jno@di.uminho.pt

Abstract. For the average programmer, *adjunctions* are (if at all known) more respected than loved. At best, they are regarded as an algebraic device of theoretical interest only, not useful in common practice.

This paper is aimed at showing the opposite: that adjunctions underlie most of the work we do as programmers, in particular those using the functional paradigm. However, functions alone are not sufficient to express the whole spectrum of programming, with its dichotomy between *specifications*—*what* is (often vaguely) required—and *implementations*—*how* what is required is (hopefully well) implemented. For this, one needs to extend functions to *relations*.

Inspired by the pioneering work of Ralf Hinze on "adjoint (un)folds", the core of the so-called (relational) Algebra of Programming is shown in this paper to arise from adjunctions. Moreover, the paper also shows how to calculate recursive programs from specifications expressed by Galois connections—a special kind of adjunction.

Because Galois connections are easier to understand than adjunctions in general, the paper adopts a tutorial style, starting from the former and leading to the latter (a path usually not followed in the literature). The main aim is to reconcile the functional programming community with a concept that is central to software design as a whole, but rarely accepted as such.

Keywords: Algebra of programming · Programming from specifications · Adjunctions

> *"(...) and Jim Thatcher proposed the name ADJ as a (terrible) pun on the title of the book that we had planned to write (...)* [recalling] *that* adjointness *is a very important concept in category theory (...)"*
> — Joseph A. Goguen, *Memories of ADJ*, EATCS nr. 36, 1989

1 Context

The notion of an *algebraic data type* is central to the theoretical advances in computer science since the 1980s—a "vintage decade" that turned *program semantics*

© Springer Nature Switzerland AG 2023
A. Madeira and M. A. Martins (Eds.): WADT 2022, LNCS 13710, pp. 25–59, 2023.
https://doi.org/10.1007/978-3-031-43345-0_2

into a branch of scientific knowledge [6,7], and the trend in which the WADT series of workshops arose. In particular, the 'ADJ group' promoted what can be regarded as the first effective use of category theory in computer science, centered upon notions such as *initiality, freeness* and *institution* [7,10].

The categorial concept of an *adjunction* [14] underlies all such techniques and is so important that the ADJ group decided to carve it in their own acronym, as quoted above. However, for the average programmer *adjunctions* are regarded (if at all known) as working at the meta-level only [10]. In fact, explicit use of adjunctions as an instrumental device for abstract reasoning in programming is relatively rare. Less rare is the use of Galois connections (a special case of adjunction) to structure relational algebra techniques [1,2], but even so the topic is not mainstream.

This contribution to the WADT series tries to show how relevant adjunctions are in explaining many things we do as programmers. In a tutorial flavour, it will try to show how practical adjunctions are by revealing their "chemistry in action".

It is common practice to introduce the adjunction concept first, and only then refer to what is regarded as a modest instance: the Galois connection (GC). That is, general concept first, instances later. Below we go in the opposite direction, which is easier to grasp: GCs are presented first, together with a set of examples and applications. Only after these are understood and appreciated does one step into full generality.

2   Galois Connections

Things in everyday life often come "in pairs", as dichotomies such as e.g. *good/bad, action/reaction, the left/the right, lower/upper, easy/hard* and so on. In a sense, each pair defines itself: one element of the pair exists... because the other also exists, and is its *opposite* (i.e. *antithesis*). Despite the circularity, common everyday language survives over such dualities.

Perfect Antithesis. The perfect antithesis (opposition, inversion) is the *bijection* or *isomorphism*. For instance, *multiplication* and *division* are inverses of each other in the positive reals: $\frac{x}{y} \times y = x$ and $\frac{x \times y}{y} = x$. That is, there is no loss of information when dividing or multiplying. In general, f and g such that

$$
B \underset{f}{\overset{g}{\cong}} A \quad \begin{cases} f\,(g\,b) = b \\ g\,(f\,a) = a \end{cases} \tag{1}
$$

hold are termed *isomorphisms* and regarded as *lossless* transformations.

Imperfect Antithesis. However, data transformations in practice are *lossy*, e.g.

$$jpg2pdf \cdot pdf2jpg \neq id$$
$$pdf2jpg \cdot jpg2pdf \neq id$$

even though our eyes can hardly spot the difference in most cases.

It is often the case that loss of information in such imperfect inversions can be expressed in this way,

$$\begin{cases} f\,(g\,b) \leqslant b \\ a \sqsubseteq g\,(f\,a) \end{cases} \tag{2}$$

telling "how bad" each *"round trip"* is. This relies on under and over *approximations* captured by two *preorders* (i.e. reflexive and transitive relations),

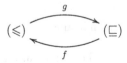

where f and g are assumed monotonic.

Handling Approximations. Let us write the arrow
$x \xrightarrow{(\leqslant)} y$ (resp. $x \xrightarrow{(\sqsubseteq)} y$) to denote $x \leqslant y$
(resp. $x \sqsubseteq y$) in (2). We shall drop the ordering
symbols, e.g. simply writing $x \longrightarrow y$, wherever these are clear from the context, as in the
Hasse diagram aside. This arrow-notation will

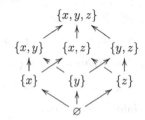

enable us to express our reasoning graphically, as in the following diagram:

$$(\sqsubseteq) \xrightarrow{\;f\;} (\leqslant) \xrightarrow{\qquad g \qquad} (\sqsubseteq)$$

$$\tag{3}$$

Let us "parse" this diagram without rushing: arrow $a \to g\,x$ means $a \sqsubseteq g\,x$. By monotonicity we get $f\,a \leqslant f\,(g\,x)$, i.e. arrow $f\,a \to f\,(g\,x)$. From (2) we get $f\,(g\,x) \to x$ and, by transitivity ("composition" of these two arrows) we get $f\,a \to x$. We are done with the first "triangle".

The triangle on the right starts with $g\,(f\,a) \to g\,x$, which follows by mono-tonicity from $f\,a \to x$ in the first one. Again from (2) and transitivity we get $a \to g\,x$ where we started from. Summing up:

$$a \sqsubseteq g\,x \Rightarrow f\,a \leqslant x \Rightarrow a \sqsubseteq g\,x$$

By circular implication, the equivalence

$$f\,a \leqslant x \;\Leftrightarrow\; a \sqsubseteq g\,x \tag{4}$$

holds for any a and x, and we say that f and g are *Galois connected*, writing $f \dashv g$ to declare so. Terminology: f is said to be the *lower* (a.k.a. *left*) adjoint of the connection and g the *upper* (a.k.a. *right*) adjoint. The intuition behind this terminology is captured by the superlatives in the following interpretation of (4):

- $f\,a$—*lowest* x such that $a \sqsubseteq g\,x$
- $g\,x$—*greatest* a such that $f\,a \leqslant x$.

Did we write *"superlatives"*? Note that we have plenty of these in *software requirements*, e.g.

- ... the *largest* prefix of x with at most n elements (i.e. the meaning of function take $n\;x$ in Haskell)
- ... the *largest* number that multiplied by y is at most x (i.e. the meaning of integer division $x \div y$).

Back to the perfect/imperfect dichotomies above, compare numeric division in the reals $(\mathbb{R})$, for $y \neq 0$,

$$a \times y = x \quad \Leftrightarrow \quad a = x\,/\,y$$

—an *isomorphism*—with (whole) division in the natural numbers $(\mathbb{N}_0)$,

$$a \times y \leqslant x \quad \Leftrightarrow \quad a \leqslant x \div y \tag{5}$$

—a Galois *connection*: $(\times y) \dashv (\div y)$.

3   The Easy and the Hard

It is the experience of every school child that $x \div y$ is much harder to calculate by hand than $x \times y$. Indeed, division is perhaps the very first "hard" problem (algorithm) that children encounter in their basic maths education. Interestingly, $(\times y) \dashv (\div y)$ bears a simple message:

hard $(\div y)$ is explained by *easy* $(\times y)$.

This pattern extends to program specifications, recall

take $n\;xs$ should yield the *longest* possible *prefix* of xs not exceeding n in *length*

from above. The corresponding *formal specification*,

$$\underbrace{\text{length } ys \leqslant n \wedge ys \sqsubseteq xs}_{easy} \quad \Leftrightarrow \quad \underbrace{ys \sqsubseteq \text{take } n\;xs}_{hard} \tag{6}$$

is another GC, where $(\sqsubseteq)$ is the list-prefix partial ordering.[1] Many other examples can be found in programming, for instance:

---

[1] The reader may wonder how (6) fits in the frame of (4). To see this, let us write (6) in the *uncurried* format: $(\text{length } ys, ys)\;((\leqslant) \times (\sqsubseteq))\;(n, xs) \;\Leftrightarrow\; ys \sqsubseteq \widehat{\text{take}}\;(n, xs)$ where, in general, $\widehat{g}\,(a, b) = g\,a\,b$. Thus $f\,x = (\text{length } x, x)$, $g = \text{take}$ and the product ordering has the expected relational meaning, which in general is: $(x, y)\;(R \times S)\;(a, b) \;\Leftrightarrow\; x\,R\,a \wedge y\,S\,b$.

- The function takeWhile p xs should yield the *longest prefix* of xs whose elements all satisfy predicate p.
- The function filter p xs should yield the *longest sublist* of xs all elements of which satisfy predicate p.

4   Indirect Equality

Back to $(\times y) \dashv (\div y)$, consider the following, well-known *implementation* of integer division:

$$x \div y = \textbf{if } x \geqslant y \textbf{ then } 1 + (x \ominus y) \div y \textbf{ else } 0 \qquad (7)$$

Can this *implementation* be derived from the *specification* (5)? Note that, because subtraction in $\mathbb{N}_0$ is not invertible, one needs to resort to "truncated subtraction" (written $x \ominus y$ below) which, as one might suspect, is an adjoint of another GC in $\mathbb{N}_0$:

$$a \ominus b \leqslant x \;\Leftrightarrow\; a \leqslant x + b \qquad (8)$$

To address the question above, one needs yet another brick in the wall: the principle of *indirect equality*, valid for any partial order [2]:

$$a = b \;\Leftrightarrow\; \langle \forall z \;::\; z \leqslant a \;\Leftrightarrow\; z \leqslant b \rangle \qquad (9)$$

This principle of indirect equality blends nicely with GCs, as the following calculation sketch suggests:

$$z \leqslant g\ a$$

$$\Leftrightarrow \quad \{ \ \dots \ \}$$

$$\dots (\text{go to the } \textit{easy} \text{ side, do things there and come back})$$

$$\Leftrightarrow \quad \{ \ \dots \ \}$$

$$z \leqslant \dots g \dots a' \dots$$

$$:: \quad \{ \ \text{indirect equality} \ \}$$

$$g\ a = \dots g \dots a' \dots$$

Note how a difficult g can in principle be calculated by *going to the* easy *side of the specification GC and coming back*.

As a simple example of using (9), let us calculate $x \div y$ (5) in case $x \geqslant y$ holds:

$z \leqslant x \div y$

$\Leftrightarrow \quad \{ (\times y) \dashv (\div y)$ and $(x \ominus y) + y = x$ for $x \geqslant y \}$

$z \times y \leqslant (x \ominus y) + y$

$\Leftrightarrow \quad \{ (\ominus y) \dashv (+y) \}$

$(z \times y) \ominus y \leqslant x \ominus y$

$\Leftrightarrow \quad \{ \text{ factoring out } y \text{ works also for } \ominus \}$

$(z \ominus 1) \times y \leqslant x \ominus y$

$\Leftrightarrow \quad \{ \text{ chain the two } GCs \}$

$z \leqslant 1 + (x \ominus y) \div y$

$:: \quad \{ \text{ recursive branch of (7) calculated thanks to indirect equality (9) } \}$

$x \div y = 1 + (x \ominus y) \div y$

□

The other case $(x < y)$ also stems from (5):

$x < y$

$\Leftrightarrow \quad \{ \text{ trivial } \}$

$\neg (y \leqslant x)$

$\Leftrightarrow \quad \{ (5), \text{ for } a := 1 \}$

$1 > x \div y$

$\Leftrightarrow \quad \{ \text{ trivial (in } \mathbb{N}_0) \}$

$x \div y = 0$

□

Altogether, we have proven that the recursive implementation (7) of $x \div y$ is correct with respect to its GC specification (5).

5   GCs as Formal Specifications

Let us now try a similar exercise for take, formally specified by (6). This time, however, no known implementation is assumed. Moreover, we wish to show how to draw properties from specification (6) *before* implementing take, i.e. *without* knowing anything about its actual implementation.

For instance, what happens if we chain two takes in a row, $(\text{take } m) \cdot (\text{take } n)$? We *calculate*:

$$ys \sqsubseteq \text{take } m \ (\text{take } n \ xs)$$

$\Leftrightarrow$ { GC (6) }

$$\text{length } ys \leqslant m \land ys \sqsubseteq \text{take } n \ xs$$

$\Leftrightarrow$ { again GC (6) }

$$\text{length } ys \leqslant m \land \text{length } ys \leqslant n \land ys \sqsubseteq xs$$

$\Leftrightarrow$ { min GC: $a \leqslant x \land a \leqslant y \Leftrightarrow a \leqslant x \text{ 'min' } y$ }

$$\text{length } ys \leqslant (m \text{ 'min' } n) \land ys \sqsubseteq xs$$

$\Leftrightarrow$ { again GC (6) }

$$ys \leqslant \text{take } (m \text{ 'min' } n) \ xs$$

$::$ { indirect equality (9) }

$$\text{take } m \ (\text{take } n \ xs)) = \text{take } (m \text{ 'min' } n) \ xs$$

Note the fully *deductive* calculation—no recursion, no *induction*. There could be none, in fact, because we have no implementation of take yet! Calculating this is the subject of the reasoning that follows.

A quick inspection of (6) invites us to consider the cases $n = 0$ and $xs = [\,]$ because they trivialize the *easy side* of the GC, as is easy to show. Case $n = 0$ first:

$$ys \sqsubseteq \text{take } 0 \ xs$$

$\Leftrightarrow$ { GC }

$$\text{length } ys \leqslant 0 \land ys \sqsubseteq xs$$

$\Leftrightarrow$ { length $ys \leqslant 0 \Leftrightarrow ys = [\,]$ }

$$ys = [\,]$$

$\Leftrightarrow$ { antisymmetry of $(\sqsubseteq)$; $[\,] \sqsubseteq ys$ holds for any ys }

$$ys \sqsubseteq [\,]$$

$::$ { indirect equality }

$$\text{take } 0 \ xs = [\,]$$

Now case $xs = [\,]$:

$$ys \sqsubseteq \text{take } n \, [\,]$$

$\Leftrightarrow$ $\{$ GC $\}$

$$\text{length } ys \leqslant n \wedge ys \sqsubseteq [\,]$$

$\Leftrightarrow$ $\{$ $ys \sqsubseteq [\,] \Leftrightarrow ys = [\,]$; length $[\,] = 0$ $\}$

$$ys = [\,]$$

$\Leftrightarrow$ $\{$ antisymmetry of $(\sqsubseteq)$; $[\,] \sqsubseteq ys$ holds for any ys $\}$

$$ys \sqsubseteq [\,]$$

$::$ $\{$ indirect equality $\}$

$$\text{take } n \, [\,] = [\,]$$

Thus we get the base cases:

$$\text{take } 0 \, \_ = [\,]$$
$$\text{take } \_ \, [\,] = [\,]$$

By pattern matching, the remaining case is $\text{take } (n+1) \, (h\!:\!xs)$. The following fact about list-prefixing,

$$s \sqsubseteq (h\!:\!t) \Leftrightarrow s = [\,] \vee \langle \exists \, s' :: s = (h\!:\!s') \wedge s' \sqsubseteq t \rangle \qquad (10)$$

will be required. This property is quite obvious but... where does it come from?[2] Let us accept it for the moment, leaving the answer to the question to Sect. 16 later on. Once again, we calculate:

$$ys \sqsubseteq \text{take } (n+1) \, (h:xs)$$

$\Leftrightarrow$ $\{$ GC (6) ; prefix (10) $\}$

$$\text{length } ys \leqslant n+1 \wedge (ys = [\,] \vee \langle \exists \, ys' :: ys = (h:ys') \wedge ys' \sqsubseteq xs \rangle)$$

$\Leftrightarrow$ $\{$ distribution ; length $[\,] = 0 \leqslant n+1$ $\}$

$$ys = [\,] \vee \langle \exists \, ys' :: ys = (h:ys') \wedge \text{length } ys \leqslant n+1 \wedge ys' \sqsubseteq xs \rangle$$

$\Leftrightarrow$ $\{$ length $(h:t) = 1 + \text{length } t$ $\}$

$$ys = [\,] \vee \langle \exists \, ys' :: ys = (h:ys') \wedge \text{length } ys' \leqslant n \wedge ys' \sqsubseteq xs \rangle$$

$\Leftrightarrow$ $\{$ GC (6) $\}$

$$ys = [\,] \vee \langle \exists \, ys' :: ys = (h:ys') \wedge ys' \sqsubseteq \text{take } n \, xs \rangle$$

$\Leftrightarrow$ $\{$ fact (10) $\}$

$$ys \sqsubseteq h : \text{take } n \, xs$$

$::$ $\{$ indirect equality over list prefixing $(\sqsubseteq)$ $\}$

$$\text{take } (n+1) \, (h:xs) = h : \text{take } n \, xs$$

---

[2] The question also applies to $ys \sqsubseteq [\,] \Leftrightarrow ys = [\,]$ which was taken for granted above.

By putting everything together we have an implementation of take, indeed the standard one in Haskell:

```
take 0 _ = []
take _ [] = []
take (n + 1) (h : xs) = h : take n xs
```

In summary, by expressing the formal specification of a particular (e.g. recursive) function in the form of a GC, not only one can prove properties but also calculate an implementation (program) without performing inductive proofs. However, the final implementation is inductive. So, the question arises:

Where does this induction come from?

The answer is not immediate and calls for the generalization from GCs to adjunctions.

6   From GCs to Adjunctions

Recall our arrow notation $a \xrightarrow{(\leqslant)} b$ for $a \leqslant b$ in (3). In the "set of pairs" interpretation of a binary relation, one might write

$$(\leqslant) (a, b) = \{(a, b)\}$$

meaning that the evidence that we have that $a \leqslant b$ holds is $\{(a, b)\}$—the singleton set made of exactly the pair $(a, b) \in (\leqslant)$.

Now compare $(\leqslant) (a, b) = \{(a, b)\}$ with something like (broadening scope):

$$\mathbf{C}(a, b) = \{ \text{ 'the things that relate } a \text{ to } b \text{ in some context } \mathbf{C}\text{' } \}$$

So, every such "thing" $m \in \mathbf{C}(a, b)$ acts as a *witness* of the $\mathbf{C}$-relationship between a and b. Moreover, assuming $\mathbf{C}$ (whatever this is), $m \in \mathbf{C}(a, b)$ can be written $m : a \to b$, recovering the arrow notation used before. (Notation $m : a \to b$ can also be read as telling that m is of *type* $a \to b$, a view that matches with some examples below.)

We thus land into a *category*—$\mathbf{C}$—where a and b are *objects* and m is said to be a *morphism*. In general, there will be more than one morphism between a and b, thus the need to name them. The set $\mathbf{C}(a, b)$ of all such morphisms is called a *homset*.

Categories are an extremely versatile concept, as the following instances of categories show,

$$\mathbf{C}(a, b) = \{ \text{ 'matrices with } a\text{-many columns and } b\text{-many rows' } \}$$

or

$$\mathbf{C}(a, b) = \{ \text{ 'Haskell functions from type } a \text{ to type } b\text{' } \}$$

or

$$C(a, b) = \{ \text{ 'binary relations in } a \times b' \}$$

among many others relevant to maths and programming.

Compared to the preorders they generalize, categories purport a "dramatic" increase in expressiveness (Fig. 1). For instance, $a \leqslant a$ always holds in a preorder (*reflexivity*), that is, homset $(\leqslant)$ (a, a) is non-empty. The categorial extension of reflexivity to an arbitrary category C also means that C (a, a) is non-empty because it always includes a special morphism, the so-called *identity* morphism id. This is written $id{:}a \to a$ wherever C is implicit from the context. For instance, in the category S of sets (objects) and functions between sets (morphisms), $id : a \to a$ is the identity function $id\ x = x$ on set a.

In turn, preorder transitivity, $a \leqslant b \wedge b \leqslant c \Rightarrow a \leqslant c$, generalizes to morphism *composition*: $m \in C$ (a, b) and $n \in C$ (b, c) generate $n{\cdot}m$ in C (a, c), called the composition of n and m, which is such that $m \cdot id = id \cdot m = m$.

What is the meaning of generalizing (3) from preorders $(\leqslant)$ and $(\sqsubseteq)$ to two categories S and D? Recall our starting point,

$$\begin{cases} f\ (g\ x) \leqslant x \\ a \sqsubseteq g\ (f\ a) \end{cases}$$

which meanwhile was written thus:

$$\begin{cases} f\ (g\ x) \to x \\ a \leftarrow g\ (f\ a) \end{cases}$$

According to the correspondence of Fig. 1, monotonic functions f and g give place to *functors* F and G, respectively:[3]

$$\begin{cases} F\ (G\ X) \xrightarrow{\ \epsilon\ } X \\ A \xleftarrow{\ \eta\ } G\ (F\ A) \end{cases} \tag{11}$$

The "core" morphisms ϵ and η will be explained later. For the moment, our aim is to "replay" (3), now in the categorial setting:

$$D \xrightarrow{\ F\ } C \xrightarrow{\qquad G \qquad\qquad} D$$

$$\tag{12}$$

---

[3] Recall that functors are available in Haskell via *fmap*, exported by the *Functor* class. As is well known, properties $F\ id = id$ and $F\ (f \cdot g) = (F\ f) \cdot (F\ g)$ hold.

Starting from some $A \xrightarrow{k} \mathsf{G}\, X$ we obtain $\epsilon{\cdot}\mathsf{F}\, k$, granted by functor F (triangle on the left). We define $\lfloor k \rfloor = \epsilon \cdot \mathsf{F}\, k$ and choose to use h to denote $\lfloor k \rfloor$ in the triangle that follows. Picking h in turn, functor G grants $\mathsf{G}\, h \cdot \eta$. We define $\lceil h \rceil = \mathsf{G}\, h \cdot \eta$, that is, $\lceil h \rceil = \lceil \lfloor k \rfloor \rceil$. In case $\lceil h \rceil = k$, h and k are in a 1-to-1 correspondence and we have the isomorphism

$$\mathsf{C}\,(\mathsf{F}\, A, X) \cong \mathsf{D}\,(A, \mathsf{G}\, X) \tag{13}$$

clearly generalizing (4). In this case we say that we have an *adjunction* and that F and G are *adjoint functors*, writing $\mathsf{F} \dashv \mathsf{G}$ as before. F is called the *left adjoint* functor and G the *right adjoint* functor.

Preorder	Category
Object pair	Morphism
Reflexivity	Identity
Transitivity	Composition
Monotonic function	Functor
Equivalence	Isomorphism
Pointwise ordering	Natural transformation
Closure	Monad
Galois connection	Adjunction
Indirect equality	Yoneda lemma

Fig. 1. From preorders to categories.

7 Adjunctions

Another way to express (13) is given below (14), where the two adjoint functors $\mathsf{F}\!:\!\mathsf{D} \to \mathsf{C}$ and $\mathsf{G}\!:\!\mathsf{C} \to \mathsf{D}$ are renamed to $\mathsf{L}\!:\!\mathsf{D} \to \mathsf{C}$ and $\mathsf{R}\!:\!\mathsf{C} \to \mathsf{D}$, respectively, to better match with the *left* and *right* qualifiers above:

$$
\begin{array}{cc}
\mathbf{C} & \mathbf{D}
\end{array}
$$

$$
\mathsf{L}\, A \to X \quad
\overset{\lceil\_\rceil}{\underset{\lfloor\_\rfloor}{\rightleftarrows}}
\quad \cong \quad A \to \mathsf{R}\, X \tag{14}
$$

It also features the two isomorphism witnesses between the two homsets, where $\lceil h \rceil$ is called the R-*transpose* of h and $\lfloor k \rfloor$ the L-*transpose* of k. This isomorphism can be expressed in the standard way,

$$k = \lceil h \rceil \quad \Leftrightarrow \quad \lfloor k \rfloor = h \tag{15}$$

capturing how one transpose is the opposite of the other. Clearly,

$$
\begin{cases}
\lfloor \lceil h \rceil \rfloor = h \\
\lceil \lfloor k \rfloor \rceil = k
\end{cases}
\tag{16}
$$

and one is back to perfect antithesis (1), but in a much richer setting, as is explained next.

From (12) we know that $\lfloor k \rfloor = \epsilon \cdot F\,k$. So we can inline this in (15) and draw a diagram to depict what is going on:

$$
\begin{array}{c}
R \\
D \overset{\longleftarrow}{\underset{\longrightarrow}{\quad \top \quad}} C \\
L
\end{array}
$$

$$
k = \lceil h \rceil \;\Leftrightarrow\; \underbrace{\epsilon \cdot L\,k = h}_{\lfloor k \rfloor}
\qquad
\begin{array}{c}
R\,X \\
k=\lceil h\rceil \Big\uparrow \\
A
\end{array}
\qquad
\begin{array}{c}
L\,(R\,X) \overset{\epsilon}{\longrightarrow} X \\
L\,k \Big\uparrow \quad \nearrow h \\
L\,A
\end{array}
\tag{17}
$$

Thus we see how the adjunction $L \dashv R$ embodies a *universal property* that tells that $\lceil h \rceil$ is the *unique solution* of the equation $\epsilon \cdot L\,k = f$ on k, for a given h. Very soon we shall see how productive (17) is. For the moment, we just inspect what happens for $k = id$. Since $L\,id = id$ and $\epsilon \cdot id = \epsilon$, we get $id = \lceil \epsilon \rceil$, equivalent to

$$
\epsilon = \lfloor id \rfloor
\tag{18}
$$

by (15), leading to the definition of ϵ. Terminology: ϵ is called the *co-unit* of the adjunction.

Dual Formulation. The term *co-unit* suggests that there might be a *unit* somewhere in the construction—and indeed there is. Above we inlined $\lfloor k \rfloor = \epsilon \cdot L\,k$ in (15). But we could do otherwise, inlining the other definition $\lceil k \rceil = R\,k \cdot \eta$. This gives us a dual formulation of the adjunction,

$$
k = \lfloor h \rfloor \;\Leftrightarrow\; \underbrace{R\,k \cdot \eta = h}_{\lceil k \rceil}
\qquad
\begin{array}{c}
L\,B \\
k=\lfloor h\rfloor \Big\downarrow \\
C
\end{array}
\qquad
\begin{array}{c}
R\,(L\,B) \overset{\eta}{\longleftarrow} B \\
R\,k \Big\downarrow \quad \swarrow h \\
R\,C
\end{array}
\tag{19}
$$

—compare with (17)—now telling that $\lfloor h \rfloor$ is the unique solution to equation $R\,k \cdot \eta = h$. Terminology:

$$
\eta = \lceil id \rceil
\tag{20}
$$

is called the *unit* of the adjunction.

Natural Transformations. Morphisms such as ϵ and η are of generic type $F\,X \to G\,X$, where functors F and G come from and go to the same categories, the identity functor $F\,X = X$ from a category to itself included. They are said to be *natural transformations*. This invites us to go back to Fig. 1, where the pointwise ordering between two functions, $f \leqslant g$ meaning $f\,x \leqslant g\,x$ for every input x, is said to scale up to such *natural transformations* between two functors F and G, i.e. morphisms of type $F\,X \to G\,X$ parametric on X.[4]

8 Examples

A rich theory arises from (17,19) which the reader can find compactly presented in laws (64) to (81) of the appendix. Before exploring such a theory, let us give some adjunction examples. Because we wish to focus on adjunctions that are relevant to programming, the examples are less general than they could be. Thus we stay within the category **S** of sets and functions in the examples that follow.

(Covariant) Exponentials: $(\_ \times K) \dashv (\_^K)$ This is perhaps the most famous adjunction, holding between category **S** and itself:

$$A \times K \to X \underset{\text{uncurry}}{\overset{\text{curry}}{\cong}} A \to X^K \quad \text{where } \begin{cases} \textbf{curry} f\ a\ b = f\,(a,b) \\ \textbf{uncurry}\ g\,(a,b) = g\ a\ b \end{cases}$$

This instantiates (17) for

$$\begin{cases} L\,X = X \times K \\ R\,X = X^K \\ \epsilon = \textbf{ev} \end{cases} \quad \begin{cases} \lceil f \rceil = \textbf{curry}\,f \\ \lfloor f \rfloor = \textbf{uncurry}\ f \end{cases} \tag{21}$$

where $X \times K$ denotes the Cartesian product of sets X and K, X^K denotes the set of all functions of type $K \to X$ and $\textbf{ev}\,(f,k) = f\ k$. Universal property (17) and its diagram become

$$k = \textbf{curry} f \iff \underbrace{\textbf{ev} \cdot (k \times id)}_{\text{uncurry } k} = f$$

in this adjunction.

Associated with the Cartesian product $X \times Y$ of two sets X and Y we have the two *projections* $\pi_1 : X \times Y \to X$ and $\pi_2 : X \times Y \to Y$ which are such

---

[4] Thus natural transformations instantiate to the *polymorphic functions* so dear to the functional programmer, together with their *theorems for free* [23] so useful in program calculation. For the correspondence between *indirect equality* and the so-called *Yoneda lemma* (still Fig. 1) please see [5].

that $\pi_1\,(x,y) = x$ and $\pi_2\,(x,y) = y$. These projections are the essence of the adjunction that follows, which captures the categorial view of *pairing*.

Pairing: $\Delta \dashv (\times)$ In this adjunction we have

$$\begin{cases} \mathsf{L}\,X = \Delta\,X = (X,X) \\ \mathsf{R}\,(X,Y) = X \times Y \\ \epsilon = (\pi_1, \pi_2) \end{cases} \quad \begin{cases} \lceil (f,g) \rceil = \langle f, g \rangle \\ \lfloor k \rfloor = (\pi_1 \cdot k, \pi_2 \cdot k) \end{cases} \tag{22}$$

where $\langle f, g \rangle\,x = (f\,x, g\,x)$ pairs up the results of two functions f and g applied to the same input.

Note how the product in the left adjoint of the previous adjunction now participates in the right adjoint of this one, but in a more general way: it takes a pair of sets and builds their Cartesian product.

What is the new left adjoint? It is the functor that duplicates sets, $\mathsf{L}\,X = (X,X)$. This means that its target category is $\mathbf{S}^2$, the category of pairs of both sets and functions. Composition in $\mathbf{S}^2$ is the expected $(f,g) \cdot (h,k) = (f \cdot h, g \cdot k)$. Using this composition rule when instantiating (17) for this adjunction, we get the universal property of pairing:

$$k = \langle f, g \rangle \Leftrightarrow \begin{cases} \pi_1 \cdot k = f \\ \pi_2 \cdot k = g \end{cases}$$

Above we have seen how components of adjoint functors can shift roles, leading to new adjunctions. Is there any adjunction in which the duplication functor Δ, which above plays the left adjoint role, becomes right adjoint? Yes, see our third example below.

Co-pairing: $(+) \dashv \Delta$ The previous adjunction $\Delta \dashv (\times)$ gave us an explanation of what it means to run two functions at the same time, in *parallel*, for the same input. Shifting Δ to the right of the $\dashv$ symbol will provide an explanation for the dual idea of running two functions not in parallel, but in *alternative*:

$$\begin{cases} \mathsf{L}\,(X,Y) = X + Y \\ \mathsf{R}\,X = \Delta\,X = (X,X) \\ \epsilon = \nabla = [id, id] \end{cases} \quad \begin{cases} \lceil k \rceil = (k \cdot i_1, k \cdot i_2) \\ \lfloor (f,g) \rfloor = [f,g] \end{cases} \tag{23}$$

The corresponding left adjoint builds the disjoint union $X + Y$ of a pair of sets (X, Y) inhabited with X and Y data via two range-disjoint injections $i_1 : X \to X + Y$ and $i_2 : Y \to X + Y$. So the equation $i_1\,x = i_2\,y$ has no solution in $X + Y$ and thus any function of type $X + Y \to Z$ is made of two independent components, one of type $X \to Z$ and the other of type $Y \to Z$, which run in *alternative* depending on which side of the sum the input is. Such an alternative is denoted by $[f, g]$ and, in symbols rather than words, we have $[f, g] \cdot i_1 = f$ and $[f, g] \cdot i_2 = g$.

By instantiating (17) with (23) one gets the universal property of alternatives:

$$\begin{cases} f = k \cdot i_1 \\ g = k \cdot i_2 \end{cases} \Leftrightarrow k = [f, g] \qquad \qquad \qquad \qquad \qquad \qquad (24)$$

$$\mathbf{S}^2 \xrightarrow[\;(+)\;]{\;\Delta\;} \mathbf{S}$$

$$\begin{array}{ccc} (A, A) & \qquad & A + A \xrightarrow{\;\nabla\;} A \\ {\scriptstyle (f,g)=(k \cdot i_1, k \cdot i_2)} \Big\uparrow & & {\scriptstyle f+g} \Big\uparrow \quad \nearrow {\scriptstyle k} \\ (C, D) & & C + D \end{array}$$

The adjunctions given so far involve the category of sets and (total) functions that provide a basis for so-called *strong* [22] functional programming. For instance, alternatives give rise to conditional computations [4] and so on.

More examples of adjunctions could be given in this setting, see e.g. [11]. We prefer to give a final example that does not fit (directly) in functional programming practice, but is essential to reasoning about functional programs. It links **S** to another category which extends it: its objects are the same (sets) but the morphisms become binary relations instead of functions. This category of relations will be denoted by **R** and its composition corresponds to relational chaining, as seen below.

Power Transpose: $\mathsf{J} \dashv \mathsf{P}$ This adjunction captures the view that every binary relation $R: A \to B$ (a morphism in **R**) can be expressed by a set-valued function $\Lambda R: A \to \mathsf{P}\,B$ (a morphism in **S**), defined by:[5]

$$(\Lambda R)\, a = \{ b \mid b\, R\, a \} \qquad\qquad\qquad\qquad (25)$$

Thus $b \in \Lambda R\, a \Leftrightarrow b\, R\, a$, which in relational pointfree notation (the "internal language" of **R**) is written $\in \cdot \Lambda R = R$, where $\in : B \leftarrow \mathsf{P}\,B$ is the set *membership* relation. Thus membership "cancels" the power-transpose Λ:

$$\begin{array}{ccc} \mathbf{R} & \quad\Lambda\quad & \mathbf{S} \\ A \to X & \xrightleftharpoons[\;(\in\cdot)\;]{\;\cong\;} & A \to \mathsf{P}\,X \end{array} \qquad\qquad (26)$$

We write $A \to X$ instead of $\mathsf{J}\, A \to X$ because the lower adjoint J is the identity on objects. It just converts a function in **S** to the corresponding relation in $\mathbf{R}$[6],

---

[5] Notation $\mathsf{P}\,B$ means the *powerset* of B, i.e. the set of all subsets of B. Also note that we write $b\, R\, a$ to express $(b, a) \in R$, keeping with the tradition of using infix notation in relational facts, e.g. $a \leqslant b$ instead of $(a, b) \in (\leqslant)$ and so on. In this vein, relation composition is expressed by $b\, (S \cdot R)\, a \Leftrightarrow \langle \exists\, c\, ::\, b\, S\, c \wedge c\, R\, a \rangle$.

[6] Interestingly, the usual presentation $y = f(x)$ of functions in maths textbooks is relational, not strictly functional.

cf.:

$$\begin{cases} \mathsf{J}\,X = X \\ y\,(\mathsf{J}\,k)\,x \Leftrightarrow y = k\,x \\ \mathsf{R}\,X = \mathsf{P}\,X = \{S \mid S \subseteq X\} \end{cases} \quad \begin{cases} \epsilon = (\in) \\ \lceil R \rceil = \Lambda R \\ y\,\lfloor k \rfloor\,x \Leftrightarrow y \in (k\,x) \end{cases} \tag{27}$$

Altogether, the adjunction expresses the universal property of power-transposition:

$$k = \Lambda R \Leftrightarrow \underbrace{\epsilon \cdot k = R}_{\lfloor k \rfloor} \tag{28}$$

This adjunction will prove specially useful later on where dealing with recursion in presence of inductive data types.

9   Properties

The main advantage of a unifying concept such as that of an adjunction is that one can express the rich theory of (17, 19) only once, covering all the particular instances by construction. As already mentioned, several properties that are easy to derive as corollaries of (17, 19) are given in the appendix. The terminology is inspired by [4], among other references that use similar names, see e.g. [18].

To illustrate their application, let us see how the actions of the functors involved in an adjunction can be recovered from the adjunction itself, laws (71) and (80). Taking $\Delta \dashv (\times)$ as example, let us use (71), $\mathsf{R}\,h = \lceil h \cdot \epsilon \rceil$, to find a definition for $f \times g$, which is $\mathsf{R}\,(f, g)$. Since $\epsilon = (\pi_1, \pi_2)$, then $(f, g) \cdot \epsilon = (f \cdot \pi_1, g \cdot \pi_2)$. Since $\lceil (x, y) \rceil = \langle x, y \rangle$, we finally get

$$f \times g = \langle f \cdot \pi_1, g \cdot \pi_2 \rangle \tag{29}$$

Similarly, for $\mathsf{J} \dashv \mathsf{P}$, by (71) we get

$$\mathsf{P}\,R = \Lambda(R \cdot (\in)) \tag{30}$$

that is, $(\mathsf{P}\,R)\,X = \{b \mid b\,R\,a \wedge a \in X\}$.[7]

Next, let us calculate $f + g$ as in the left-adjoint of $(+) \dashv \Delta$ (23) using (80), $\mathsf{L}\,g = \lfloor \eta \cdot g \rfloor$. In the same way as above, $f + g = \mathsf{L}\,(f, g) = \lfloor \eta \cdot (f, g) \rfloor$. Since $\eta = \lceil id \rceil$ (74), i.e. $\eta = (i_1, i_2)$ by (23), we get $f + g = \lfloor i_1 \cdot f, i_2 \cdot g \rfloor$ and finally:

$$f + g = [i_1 \cdot f, i_2 \cdot g] \tag{31}$$

---

[7] Note that P is not a relational functor (in $\mathbf{R}$) but rather another way of expressing relations by functions in $\mathbf{S}$. It is often referred to as the *existential image functor* [4]. Interestingly, (30) captures the way the so-called *navigation style* of Alloy [12] works, enabling an (essentially) functional execution of its relational core.

All such properties and those of the appendix involve only one adjunction at a time. Perhaps more interesting are those that arise by composing adjunctions, to be seen shortly. Before this, we address a topic that is very relevant to programming and bears a strong link to adjunctions.

10 Monads

The categorial view of functional programming had a big "push forward" when the concept of a *monad* was incorporated in languages such as e.g. Haskell, making it possible to have purely functional implementations of computations that were regarded as non-functional before. Since the pioneering work by Moogi [15], the concept has gained wider and wider acceptance from both the theory and practice cohorts of the programming community, see e.g. [9,24] among many other references.

The question is: where do monads come from? It turns out that monads arise from adjunctions. Put simply, for every adjunction $L \dashv R$, the composition $M = R \cdot L$ is a monad, meaning that M comes equipped with natural transformations η and μ,

$$A \xrightarrow{\ \eta\ } MA \xleftarrow{\ \mu\ } M^2 A$$

such that

$$\mu \cdot \eta = id = \mu \cdot M\,\eta \qquad (32)$$
$$\mu \cdot \mu = \mu \cdot M\,\mu \qquad (33)$$

hold. Definitions

$$\eta = \lceil id \rceil \qquad (34)$$
$$\mu = R\,\epsilon \qquad (35)$$

show how the so-called *multiplication* (μ) and *unit* (η) of monad $M = R \cdot L$ arise from $L \dashv R$. Proofs that (32, 33) follow from definitions (34, 35) and adjunction properties can be found in the appendix.

As an example, recall the adjunction $J \dashv P$ (27). Because J is the identity on objects, it turns out that P, the powerset functor, is a monad. By (34) and (25), its unit is $\eta\,a = \{a\}$. By (35) and (71), its multiplication $\mu = \Lambda(\in) \cdot (\in)$ is distributed union,

$$\mu\,S = \{a \mid \langle \exists\,x\ :\ a \in x :\ x \in S \rangle\}$$

where S is a set of sets. (The usual notation for $\mu\,S$ is $\bigcup S$.)

In the interest of programming, one may wonder whether, in this powerset adjunction $J \dashv P$ (28), one can interpret relational expressions in **R** by set-valued functions in **S**. In particular, one may be interested in implementing relational composition $R \cdot S$ by somehow running their set-valued function counterparts ΛR and ΛS as functional programs.

This is possible as instance of the so-called *monadic* (or *Kleisli*) composition,[8] defined for any adjunction L ⊣ R as follows,

$$f \bullet g = \mu \cdot M f \cdot g \tag{36}$$

where M = R · L as seen above. One has

$$\lceil f \cdot g \rceil = \lceil f \rceil \bullet \lceil g \rceil \tag{37}$$

as proved in the appendix.

As a well-known example, Kleisli composition enables one to sequence state-based computations in a purely functional, elegant way using the so-called *state monad* which arises from the $(\_ \times K) \dashv (\_^K)$ adjunction (21).[9]

11 Composing Adjunctions

Above we saw the example of a functor (Δ) being at the same time a left adjoint and a right adjoint of a different adjunction. Let us study the situation in which two such adjunctions are chained: L ⊣ M ⊣ R.

A quick inspection of how a morphism $L\,A \xrightarrow{\ k\ } R\,B$ can be transformed unveils the composite adjunction (M L) ⊣ (M R):[10]

$$\mathsf{M\,L}\,A \to B$$
$$\cong \quad \{\ \mathsf{M} \dashv \mathsf{R}\ \}$$
$$\mathsf{L}\,A \to \mathsf{R}\,B$$
$$\cong \quad \{\ \mathsf{L} \dashv \mathsf{M}\ \}$$
$$A \to \mathsf{M\,R}\,B$$

Given $L\,A \xrightarrow{\ k\ } R\,B$, $k = \lceil f \rceil_{\mathsf{R}}$ holds for exactly one $M\,L\,A \xrightarrow{\ f\ } B$. (See the diagram aside.) On the other hand, $k = \lfloor g \rfloor_{\mathsf{L}}$ holds for exactly one $A \xrightarrow{\ g\ } M\,R\,B$. So the *exchange law*

$$\lceil f \rceil_{\mathsf{R}} = \lfloor g \rfloor_{\mathsf{L}} \tag{38}$$

holds for such $M\,L\,A \xrightarrow{\ f\ } B$ and $A \xrightarrow{\ g\ } M\,R\,B$. Observe in the diagram that f and g in (38) live in the same category (**D**).

---

[8] This is the way relational specifications are handled in [4], for instance.

[9] For more details about this monad and how to calculate with it please see e.g. [18].

[10] In the sequel we adopt the usual shortcut for functor composition, e.g. M L instead of M · L and so on.

The Product-Coproduct "Mix". Let us see an instance of (38) that emerges from composing $(+) \dashv \Delta \dashv (\times)$ and is dear to algebra of programming practitioners [4]: in this case, $\mathsf{M L}\ A \xrightarrow{\ f\ } B$ is of type $\Delta\,(+)\,(A, C) \to (B, D)$,

$$f = (A + C, A + C) \xrightarrow{(m,n)} (B, D)$$

and $A \xrightarrow{\ g\ } \mathsf{M R}\ B$ is of type $(A, C) \to \Delta\,(\times)\,(B, D)$:

$$g = (A, C) \xrightarrow{(i,j)} (B \times D, B \times D) \tag{39}$$

So, $\lceil f \rceil_\mathsf{R} = \lfloor g \rfloor_\mathsf{L}$ becomes $\langle m, n \rangle = [i, j]$, which we want to solve next. Looking at (39), we have $i = \langle h, k \rangle$ and $j = \langle p, q \rangle$ for some h, k, p, q. Then:

$$\langle m, n \rangle = [\langle h, k \rangle, \langle p, q \rangle]$$

$\Leftrightarrow \qquad \{\ (+) \dashv \Delta\ \}$

$$\begin{cases} (m, n) \cdot (i_1, i_1) = (h, k) \\ (m, n) \cdot (i_2, i_2) = (p, q) \end{cases}$$

$\Leftrightarrow \qquad \{\ \text{re-arranging}\ \}$

$$\begin{cases} (m, m) \cdot (i_1, i_2) = (h, p) \\ (n, n) \cdot (i_1, i_2) = (k, q) \end{cases}$$

$\Leftrightarrow \qquad \{\ \Delta \dashv (\times)\ \}$

$$\begin{cases} m = [h, p] \\ n = [k, q] \end{cases}$$

The composite adjunction $(+) \dashv \Delta \dashv (\times)$ therefore yields the well-known *exchange law* [4],

$$\langle [h, p], [k, q] \rangle = [\langle h, k \rangle, \langle p, q \rangle] \tag{40}$$

which is very useful in handling functions that input sums and output products. As will be seen in the sequel, (40) will play an important role

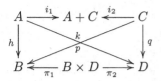

when dealing with mutual recursion.

$(+) \dashv \Delta$ *meets* $\mathsf{L} \dashv \mathsf{R}$. As we have seen, adjunction (24) brings with it the possibility of expressing alternative computations. One wonders whether such a possibility can be extended "across" other adjunctions via the composition

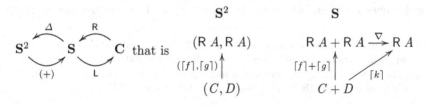

meaning:[11]

$$\begin{cases} \lceil f \rceil = \lceil k \rceil \cdot i_1 \\ \lceil g \rceil = \lceil k \rceil \cdot i_2 \end{cases} \Leftrightarrow \lceil k \rceil = [\lceil f \rceil, \lceil g \rceil] \tag{41}$$

Clearly, the right side of (41) can be written $k = \lfloor [\lceil f \rceil, \lceil g \rceil] \rfloor$. Concerning the left side:

$$\begin{cases} \lceil k \rceil \cdot i_1 = \lceil f \rceil \\ \lceil k \rceil \cdot i_2 = \lceil g \rceil \end{cases}$$

$\Leftrightarrow$ { fusion (67) and isomorphism (72) (twice) }

$$\begin{cases} k \cdot \mathsf{L}\, i_1 = f \\ k \cdot \mathsf{L}\, i_2 = g \end{cases}$$

In summary, (41) re-writes to the universal property

$$k = \lfloor [\lceil f \rceil, \lceil g \rceil] \rfloor \Leftrightarrow \begin{cases} k \cdot \mathsf{L}\, i_1 = f \\ k \cdot \mathsf{L}\, i_2 = g \end{cases} \tag{42}$$

that is, we have coproducts in **C** induced by the lower adjoint L.

Relational Coproducts. Let us inspect (42) for $\mathsf{L} \dashv \mathsf{R} := \mathsf{J} \dashv \mathsf{P}$ (27). In this case, $\lfloor k \rfloor = (\in) \cdot k$ and $\mathsf{L}\, i_1 = \mathsf{J}\, i_1$ is injection i_1 regarded as a relation, $y\, i_1\, x \Leftrightarrow y = i_1\, x$, which is usually abbreviated to i_1 (similarly for i_2):

$$X = \underbrace{(\in) \cdot [\Lambda R, \Lambda S]}_{[R,S]} \Leftrightarrow \begin{cases} X \cdot i_1 = R \\ X \cdot i_2 = S \end{cases} \tag{43}$$

Thus relational coproducts are born, in which *alternatives* are still denoted by $[R, S]$, as in the functional case, since types always tell us whether we are in **S** or **R**.

As another example, this time concerning $(\_ \times K) \dashv (\_^K)$ (21), we get

$$k = \textbf{uncurry}\ [\textbf{curry}\, f, \textbf{curry}\, g] \Leftrightarrow \begin{cases} k \cdot (i_1 \times id) = f \\ k \cdot (i_2 \times id) = g \end{cases}$$

and so on and so forth for other $\mathsf{L} \dashv \mathsf{R}$.[12]

12   More About R

We have just seen that the category of relations **R** has coproducts. In fact, it has a much richer structure which stems from the powerset construction in **S** (27).

---

[11] The $\lceil \_ \rceil$ and $\lfloor \_ \rfloor$ that occur in (41) and (42) have to do with $\mathsf{L} \dashv \mathsf{R}$, since the corresponding transposes of $(+) \dashv \nabla$ are spelt out via (23).

[12] These facts are actually instances of a more general result: coproducts generalize to so-called *colimits* and these are preserved by left adjoints [14].

The fact that powersets are ordered by set inclusion induces a partial order on relations in $\mathbf{R}$ easy to define:[13]

$$R \subseteq S \iff \langle \forall\, a :: (\Lambda R\, a) \subseteq (\Lambda S\, a) \rangle \tag{44}$$

Put in another way, every homset $\mathbf{R}(A, B)$ is partially ordered and we say that $\mathbf{R}$ is *order-enriched*.

This enrichment is actually "richer": (44) carries with it a complete Boolean algebra and therefore relation union $(R \cup S)$ and intersection $(R \cap S)$ are defined within the same homset $\mathbf{R}\,(A, B)$ by construction, whose least element is usually denoted by $\perp$ and the largest by $\top$.

The other interesting structural property is that homsets $\mathbf{R}(A, B)$ and $\mathbf{R}(B, A)$ are isomorphic, that is, $\mathbf{R}$ is *self dual*. For each $R \in \mathbf{R}(A, B)$, the corresponding relation in $\mathbf{R}\,(B, A)$ is denoted by R° (the *converse* of R) and we have:[14]

$$b\, R\, a \iff a\, R^\circ\, b$$

This is a major advantage of $\mathbf{R}$ when compared to $\mathbf{S}$, where only isomorphisms can be reversed. Moreover, it turns out that converses of functions play a major role in $\mathbf{R}$. In particular, the useful rule

$$b\, (f^\circ \cdot R \cdot g)\, a \iff (f\, b)\, R\, (g\, a) \tag{45}$$

holds, for suitably typed functions f and g and relation R,[15] please see the type diagram below.

The use of this rule can be appreciated by applying it to both sides of a Galois connection, recall (4): term $f\, a \leqslant x$ becomes $a\, (f^\circ \cdot (\leqslant))\, x$ and term $a \sqsubseteq g\, x$ becomes $a\, ((\sqsubseteq) \cdot g)\, b$. That is, the logical equivalence of a GC (4) becomes the relational *equality*:

$$f^\circ \cdot (\leqslant) = (\sqsubseteq) \cdot g \tag{46}$$

$$
\begin{array}{ccc}
C & \xleftarrow{\;\;R\;\;} & D \\
{\scriptstyle f}\big\uparrow & & \big\uparrow{\scriptstyle g} \\
B & \xleftarrow[f^\circ \cdot R \cdot g]{} & A
\end{array}
$$

This version of (4) is said to be *pointfree* in the sense that it dispenses with variables, or *points*, a and x.[16] The question arises: how does one describe the preorders $(\leqslant)$ and $(\sqsubseteq)$ at such a *pointfree* level? This is related to a previous question: how does a recursive program such as e.g. take get generated from an equality like (46)? With no further delay we need to bring recursion into our framework of reasoning.

---

[13] The fact that we use the same symbol to order relations and order powersets should not be a problem, as types disambiguate its use.

[14] Self-duality in $\mathbf{R}$ arises from isomorphism $\mathsf{P}\, X \cong 2^X$ ("sets are predicates") in $\mathbf{S}$. By this and uncurrying, $A \to \mathsf{P}\, B \cong 2^{A \times B}$. Since $A \times B \cong B \times A$, we can go in reverse order and obtain $B \to \mathsf{P}\, A$, etc.

[15] Following a widely adopted convention [4] to save text, we denote "relations that are functions" by lowercase letters.

[16] This is the way (in $\mathbf{R}$) Galois connections are handled in e.g. [1,16].

13 Recursion Comes In

For a given (endo)functor F, any morphism $A \xleftarrow{\;a\;} F\,A$ is said to be an F-algebra, where A is said to be the *carrier* of the algebra. F-algebras form a category provided its morphisms $a \xrightarrow{\;f\;} b$ satisfy a particular property,

$$f \cdot a = b \cdot F\,f \qquad\qquad (47)$$

captured in the diagram aside.[17] Property (47) states that A-elements are mapped to B-elements in a structural way. Think for instance of $A = B = \mathbb{N}_0$ being the natural numbers, $F\,X = X \times X$, $a\,(n,m) = n + m$, $b\,(x,y) = x \times y$ and $f\,x = c^x$, for some fixed c. Then (47) becomes $f\,(a\,(n,m)) = b\,(f\,n, f\,m)$, then $f\,(n+m) = (f\,n) \times (f\,m)$ and finally $c^{n+m} = c^n \times c^m$, which holds in $\mathbb{N}_0$. Thus $(+) \xrightarrow{\;c^{(-)}\;} (\times)$ is a F-algebra morphism.

Some situations arise in which a is such that, for every b, f is unique. In such cases, a is an isomorphism[18], that is, there exists some morphism a° such that $a^\circ \cdot a = id$ and $a \cdot a^\circ = id$. Such algebras a are said to be *initial* and usually denoted by in, i.e. $F\,T \xrightarrow{\;in\;} T$ assuming their carrier set denoted by T. The uniqueness of f wrt. b is written $f = (\!|\,b\,|\!)$ and we have the universal property:

$$k = (\!|\,b\,|\!) \;\Leftrightarrow\; k \cdot in = b \cdot F\,k$$

Due to the tight relationship between in and F, it is common to write μ_F instead of T and in_F instead of in:

$$k = (\!|\,b\,|\!) \;\Leftrightarrow\; k \cdot in_F = b \cdot F\,k \qquad\qquad (48)$$

In words, $(\!|\,b\,|\!)$ is referred to as *the*[19] F-*catamorphism* induced by algebra b. As illustrated in the sequel, it is a generic, recursive construct expressing the transformation of μ_F into B in a "recursive-descent" manner dictated by functor F.

---

[17] Such F-algebra morphisms are often called F-homomorphisms. Note the overloading of f in $a \xrightarrow{\;f\;} b$, a F-algebra morphism; and f in (47), a function between the corresponding carriers.

[18] This is known as the *Lambek lemma* [4].

[19] Definite article because it is unique.

A very simple example of catamorphism is the "for-loop" combinator defined over the natural numbers ($\mu_F = \mathbb{N}_0$) in which $F\,X = 1 + X$:

$$\text{for } b\ i = (\!|\,[\underline{i}, b]\,|\!) \tag{49}$$

In this case,

$$\text{in}_F = [\text{zero}, \text{succ}] \tag{50}$$

is the so-called *Peano algebra* which builds natural numbers, where $1 \xrightarrow{\text{zero}} \mathbb{N}_0 = \underline{0}$ generates 0 and $\mathbb{N}_0 \xrightarrow{\text{succ}} \mathbb{N}_0$, the successor function $\text{succ } n = n + 1$, generates all other numbers. (By $1 \xrightarrow{k} X$ we mean the constant function $\underline{k}\ \_ = k$, where 1 is a singleton object.)

By unfolding (49) through (48) one derives

$$\text{for } b\ i\ 0 = i$$
$$\text{for } b\ i\ (n + 1) = b\ (\text{for } b\ i\ n)$$

clearly showing that b is the loop-body and i is the loop-initialization.[20]

Due to its genericity, the catamorphism concept has proved very useful in studying functional recursion. Similarly to [11], but extending this work towards the relational setting, the remainder of this paper addresses the "chemistry" between adjunctions and catamorphisms.

$(\!|\,\_\,|\!)$ *meets* $L \dashv R$. As a first step in the investigation of such "chemistry", we set ourselves the task of solving the equation $\lceil f \rceil = (\!|\lceil h \rceil|\!)$, where $\lceil \_ \rceil$ is the R-transpose of some adjunction $L \dashv R$, $\lceil f \rceil : \mu_F \to R\,A$ and $\lceil h \rceil : F\,R\,A \to R\,A$:

$$\lceil f \rceil = (\!|\lceil h \rceil|\!)$$

$\Leftrightarrow$ { cata-universal (48) }

$$\lceil f \rceil \cdot \text{in}_F = \lceil h \rceil \cdot F\,\lceil f \rceil$$

$\Leftrightarrow$ { fusion (67) twice }

$$\lceil f \cdot L\,\text{in}_F \rceil = \lceil h \cdot L\,F\,\lceil f \rceil \rceil$$

$\Leftrightarrow$ { isomorphism $\lceil \_ \rceil$ (72) }

$$f \cdot L\,\text{in}_F = h \cdot L\,F\,\lceil f \rceil$$

Altogether,

$$f \cdot L\,\text{in}_F = h \cdot L\,F\,\lceil f \rceil \quad \Leftrightarrow \quad \lceil f \rceil = (\!|\lceil h \rceil|\!) \tag{51}$$

---

[20] In spite of its elementary nature, the for-loop combinator is very useful in programming, see e.g. [8,19]. The unfolding of (49) down to the given pointwise definition is routine work in algebra of programming practice, see e.g. [18]. Starting from (48), it mainly uses the laws of the $(+) \dashv \nabla$ adjunction.

cf. the diagrams:

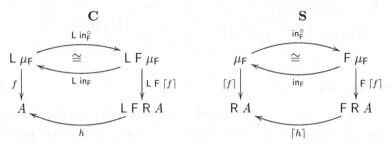

Although we did not get rid of $\lceil \_ \rceil$ from the left side of (51), this result already offers us something useful, as the following example shows.

Let us see how $(\!(\_)\!)$ meets $\Delta \dashv (\times)$, the pairing adjunction (22) where (recall) $\mathsf{L}\,f = \Delta\,f = (f,f)$, $\epsilon = (\pi_1, \pi_2)$ and $\lceil (f,g) \rceil = \langle f, g \rangle$. In this case, the left-hand side of (51) becomes:

$$(f,g) \cdot \mathsf{L}\, \mathsf{in_F} = (h,k) \cdot \mathsf{L}\, (\mathsf{F}\, \lceil (f,g) \rceil)$$

$$\Leftrightarrow \quad \{\ \mathsf{L}\,f = (f,f)\ ;\ \lceil (f,g) \rceil = \langle f,g \rangle\ \}$$

$$(f,g) \cdot (\mathsf{in_F}, \mathsf{in_F}) = (h,k) \cdot (\mathsf{F}\, \langle f,g \rangle, \mathsf{F}\, \langle f,g \rangle)$$

$$\Leftrightarrow \quad \{\ \text{composition and equality of pairs of functions}\ \}$$

$$\begin{cases} f \cdot \mathsf{in_F} = h \cdot \mathsf{F}\, \langle f,g \rangle \\ g \cdot \mathsf{in_F} = k \cdot \mathsf{F}\, \langle f,g \rangle \end{cases}$$

Concerning the right-hand side:

$$\lceil (f,g) \rceil = (\!(\, \lceil (h,k) \rceil \,)\!)$$

$$\Leftrightarrow \quad \{\ \lceil (f,g) \rceil = \langle f,g \rangle\ \text{twice}\ \}$$

$$\langle f,g \rangle = (\!(\, \langle h,k \rangle \,)\!)$$

Putting both sides together we get the so-called *mutual recursion* law:

$$\langle f,g \rangle = (\!(\, \langle h,k \rangle \,)\!) \Leftrightarrow \begin{cases} f \cdot \mathsf{in_F} = h \cdot \mathsf{F}\, \langle f,g \rangle \\ g \cdot \mathsf{in_F} = k \cdot \mathsf{F}\, \langle f,g \rangle \end{cases} \tag{52}$$

This first outcome of the interplay between recursion and adjunctions is already useful in programming, as it can help reduce the complexity of some dynamic programming (DP) problems by calculation. In particular, it can be used to convert complex multiple recursion into Peano-recursion, i.e., for-loops (49).

Many examples of application of (52) could be given.[21] Perhaps the most famous (and shortest to explain) is the Fibonacci series, a classic in *DP*:

---

[21] See e.g. [18], where examples include the derivation of efficient implementations of $\mathbb{R}$-valued functions from their Taylor series expansion into mutually recursive functions that are "packed together" via (52).

$$fib\ 0 = 1$$
$$fib\ 1 = 1$$
$$fib\ (n + 2) = fib\ (n + 1) + fib\ n$$

By defining $f\ n = fib\ (n + 1)$ and expanding it through the Peano-algebra, one gets,

$$\begin{cases} f\ 0 = 1 \\ f\ (n + 1) = f\ n + fib\ n \end{cases}$$
$$\begin{cases} fib\ 0 = 1 \\ fib\ (n + 1) = f\ n \end{cases}$$

that is:

$$\begin{cases} f \cdot [\text{zero}, \text{succ}] = [\underline{1}, \text{add}] \cdot \langle f, fib \rangle \\ fib \cdot [\text{zero}, \text{succ}] = [\underline{1}, \pi_1] \cdot \langle f, fib \rangle \end{cases}$$

By (52) and the *exchange law* (40), this leads to the for-loop

$$\langle f, fib \rangle = (\! [(1, 1), \langle \text{add}, \pi_1 \rangle] \!)$$

that is (in Haskell syntax):

$$fib = \pi_2 \cdot \text{for } loop\ (1, 1)\ \textbf{where}$$
$$loop\ (x, y) = (x + y, x)$$

In retrospect, note how the main ingredients of the calculation above rely mainly on adjunctions: law (52), which instantiates (51) for $\Delta \dashv (\times)$, and law (40), which arises from $(+) \dashv \Delta \dashv (\times)$.

14   Towards Adjoint-Recursion

The relevance of (51) is, as already seen in (52), the possibility of "converting" a non-standard recursive construct (f) into a catamorphism by right-adjoint transposition. However, (51) still needs the transpose $\lceil f \rceil$ on the left side of the equivalence. Can we do without this transpose?

For this to happen, we need to get rid of $\lceil f \rceil$ in the recursive call $\mathsf{L}\ \mathsf{F}\ \lceil f \rceil$. The resource we have for this is the *cancellation* law (66), $\epsilon \cdot \mathsf{L}\ \lceil f \rceil = f$. However, L in $\mathsf{L}\ \mathsf{F}\ \lceil f \rceil$ is in the wrong position and needs to commute with F. So we need a *distributive* law $\mathsf{L}\ \mathsf{F} \to \mathsf{F}\ \mathsf{L}$ or, more generally, a *natural transformation*

$$\phi : \mathsf{L}\ \mathsf{F} \to \mathsf{G}\ \mathsf{L} \tag{53}$$

enabling such a commutation over some other functor G. Still, for $\epsilon \cdot \mathsf{L}\ \lceil f \rceil = f$ to be of use, we need $\mathsf{G}\ \epsilon$ somewhere in the pipeline. We thus refine $h := h \cdot \mathsf{G}\ \epsilon \cdot \phi$ in (51) and carry on:

$$\lceil f \rceil = (\!|\lceil h \cdot G \, \epsilon \cdot \phi \rceil |\!)$$

$\Leftrightarrow$ $\{$ (51) $\}$

$$f \cdot L \, in_F = h \cdot G \, \epsilon \cdot \phi \cdot L \, F \, \lceil f \rceil$$

$\Leftrightarrow$ $\{$ natural-ϕ: $\phi \cdot L \, F \, f = G \, L \, f \cdot \phi$ $\}$

$$f \cdot L \, in_F = h \cdot G \, \epsilon \cdot G \, L \, \lceil f \rceil \cdot \phi$$

$\Leftrightarrow$ $\{$ functor G; cancellation $\epsilon \cdot L \, \lceil f \rceil = f$ (66) $\}$

$$f \cdot L \, in_F = h \cdot G \, f \cdot \phi$$

We thus reach

$$f \cdot (L \, in_F) = h \cdot G \, f \cdot \phi \quad \Leftrightarrow \quad \lceil f \rceil = (\!|\lceil h \cdot G \, \epsilon \cdot \phi \rceil |\!) \tag{54}$$

where natural transformation $\phi : L \, F \to G \, F$ captures a switch of recursion-pattern between f and the F-catamorphism $\lceil f \rceil$, through L.

What kind of function is f? Because in_F is an isomorphism, f can also be written as

$$f = h \cdot G \, f \cdot \phi \cdot L \, in_F^\circ$$

that is, f is a fixpoint. It is an instance of the recursive scheme

$$f = c \cdot G \, f \cdot d \tag{55}$$

which is often termed *hylomorphism* [4] and generalizes the catamorphism combinator. (For $d = in_{\mu F}^\circ$ one would have, by (48), $f = (\!| c |\!)$.) Altogether, (54) shows the equivalence of a G-hylomorphism and an F-catamorphism made possible by natural transformation $\phi : L \, F \to G \, F$:

$$\underbrace{f \cdot (L \, in_F) = h \cdot G \, f \cdot \phi}_{\text{G-hylomorphism}} \quad \Leftrightarrow \quad \underbrace{\lceil f \rceil = (\!|\lceil h \cdot G \, \epsilon \cdot \phi \rceil |\!)}_{\text{adjoint F-catamorphism}}$$

Note that, in general, they sit in different categories. The G-hylomorphism (in say **C**) is depicted in a diagram by:

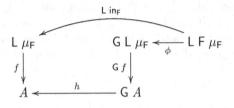

The diagram of its adjoint F-catamorphism (in **S**) is:

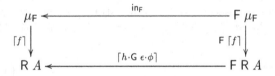

$$A \xleftarrow{\;h\;} G\,A \xleftarrow{\;G\,\epsilon\;} G\,L\,R\,A \xleftarrow{\;\phi\;} L\,F\,R\,A$$

We shall refer to (54) as the *adjoint-cata* theorem. Its main interest is that one can use the "*cata*-artillery" that stems from universal property (48) to reason about hylomorphism f by converting f to $\lceil f \rceil$.[22] But not necessarily: by (17) on the right side of (54), we get

$$\underbrace{f \cdot (\mathsf{L}\, \mathrm{in_F}) = h \cdot \mathsf{G}\,f \cdot \phi}_{\text{G-hylomorphism}} \;\Leftrightarrow\; f = \underbrace{\lfloor (\!\lceil h \cdot \mathsf{G}\,\epsilon \cdot \phi \rceil\!) \rfloor}_{(\!\langle h \rangle\!)} \tag{56}$$

giving birth to a new recursion combinator with *universal property*:

$$f = (\!\langle h \rangle\!) \;\Leftrightarrow\; f \cdot \mathsf{L}\, \mathrm{in_F} = h \cdot \mathsf{G}\,f \cdot \phi$$

In case ϕ is invertible, i.e. an isomorphism, the above converts to

$$f = (\!\langle h \rangle\!) \;\Leftrightarrow\; f \cdot \underbrace{\mathsf{L}\, \mathrm{in_F} \cdot \phi^{\circ}}_{\alpha} = h \cdot \mathsf{G}\,f \tag{57}$$

which shares the structure of (48), where we started from. Indeed, for the trivial adjunction in which L and R are the identity functors, $\phi = id$, F = G and $(\!\langle h \rangle\!)$ coincides with $(\!| h |\!)$. But, in general, (57) has a much wider scope as it enables us to handle recursive structures (μ_F) "embraced" by some contex information (L μ_F), a quite common situation in programming.

For instance, f may be applied to a recursive structure x paired with some data k, $f\,(x, k)$. While this falls off the scope of (48), it is handled by (56) for L $X = X \times K$, the lower adjoint of the exponentials adjunction (21). This is precisely the situation in a result known as the *Structural Recursion Theorem* which is proved in [4] with no explicit connection to the underlying adjunction.[23]

Clearly, (56) is much wider in scope. And, as it turns out, it also covers another result in [4] as special case, this time involving the already mentioned category of relations **R**. This is addressed in the following section.

---

[22] As explained extensively in [26], the expressive power of hylomorphisms (55) comes at the cost of being more difficult to reason with when compared to catamorphisms, as they lack, in general, a universal property.

[23] See Theorem 3.1 in [4], which we can now regard as a corollary of (56).

15 Going Relational

Let us inspect what (56) means in presence of the power-transpose adjunction $J \dashv P$ (27). Thanks to J being the identity on objects, we may choose G (in $\mathbf{R}$) as defined by:

$$y \; G \; (L \, f) \; x \;\; \Leftrightarrow \;\; y = F \, f \, x \tag{58}$$

In words, G establishes a structural relationship between object structures x and y, via the relation $L \, f$, iff y is the outcome of mapping f over x in $\mathbf{S}$. That is, G is the *relator* [3] that models $F \, f$ in $\mathbf{R}$. Moreover, (58) is nothing but (53) written pointwise, for $\phi = id$.

Given the close association of G to F expressed by (58), there is no harm in writing only one such symbol (e.g. F) knowing that F in a relational context means G. Assuming this notation convention, and knowing that ϕ "is" the identity, (54) instantiates to

$$X \cdot in_F = R \cdot F \, X \;\; \Leftrightarrow \;\; \Lambda X = (\!| \Lambda (R \cdot F \in) |\!) \tag{59}$$

depicted by diagrams as follows:[24]

Finally, there is little harm in denoting the new combinator of (56) by $(\!| R |\!)$ instead of $(\!\langle R \rangle\!)$, giving birth to the *relational catamorphism* combinator:

$$X \cdot in_F = R \cdot F \, X \;\; \Leftrightarrow \;\; X = \underbrace{\in \cdot (\!| \Lambda (R \cdot F \in) |\!)}_{(\!| R |\!)} \tag{60}$$

Thus "banana-brackets" are extended to *relations*, giving birth to *inductive relations*. Note that R is a *relational* F-algebra, which is checked in every recursive descent of $(\!| R |\!)$ across the input data.

Before proceeding to examples, it should be mentioned that the equivalence

$$X = (\!| R |\!) \Leftrightarrow \Lambda X = (\!| \Lambda (R \cdot F \in) |\!) \tag{61}$$

—which is another way of expressing (60)—is known in the literature as the *Eilenberg-Wright* Lemma [4]. So we have just shown that this lemma follows from the more general "adjoint-cata" theorem (54) via the *power-transpose* adjunction $J \dashv P$.

$(\!| \_ |\!)$*-reflection and More.* As a first introduction to reasoning about inductive relations in $\mathbf{R}$, let us see what we get from (60) when $X = id$. Put in another

---

[24] Note that the left diagram lives in $\mathbf{R}$ while the right one lives in $\mathbf{S}$.

way, we wish to solve $id = (\!|\,R\,|\!)$ for R. Since $\mathsf{F}\,id = id$, (60) immediately gives us $\mathsf{in_F} = R \Leftrightarrow id = (\!|\,R\,|\!)$, meaning that the equation $id = (\!|\,R\,|\!)$ has one sole solution, $R = \mathsf{in_F}$. Substituting, we get

$$(\!|\,\mathsf{in_F}\,|\!) = id \tag{62}$$

known as the *reflection* law [4]. In words, it means that recursively dismantling a tree-structure into its parts and assembling these back again yields the original tree-structure.

Taking the case of the Peano algebra $\mathsf{in_F} = [\mathsf{zero}, \mathsf{succ}]$ (50), where $\mathsf{F}\,X = 1 + X$, as example, we get $(\!|\,[\mathsf{zero}, \mathsf{succ}]\,|\!) = $ for succ $0 = id$. Note that $[\mathsf{zero}, \mathsf{succ}]$ is a function, and so we actually do not need (60) for this, (48) where we started from is enough.

Now, since we can plug relations into (60), how about going for something larger than $[\mathsf{zero}, \mathsf{succ}]$, for instance $(\!|\,[\mathsf{zero}, \mathsf{zero} \cup \mathsf{succ}]\,|\!)$? (Recall from (43) that relation union and alternatives involving relations are well-defined.)

Let us first of all see what kind of relation $X = (\!|\,[\mathsf{zero}, \mathsf{zero} \cup \mathsf{succ}]\,|\!)$ is, governed by universal property (60):

$X = (\!|\,[\mathsf{zero}, \mathsf{zero} \cup \mathsf{succ}]\,|\!)$

$\Leftrightarrow$ $\{$ (60) for $\mathsf{F}\,X = id + X$ $\}$

$X \cdot [\mathsf{zero}, \mathsf{succ}] = [\mathsf{zero}, \mathsf{zero} \cup \mathsf{succ}] \cdot (id + X)$

$\Leftrightarrow$ $\{$ (+) $\dashv \Delta$ in $\mathbf{R}$: fusion (76) and absorption (77) $\}$

$[X \cdot \mathsf{zero}, X \cdot \mathsf{succ}] = [\mathsf{zero}, (\mathsf{zero} \cup \mathsf{succ}) \cdot X]$

$\Leftrightarrow$ $\{$ (+) $\dashv \Delta$ in $\mathbf{R}$: isomorphism $\}$

$\begin{cases} X \cdot \mathsf{zero} = \mathsf{zero} \\ X \cdot \mathsf{succ} = (\mathsf{zero} \cup \mathsf{succ}) \cdot X \end{cases}$

$\Leftrightarrow$ $\{$ go pointwise in $\mathbf{R}$ via relation composition and (45), several times $\}$

$\begin{cases} n\,X\,0 \Leftrightarrow n = 0 \\ m\,X\,(n+1) = \langle \exists\,k\ :\ k\,X\,n:\ m = 0 \vee m = k+1 \rangle \end{cases}$

$\Leftrightarrow$ $\{$ simplify $\}$

$\begin{cases} n\,X\,0 \Leftrightarrow n = 0 \\ m\,X\,(n+1) \Leftrightarrow m = 0 \vee (m-1)\,X\,n \end{cases}$

By inspection, it can be seen that X is the *less-or-equal* relation in $\mathbb{N}_0$. Indeed, by replacing X by $\leqslant$ we get:

- base clause—$n \leqslant 0 \Leftrightarrow n = 0$, which means that 0 is the infimum of the ordering.
- inductive clause—$m \leqslant n + 1$, which means that either $m = 0$ (the infimum of the ordering again) or, for $m \neq 0$, we have $m \leqslant n + 1 \Leftrightarrow m - 1 \leqslant n$, something we have seen many times in school algebra.

All in all, our calculations show that the ($\leqslant$) ordering on the natural numbers is an *inductive relation*. Note, however, this is not a privilege of ($\leqslant$) : $\mathbb{N}_0 \to \mathbb{N}_0$, as we shall see next.

16   Back to Galois Connections

Recall from Sect. 5 that the prefix ($\sqsubseteq$) ordering over finite lists was handled assuming basic "axiom" (10),

$$s \sqsubseteq (h : t) \Leftrightarrow s = [] \lor \langle \exists s' :: s = (h : s') \land s' \sqsubseteq t \rangle$$

as well as the assumption that the empty sequence [] is the infimum of the ordering. (Further recall that these assumptions were needed where e.g. calculating take from its Galois connection specification.)

Let us work out ($\sqsubseteq$) in the same way as ($\leqslant$) above. There are two constructors of finite lists, either nil _ = [] generating the empty list; or cons $(a, x) = a : x$ generating a new list $a : x$ from an existing one (x) by placing a new element (a) at the front of x.

Thus the initial algebra in this case is $in_F = [\text{nil}, \text{cons}]$, giving way to catamorphisms over a slightly more complex relator, $F\,R = id + id \times R$, where $id \times R$ has to do with the fact that cons requires two arguments.

The parallel between [zero, succ] and [nil, cons] is obvious, and so we move straight to defining ($\sqsubseteq$) as the *inductive relation* (a.k.a. relational catamorphism):

$$(\sqsubseteq) = (\![[\text{nil}, \text{nil} \cup \text{cons}]]\!) \tag{63}$$

The reader can easily replay the calculation of ($\leqslant$) this time for ($\sqsubseteq$) and conclude that "axioms" (10) and $x \sqsubseteq [] \Leftrightarrow x = []$ are indeed the *pointwise equivalent* to defining the list-catamorphism (63) in $\mathbf{R}$.

Eventually, we are in position to answer the main question in Sect. 5, raised by the calculation of recursive right-adjoints such as integer division and take:

"Where does this induction come from?"

It is now clear that what turns such adjoints into recursive (inductive) functions is the very nature of the partial orderings that express them as "best solutions", which are bound to be inductive relations as dictated by the inductive structure of the underlying data.

Last but not least, there is yet another advantage: in $\mathbf{R}$ we can resort to the pointfree version of Galois connections (46), where all the components of the connections are homogeneous—all of them are *morphisms* of a (single) category, $\mathbf{R}$—be them functions, orderings or other relations. By catamorphism algebra, the reasonings of Sect. 5 can be performed at *pointfree* level, in a more calculational style, possibly assisted by GC-oriented proof assistants [21], as detailed below.

17   Related and Current Work

In his landmark paper [11] on "adjoint folds and unfolds", Ralf Hinze leaves the following suggestion:

> (...) Finally, we have left the exploration of **relational** adjoint (un)folds to future work.

Following this hint was the main motivation for the research reported in this paper. The main outcome is a unified view of the relational algebra of programming, in particular concerning results in the literature [4] that now fit together as outcomes of the generic *adjoint-cata* theorem of Sect. 14.

The paper is also aimed at framing, in a wider setting, the author's long standing interest in Galois connections as a generic reasoning device [16,17,21]. Previous work also includes the use of adjunctions in a categorial approach to linear algebra [13] and in calculating tail-recursive programs by "left Peano recursion" [8,19].

Current work is going in two main directions. On the applications' side, trying to evaluate how generic and useful the idea of deriving programs from Galois connections is (recall Sect. 5) and whether this can be (semi)automated by tools such as the Galculator [21]. This would have the advantage over e.g. [16] of not requiring in-depth knowledge of the algebra of relational operators such as e.g. *shrinking*.

On the side of foundations of program semantics, we would like to explore the hint in [20] of working out the relationship between *denotational semantics* and *structured operational semantics* (SOS, regarded as an inductive relation) [25] as an instance of the adjoint-cata theorem. This is expected to enable a calculational flavour in programming language semantics theory.

18   Summary

Science proceeds from the particular to the general. Scientific maturity is achieved when convincing explanations are given around simple (but expressive) concepts, generic enough to encompass an entire theoretical framework. Simplicity and elegance in science enhance scientific communication, make concepts more understandable and knowledge more lasting.

Adjunctions are one such concept, expressive and general enough to capture much of mathematics and theory of programming.

Throughout this work, the author learned to appreciate "adjoint folds" even more and to regard *adjunctions* as a very fertile device for explaining programming as a whole. So important that *teaching* them (inc. *Galois connections*) should be mainstream. May the tutorial flavour of the current paper contribute, however little, to this end.

Acknowledgments. The author wishes to thank the organizers of WADT'22 for inviting him to give the talk which led to this paper. His work is financed by National Funds through the FCT - Fundação para a Ciência e a Tecnologia, I.P. (Portuguese Foundation for Science and Technology) within the IBEX project, with reference PTDC/CCI-COM/4280/2021.

A   Properties of Adjunctions and Monads

Corollaries of $k = \lceil f \rceil \Leftrightarrow \epsilon \cdot \mathsf{L}\, k = f$ *(17)*

reflection:

$$\lceil \epsilon \rceil = id \tag{64}$$

that is,

$$\epsilon = \lfloor id \rfloor \tag{65}$$

cancellation:

$$\epsilon \cdot \mathsf{L} \lceil f \rceil = f \tag{66}$$

fusion:

$$\lceil h \rceil \cdot g = \lceil h \cdot \mathsf{L}\, g \rceil \tag{67}$$

absorption:

$$(\mathsf{R}\, g) \cdot \lceil h \rceil = \lceil g \cdot h \rceil \tag{68}$$

naturality:

$$h \cdot \epsilon = \epsilon \cdot \mathsf{L}\, (\mathsf{R}\, h) \tag{69}$$

closed definition:

$$\lfloor k \rfloor = \epsilon \cdot (\mathsf{L}\, k) \tag{70}$$

functor:

$$\mathsf{R}\, h = \lceil h \cdot \epsilon \rceil \tag{71}$$

isomorphism:

$$\lceil f \rceil = \lceil g \rceil \Leftrightarrow f = g \tag{72}$$

Dual corollaries of $k = \lfloor f \rfloor \Leftrightarrow \mathsf{R}\, k \cdot \eta = f$ *(19)*

reflection:

$$\lfloor \eta \rfloor = id \tag{73}$$

that is,

$$\eta = \lceil id \rceil \tag{74}$$

cancellation:

$$R \lfloor f \rfloor \cdot \eta = f \tag{75}$$

fusion:

$$g \cdot \lfloor h \rfloor = \lfloor R\, g \cdot h \rfloor \tag{76}$$

absorption:

$$\lfloor h \rfloor \cdot L\, g = \lfloor h \cdot g \rfloor \tag{77}$$

naturality:

$$h \cdot \epsilon = \epsilon \cdot L\, (R\, h) \tag{78}$$

closed definition:

$$\lceil g \rceil = (R\, g) \cdot \eta \tag{79}$$

functor

$$L\, g = \lfloor \eta \cdot g \rfloor \tag{80}$$

cancellation (corollary):

$$\epsilon \cdot L\, \eta = id \tag{81}$$

Monads. Proof of (32):

$$\mu \cdot \mu = \mu \cdot M\, \mu$$

$\Leftrightarrow \qquad \{\ \mu = R\, \epsilon\ (35);\ \text{functor } R\ \}$

$$R\, (\epsilon \cdot \epsilon) = (R\, \epsilon) \cdot (R\, (L\, (R\, \epsilon)))$$

$\Leftrightarrow \qquad \{\ \text{functor } R\ \}$

$$R\, (\epsilon \cdot \epsilon) = R\, (\epsilon \cdot L\, (R\, \epsilon))$$

$\Leftrightarrow \qquad \{\ \text{natural-}\epsilon\ (69)\ \}$

$$R\, (\epsilon \cdot \epsilon) = R\, (\epsilon \cdot \epsilon)$$

$\square$

Proof of (33):

$$\mu \cdot \eta = id = \mu \cdot M\, \eta$$

$\Leftrightarrow \qquad \{\ \mu = R\, \epsilon,\ \eta = \lceil id \rceil\ \text{etc}\ \}$

$$R\, \epsilon \cdot \lceil id \rceil = id = R\, \epsilon \cdot (R\, L\, \eta)$$

$\Leftrightarrow \qquad \{\ \text{absorption } (68);\ \text{functor } R\ \}$

$$\lceil \epsilon \rceil = id = R\, (\epsilon \cdot L\, \eta)$$

$\Leftrightarrow \qquad \{\ \text{reflection } (64);\ \text{cancellation } (81)\ \}$

true

$\square$

Proof of (37):

$$f \bullet g$$

$$= \quad \{ \ f \bullet g = \mu \cdot \mathsf{M} \, f \cdot g \ \}$$

$$\mu \cdot \mathsf{M} \, f \cdot g$$

$$= \quad \{ \ \mathsf{M} = \mathsf{R} \, \mathsf{L}; \mu = \mathsf{R} \, \epsilon \ \}$$

$$\mathsf{R} \, \epsilon \cdot (\mathsf{R} \, (\mathsf{L} \, f)) \cdot g$$

$$= \quad \{ \ \text{functor } \mathsf{R} \ \}$$

$$\mathsf{R} \, (\epsilon \cdot \mathsf{L} \, f) \cdot g$$

$$= \quad \{ \ \text{cancellation: } \epsilon \cdot \mathsf{L} \, f = \lfloor f \rfloor; g = \lceil \lfloor g \rfloor \rceil \ \}$$

$$\mathsf{R} \, \lfloor f \rfloor \cdot \lceil \lfloor g \rfloor \rceil$$

$$= \quad \{ \ \text{absorption: } (\mathsf{R} \, g) \cdot \lceil h \rceil = \lceil g \cdot h \rceil \ \}$$

$$\lceil \lfloor f \rfloor \cdot \lfloor g \rfloor \rceil$$

$$\square$$

References

1. Backhouse, K., Backhouse, R.C.: Safety of abstract interpretations for free, via logical relations and Galois connections. SCP **15**(1–2), 153–196 (2004)
2. Backhouse, R.C.: Mathematics of Program Construction, p. 608. University of Nottingham. Unpublished Book Draft (2004)
3. Backhouse, R.C., de Bruin, P., Hoogendijk, P., Malcolm, G., Voermans, T.S., van der Woude, J.: Polynomial relators. In: Nivat, M., Rattray, C.S., Rus, T., Scollo, G. (eds.) Proceedings of the 2nd Conference on Algebraic Methodology and Software Technology, AMAST 1991, pp. 303–326. Springer, Heidelberg (1991). Workshops in Computing (1992)
4. Bird, R., de Moor, O.: Algebra of Programming. Prentice-Hall, Upper Saddle River (1997)
5. Boisseau, G., Gibbons, J.: What you Needa know about Yoneda: profunctor optics and the Yoneda lemma (functional pearl). Proc. ACM Program. Lang. **2**(ICFP), 84:1–84:27 (2018)
6. Burstall, R., Lampson, B.: A Kernel language for abstract data types and modules. In: Kahn, G., MacQueen, D.B., Plotkin, G. (eds.) SDT 1984. LNCS, vol. 173, pp. 1–50. Springer, Heidelberg (1984). https://doi.org/10.1007/3-540-13346-1_1
7. Burstall, R.M., Goguen, J.A.: Algebras, theories and freeness. Technical report CSR-101-82, University of Edinburgh, February 1982
8. Danvy, O.: Folding left and right matters: direct style, accumulators, and continuations. J. Funct. Program. **33**, e2 (2023)
9. Gibbons, J., Hinze, R.: Just do it: simple monadic equational reasoning. In: Proceedings of the 16th ACM SIGPLAN International Conference on Functional Programming, ICFP 2011, pp. 2–14. ACM, New York (2011)

10. Goguen, J.A., Burstall, R.M.: Institutions: abstract model theory for specification and programming. J. ACM **39**(1), 95–146 (1992)
11. Hinze, R.: Adjoint folds and unfolds – an extended study. SCP **78**(11), 2108–2159 (2013)
12. Jackson, D.: Software Abstractions: Logic, Language, and Analysis. The MIT Press, Cambridge (2012). Revised edition, ISBN 0-262-01715-2
13. Macedo, H.D., Oliveira, J.N.: Typing linear algebra: a biproduct-oriented approach. SCP **78**(11), 2160–2191 (2013)
14. Mac Lane, S.: Categories for the Working Mathematician. GTM, vol. 5. Springer, New York (1978). https://doi.org/10.1007/978-1-4757-4721-8
15. Moggi, E.: Notions of computation and monads. Inf. Comput. **93**(1), 55–92 (1991)
16. Mu, S.-C., Oliveira, J.N.: Programming from Galois connections. In: de Swart, H. (ed.) RAMICS 2011. LNCS, vol. 6663, pp. 294–313. Springer, Heidelberg (2011). https://doi.org/10.1007/978-3-642-21070-9_22
17. Oliveira, J.N.: Biproducts of Galois connections. Presentation at the IFIP WG 2.1 #79 Meeting, Otterlo, NL, January 2019
18. Oliveira, J.N.: Program Design by Calculation (2021). Unpublished book draft, February 2021. Informatics Dept., U. Minho (pdf)
19. Oliveira, J.N.: A note on the under-appreciated for-loop. Technical report TR-HASLab:01:2020 (2020). (pdf), HASLab/U.Minho and INESC TEC
20. Oliveira, J.N.: On the power of adjoint recursion. Presentation at the IFIP WG 2.1 #06 Meeting (Online), October 2021
21. Silva, P.F., Oliveira, J.N.: 'Galculator': functional prototype of a Galois-connection based proof assistant. In: PPDP 2008, pp. 44–55. ACM (2008)
22. Turner, D.A.: Elementary strong functional programming. In: Hartel, P.H., Plasmeijer, R. (eds.) FPLE 1995. LNCS, vol. 1022, pp. 1–13. Springer, Heidelberg (1995). https://doi.org/10.1007/3-540-60675-0_35
23. Wadler, P.L.: Theorems for free! In: 4th International Symposium on Functional Programming Languages and Computer Architecture, London, pp. 347–359. ACM, September 1989
24. Wadler, P.L.: Comprehending monads. In: Proceedings of the 1990 ACM Conference on Lisp and Functional Programming, Nice, France (1990)
25. Winskel, G.: The Formal Semantics of Programming Languages: An Introduction. MIT Press, Cambridge (1993)
26. Yang, Z., Wu, N.: Fantastic morphisms and where to find them - a guide to recursion schemes. In: MPC 2022. LNCS, vol. 13544, pp. 222–267. Springer, Cham (2022)

Standard Contributions

A Computability Perspective on (Verified) Machine Learning

Tonicha Crook[1] , Jay Morgan[2] , Arno Pauly[1] ,
and Markus Roggenbach[1(✉)]

[1] Department of Computer Science, Swansea University, Swansea, Wales, UK
m.roggenbach@swansea.ac.uk
[2] Université de Toulon, Aix Marseille Univ, CNRS, LIS, Marseille, France
jay.morgan@univ-tln.fr

Abstract. In Computer Science there is a strong consensus that it is highly desirable to combine the versatility of Machine Learning (ML) with the assurances formal verification can provide. However, it is unclear what such 'verified ML' should look like.

This paper is the first to formalise the concepts of classifiers and learners in ML in terms of computable analysis. It provides results about which properties of classifiers and learners are computable. By doing this we establish a bridge between the continuous mathematics underpinning ML and the discrete setting of most of computer science.

We define the computational tasks underlying the newly suggested verified ML in a model-agnostic way, i.e., they work for all machine learning approaches including, e.g., random forests, support vector machines, and Neural Networks. We show that they are in principle computable.

Keywords: Machine Learning · adversarial examples · formal verification · computable analysis

1 Introduction

Machine Learning (ML) concerns the process of building both predictive and generative models through the use of optimisation procedures. The remarkable success of ML methods in various domains raises the question of how much trust one can put into the responses that an ML model provides. As ML models are also applied in critical domains, some form of verification seems essential (e.g. eloquently argued by Kwiatkowska [9]).

However, due to the widespread use of non-discrete mathematics in ML, traditional verification techniques are hard to apply to its artefacts. Furthermore, many ML applications lack specifications in the form of, say, an input/output relationship, on which 'classical' verification approaches are often based. A typical example of this would be an ML application that shall decide if a given picture depicts a cat. Lacking a specification, what kind of properties can be verified? We will take the view that, like in classical verification, it is useful to expand the range of properties beyond simple input/output relations.

© Springer Nature Switzerland AG 2023
A. Madeira and M. A. Martins (Eds.): WADT 2022, LNCS 13710, pp. 63–80, 2023.
https://doi.org/10.1007/978-3-031-43345-0_3

By employing the toolset of computable analysis (the field concerned with computation on continuous data types), we are using the same continuous mathematics underpinning the theory of machine learning, and avoids any ad-hoc discretization.

We present an investigation into what kind of verification questions are answerable in principle about ML models – irrespective of the particular ML framework applied. We see these questions as basic building blocks for a future ML property specification language. Discretization, as far as it may be necessary for the sake of efficiency, can then be left to the implementation; without impacting correctness.

We use the language of computable analysis to formally define the computational questions we want to ask. We can prove that they are solvable in general (by exhibiting algorithms for them), while remaining independent of any concrete ML methodology. The semi-decision procedures in this paper are not meant for implementation. We are also not making any claims about computational complexity.

Our paper is organised as follows: in Sect. 2 we provide a gentle summary of our results. In Sect. 3, we provide definitions and key properties from computable analysis. Section 4 develops our theory with mathematical precision. Finally, Sect. 5 discusses related work.

2   A Gentle Summary of Our Results

In this section, we provide a gentle introduction to our results. The technical details and proofs, which are using concepts of Computable Analysis, are provided later in the paper. The main results are of the nature that specific functions model aspects of interest in ML (verification), and are computable.

We first model classifiers, define elementary questions on them and explore when they are computable. Then we formalise the idea of adversarial examples for a classifier utilising metric spaces. We show that detecting adversarial examples or proving their absence is computable. Next, we consider the process of learning itself. One question of interest here is the robustness of the results of a learned classifier depending on changes of the training data. We study this in two settings within Subsect. 2.3.

2.1   Classifiers

One basic notion of ML is that of a classifier. A classifier takes as an input some description of an object, say, in the form of a vector of real numbers, and outputs either a colour or does not give an answer. This makes classifiers a generalisation of semi-decision procedures.

Computable Analysis is developed as the theory of functions on the real numbers and other sets from analysis, which can be computed by machines. The first step in formalising a classifier in Computable Analysis is to discuss its domain and codomain. To this end Computable Analysis uses the notion of a represented space (to be formalised later in this paper, as are the other technical notions). The domain of a classifier can in general be an arbitrary represented space, while the codomain is defined as follows:

Definition 1. *The represented space* $\mathbf{k}_\perp$ *contains the elements* $\{0,\ldots,k-1,\perp\}$, *where* $0,\ldots,k-1$ *are discrete points and* $\perp$ *is an additional point specified by no information at all/represents 'no information'.*

Including the bottom element $\perp$ in our framework is essential to obtain a satisfactory theory. It can represent uncertainty. When we are modelling an ML-classifier that outputs probabilities attached to the colours, we could e.g. consider $n \in \mathbf{k}$ to be the answer if the assigned probability exceeds 0.5, and $\perp$ to be the answer if no individual colour exceeds 0.5.

A classifier has to be a computable function in order to be implementable. A key observation of Computable Analysis is that computable functions are by necessity continuous[1]. In fact, it turns out that the most suitable notion of function space in Computable Analysis is the space $\mathcal{C}(\mathbf{X}, \mathbf{Y})$ of continuous functions from $\mathbf{X}$ to $\mathbf{Y}$. This justifies the following definition:

Definition (Definition 8). *A* classifier *is a continuous function that takes some* $x \in \mathbf{X}$ *as input, and either outputs a colour* $j \in \mathbf{k}$, *or diverges (which is seen as outputting* $\perp$*). The collection of classifiers is the space* $\mathcal{C}(\mathbf{X}, \mathbf{k}_\perp)$.

Any concrete classifier we would care about will actually be computable. However, the definition includes also non-computable (but continuous) ones.

Example 1. A support vector machine produces separating hyperplanes, which act as classifier by returning one colour on one side of the hyperplane, another colour on the other side, and no answer for points on the hyperplane.

Given a classifier, what verification questions could we ask? We may want to confirm individual requirements or look at assertions regarding the behaviour of the classifier on an entire set or region A. These could be used for verification, where we desire to obtain a guarantee that the system is working correctly, or to identify potential errors. Concrete question include:

1. existsValue which answers true on input (n, A, f) iff $\exists x \in A\ f(x) = n$. Otherwise, there is no answer.

---

[1] Arguing informally, continuity means that sufficiently good approximations of the input specify approximations of the output to desired precision. Computability means that we can actually compute the desired approximations of the output from sufficiently good approximations of the input. The latter cannot be possible for discontinuous function.

Example 2. Consider a DDOS-attack detection system realized as a classifier f. The region A consists of data indicating an attack is happening, and the colour n means that the system concludes there is no attack. If existsValue(n, A, f) returns true, we have identified a false negative in f.

2. forallValue which answers true on input (n, A, f) iff $\forall x \in A\ f(x) = n$. Otherwise, there is no answer.

Example 3. Continuing with Example 2, here we may consider the property that for every data point in the region A the presence of the attack is successfully identified. If forallValue(n, A, f) returns true, we have verified that all points in the set A are classified as expected.

3. fixedValue, which on input (n, A, f) answers 1 iff $\forall x \in A\ f(x) = n$, and answer 0 iff $\exists x \in A\ f(x) \in \mathbf{k} \setminus \{n\}$. The answer $\bot$ is given if the classifier returns $\bot$ for at least one point in A, but does not return any colour except n on points from A.

Example 4. Consider an automated stock trading system which makes decisions to buy, sell or hold a particular stock based on its technical indicators. Deciding to buy or sell is represented as a colour (as it is an active decision), while $\bot$ means to hold the current position. Given a region A of very positive technical indicator values, we may want to ideally be assured that the system will always buy, while the decision to sell would be a clear mistake. If fixedValue(buy, A, f) returns 1, we know that the system meets the ideal requirement. If it returns 0, we have found a mistake. Answer $\bot$ means that the system falls short of its target without making a clear mistake.

4. constantValue which on input (A, f) answers 1 iff there is some $n \in \mathbf{k}$ such that fixedValue(n, A, f) answers 1, and which answers 0 iff fixedValue(n, A, f) answers 0 for all $n \in \mathbf{k}$.

The question constantValue is a first approximation of how to deal with adversarial examples.

Example 5. Assume we have reason to believe that all points in the region A are very similar, and should thus be classified in the same way by the classifier f. If constantValue(A, f) returns 1, we have the confirmation that this indeed happens. Obtaining the answer 0 suggests that a mistake might have happened, as two similar data points get assigned different colours. No answer (i.e. $\bot$) means that some points in A remain unclassified by f.

It remains to specify what regions A are considered and how they are represented. Two familiar notions from computable analysis are exactly what we need to make these questions computable, namely the compact sets $\mathcal{K}(\mathbf{X})$ and the overt sets $\mathcal{V}(\mathbf{X})$ (see Proposition 2). Finite sets are both compact and overt. This means that for any finite sample of data all four questions are computable. The far more interesting applications however concern infinite sets, e.g. all points belonging to a geometrically defined region, as they go beyond testing a classifier for a finite number of inputs.

2.2 Adversarial Examples

One specific verification task that has caught the attention of the ML community is to find *adversarial examples* [5,7,22] or to prevent them from occurring. One says that an adversarial example occurs when a 'small' change to the input results in an 'unreasonably large' change in the output (i.e. akin our fourth task above). For example, given a correctly classified image, small, even unnoticeable changes to the pixels in the image can vastly change the classification output.

Example 6. In particular image-based Deep Neural Networks (DNNs) can be easily fooled with precise pixel manipulation. The work in [23] uses a Gaussian mixture model to identify keypoints in images that describe the saliency map of DNN classifiers. Modifying these keypoints may then change the classification label made by said DNN. They explore their approach on 'traffic light challenges' (publicly available dashboard images of traffic lights with red/green annotations). In this challenge, they find modifying a single pixel is enough to change neural network classification.

If we want to discuss *small* changes in data, say, in an image, we need to assume a notion of distance. We will thus assume that our domain $\mathbf{X}$ comes equipped with a metric $d : \mathbf{X} \times \mathbf{X} \to \mathbb{R}_{\geq 0}$, specifically, that $(\mathbf{X}, d)$ is a computable metric space (which covers nearly any metric space considered in real analysis). Detecting the presence or the absence of adversarial examples can be explored using the following function:

Definition 2. *Let $(\mathbf{X}, d)$ be a computable metric space, and $\mathcal{C}(\mathbf{X}, \mathbf{k}_\perp)$ the space of classifiers. The map* locallyConstant $: \mathbf{X} \times \mathbb{R}^+ \times \mathcal{C}(\mathbf{X}, \mathbf{k}_\perp) \to \mathbf{2}_\perp$ *returns 1 on input (x, ε, f) iff f returns the same colour $n \in \mathbf{k}$ for all $y \in \mathbf{X}$ with $d(x, y) \leq \varepsilon$. It returns 0 if there exists some $y \in \mathbf{X}$ with $d(x, y) < \varepsilon$ such that f returns distinct colours on x and y. It returns $\perp$, if some points ε-close to x remain unclassified by f (such as in the cases of the global-robustness property [10]), but no distinct colours appear; or if there is a distinct colour appearing at a distance of exactly ε to x.*

The map locallyConstant is illustrated in Fig. 1. Consider the (closed) ε-ball around a point x. For a classifier f, locallyConstant outputs 1 if everything in the ball yields the same answer under f. The answer is 0 if there are two points (depicted as a red and a blue star in the figure) that yield distinct answers in the ball. The answer $\perp$ appears in two cases: If there are unclassified points inside the open ε-ball around x (the white region inside the ball on the right), or if another colour appears on the boundary of the ball, but not inside it (blue star).

We prove in Theorem 1 below that locallyConstant is computable under mild assumptions, namely that every closed ball $\overline{B}(x, \varepsilon)$ is compact (which implies that $(\mathbf{X}, d)$ is locally compact). The Euclidean space $\mathbb{R}^n$ is both a typical example for an effectively locally compact computable metric space where all closed balls are compact, and the predominant example relevant for ML.

To relate back to adversarial examples, locallyConstant tells us whether a classifier admits an adversarial example close to a given point x.

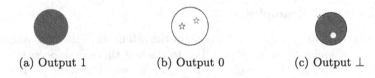

(a) Output 1   (b) Output 0   (c) Output $\perp$

Fig. 1. Illustrating the map locallyConstant (Color figure online)

Example 7. In the context of fully-autonomous vehicles that use sensor-captured data as input for DNN models, [7] explains how lighting conditions and angles, as well as defects in sensor equipment themselves, yield realistic adversarial examples. Assume the metric to be chosen to model the impact of these issues on the sensor data. Then one could deploy locallyConstant on a fully-autonomous vehicle in order to detect if one can trust the classifier on the current input data (answer 1) or not (answer 0).

2.3 Learners

Up to now, we considered already trained ML procedures. Now we discuss the process of learning itself, and introduce the concept of a *learner*. A learner takes a sample of points with corresponding labels and outputs a trained model:

Definition 3. *A* learner *is a (computable) procedure that takes as an input a tuple* $((x_0, n_0), \ldots, (x_\ell, n_\ell)) \in (\mathbf{X} \times \mathbf{k})^*$ *and outputs a classifier* $f \in C(\mathbf{X}, \mathbf{k}_\perp)$. *The collection of all learners is the space* $C((\mathbf{X} \times \mathbf{k})^*, C(\mathbf{X}, \mathbf{k}_\perp))$.

Note that we not only consider classifiers to be continuous functions, but that also learning itself is assumed to be continuous. As discussed above, this is a consequence of demanding that learning is a computable process. Continuity here means in essence[2] that if the data sample is altered by changing some x_k to some very close x_k' instead, the resulting classifiers f and f' cannot assign distinct colours to the same point y (though they may still differ in the use of $\perp$).

Now we can ask how 'robust' the classifier we are learning with the training data actually is. This phenomenon has recently attracted attention in the ML literature under the term of underspecification [4]. Whether we view the phenomenon as robustness of learning or underspecification of the desired outcome is a matter of perspective: A failure of robustness is tied to the existence of (almost) equally good alternative classifiers.

Our first question on a classifier is: is it possible by adding one extra point to the training data to change the classification? In other words, can a small addition to the training data lead to a change in classification (this is not already guaranteed by continuity of learning; the size of training data is a discrete value).

---

[2] By uncurrying, we can move from a learner L to the function $\ell : (\mathbf{X} \times \mathbf{k})^* \times \mathbf{X} \to \mathbf{k}_\perp$ such that $L((x_i, n_i)_{i \leq j})(x) = \ell((x_i, n_i)_{i \leq j}, x)$. One of them is continuous iff the other is. Now we can see that if ℓ returns a colour, it returns the same colour on an open neighbourhood of both training sample and test point.

1. robustPoint takes as input a point x, a learner and some training data. It answers 1 if every extension of the training data by one more sample point leads to x still receiving the same colour. It answers 0, if there exists an extension of the training data by a single sample point leading to x receiving a different colour. The case $\bot$ covers if x is unclassified for the original data or some of its extensions.
2. robustArea takes as input an area A, a learner and some training data. It yields 1 if every point in A is recognized as robust by robustPoint, it yields 0 if there exists a point $x \in A$ where robustPoint returns 0, and $\bot$ otherwise.

If $\mathbf{X}$ is computably compact and computably overt, and we take the regions A to be themselves compact and overt sets, then both operations are computable.

Allowing to add more than one point does not genuinely complicate the theory. However, it is useful to also ask the question where the additional points are added. Again, we consider a metric expressing the distance between the points added to the training set and the point whose classification we are interested in.

We will call training data *dense* at a point x, if adding a small number of additional data points sufficiently far from x does not change its classification under the learned classifier. It is *sparse* if the classification can be changed.

We will show that the operation SprsOrDns is computable (if the computable metric space $\mathbf{X}$ is computably compact). This operation has a number of parameters: a learner L, the number N of permitted additional data points, the distance ε, the training data $(x_i, n_i)_{i \leq \ell}$ and the point x of interest. It answers 0 iff $(x_i, n_i)_{i \leq \ell}$ is sparse at x, and answers 1 if $(x_i, n_i)_{i \leq \ell}$ is dense at x.

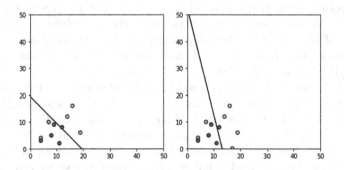

Fig. 2. Illustrating lack of robustness. Left: Original data, Right: Changed separating line due to one added data point (at (18,0)). (Color figure online)

Figures 2 and 3 illustrate the notions of robustness and sparsity/density on the same data set[3] – see https://github.com/Roggenbach/PublishedSoftware/blob/main/robust_sparse.py for the Python implementation used to produce these two figures. In Fig. 2 we show a classification example: our algorithm utilises

---

[3] Our overall algorithms are theoretical and not easily put into code. However, the individual concepts can be, in order to help the understanding of mathematical concepts such as robustness/sparsity and density.

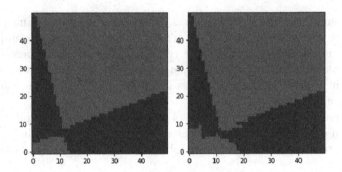

Fig. 3. Illustration of predicates concerning the original classifier. Left: Robustness (Red: Robustness, Blue: Not Robust), Right: Sparsity/Density (Red: Dense, Blue: Sparse) – note: ⊥ is at the boundaries between the coloured areas. (Color figure online)

a Support Vector Machine to create a separating line between the grey and red dots. The left side shows the original data set, and the right side shows the data set after the addition of another grey dot. We point out that the separating line has moved significantly.

In the left image of Fig. 3 one can see which areas of the input space can be affected in the classification due to adding one point to the training data. The algorithm adds the extra data point, calculates the separating line, and then checks whether each point in the graph is on the left or right of the separating line. It continues to do this for all possible addition data points in order to see what points of the graph never change sides of the line (robust) and which do. The blue area consists of all points which are not robust, i.e. can fall on either side of the separating line depending on the additional point. The red area consists of all robust points, i.e., they always fall on the same side of the separating line independent of the additional point.

The right image of Fig. 3 then shows the notion of sparsity/density: As before, we consider whether a point could fall on either side of the separating line after the addition of another sample point. However, we only consider sample points further than 5 units away from the point under consideration. There can be points which are dense, but not robust (see the area directly above (10, 0) and (20, 0)). This can be explained as follows: To obtain a very steep separating line, the extra data point needs to be placed in the area around (15, 0). Thus, the steep separating lines contribute to the pattern at the top of the picture, but do not affect the red component at the bottom.

Density implies robustness, but not the converse, as for the former we exclude additional training data too close to the point under discussion. It depends on the application which notion is more suitable. Lack of robustness under addition of a single data point indicates a too small set of training data. If we consider adding a more significant fraction of additional training data, robustness may be a too demanding notion. In this case, dense points are still those where only very similar counterexamples would challenge the response of the classifier.

3 Computing with Real Numbers and Other Non-discrete Data Types

The following summarises the formal definitions and key properties of the most important notions for our paper. It is taken near verbatim from [2]. A more comprehensive treatment is found in [16].

Definition 4. *A represented space is a pair* $\mathbf{X} = (X, \delta_{\mathbf{X}})$ *where* X *is a set and* $\delta_{\mathbf{X}} :\subseteq \mathbb{N}^{\mathbb{N}} \to X$ *is a partial surjection (the notation* $:\subseteq$ *denotes partial functions,* $\mathbb{N}^{\mathbb{N}}$ *is the space of infinite sequences of natural numbers). A function between represented spaces is a function between the underlying sets.*

For example, we will consider the real numbers $\mathbb{R}$ as a represented space $(\mathbb{R}, \rho)$ by fixing a standard enumeration $\nu : \mathbb{N} \to \mathbb{Q}$ of the rational numbers, and then letting $\rho(p) = x$ iff $\forall k \in \mathbb{N} \; |\nu(p(k)) - x| < 2^k$. In words, a name for a real number encodes a sequence of rational numbers converging to it with speed 2^{-k}. Likewise, the spaces $\mathbb{R}^n$ can be considered as represented spaces by encoding real vectors as limits of sequences of rational vectors converging with speed 2^{-k}. This generalises to the following:

Definition 5. *A computable metric space is a metric space* (X, d) *together with a dense sequence* $(a_n)_{n \in \mathbb{N}}$ *(generalizing the role of the rational numbers inside* $\mathbb{R}$*) which makes the map* $(n, m) \mapsto d(a_n, a_m) : \mathbb{N}^2 \to \mathbb{R}$ *computable. The induced representation of* X *is* δ_d *mapping* $p \in \mathbb{N}^{\mathbb{N}}$ *to* $x \in \mathbf{X}$ *iff* $\forall n \in \mathbb{N} \; d(x, a_{p(n)}) < 2^{-n}$.

An important facet of computable analysis is that equality is typically not decidable; in particular, it is not for the spaces $\mathbb{R}^n$. For these, inequality is semidecidable though (which makes them computably Hausdorff by definition). If equality is also semidecidable, a space is called computably discrete.

Definition 6. *For* $f :\subseteq \mathbf{X} \to \mathbf{Y}$ *and* $F :\subseteq \mathbb{N}^{\mathbb{N}} \to \mathbb{N}^{\mathbb{N}}$*, we call* F *a realizer of* f *(notation* $F \vdash f$*), iff* $\delta_{\mathbf{Y}}(F(p)) = f(\delta_X(p))$ *for all* $p \in \mathrm{dom}(f\delta_X)$*. A map between represented spaces is called computable (continuous), iff it has a computable (continuous) realizer.*

Two represented spaces of particular importance are the integers $\mathbb{N}$ and the Sierpiński space $\mathbb{S}$. The represented space $\mathbb{N}$ has as underlying set $\mathbb{N}$ and the representation $\delta_{\mathbb{N}} : \mathbb{N}^{\mathbb{N}} \to \mathbb{N}$ defined by $\delta_{\mathbb{N}}(p) = p(0)$, i.e., we take the first element of the sequence p. The Sierpiński space $\mathbb{S}$ has the underlying set $\{\top, \bot\}$ and the representation $\delta_{\mathbb{S}} : \mathbb{N}^{\mathbb{N}} \to \mathbb{S}$ with $\delta_{\mathbb{S}}(0^\omega) = \bot$ and $\delta_{\mathbb{S}}(p) = \top$ for $p \neq 0^\omega$.

Represented spaces have binary products, defined in the obvious way: The underlying set of $\mathbf{X} \times \mathbf{Y}$ is $X \times Y$, with the representation $\delta_{\mathbf{X} \times \mathbf{Y}}(\langle p, q \rangle) = (\delta_{\mathbf{X}}(p), \delta_{\mathbf{Y}}(q))$. Here $\langle \, , \, \rangle : \mathbb{N}^{\mathbb{N}} \times \mathbb{N}^{\mathbb{N}} \to \mathbb{N}^{\mathbb{N}}$ is the pairing function defined via $\langle p, q \rangle(2n) = p(n)$ and $\langle p, q \rangle(2n+1) = q(n)$.

A central reason why the category of represented spaces is such a convenient setting lies in the fact that it is cartesian closed. We have available a function space construction $\mathcal{C}(\cdot, \cdot)$, where the represented space $\mathcal{C}(\mathbf{X}, \mathbf{Y})$ has as underlying set the continuous functions from $\mathbf{X}$ to $\mathbf{Y}$, represented in such a way that the evaluation map $(f, x) : \mathcal{C}(\mathbf{X}, \mathbf{Y}) \times \mathbf{X} \to \mathbf{Y}$ becomes computable.

Having available the space $\mathbb{S}$ and the function space construction, we can introduce the spaces $\mathcal{O}(\mathbf{X})$ and $\mathcal{A}(\mathbf{X})$ of open and closed subsets respectively of a given represented space $\mathbf{X}$. For this, we identify an open subset U of $\mathbf{X}$ with its (continuous) characteristic function $\chi_U : \mathbf{X} \to \mathbb{S}$, and a closed subset with the characteristic function of the complement. As countable join (or) and binary meet (and) on $\mathbb{S}$ are computable, we can conclude that open sets are uniformly closed under countable unions, binary intersections, and preimages under continuous functions by merely using elementary arguments about function spaces.

Note that neither negation $\neg : \mathbb{S} \to \mathbb{S}$ (i.e. mapping $\top$ to $\bot$ and $\bot$ to $\top$) nor countable meet (and) $\bigwedge : \mathcal{C}(\mathbb{N}, \mathbb{S}) \to \mathbb{S}$ (i.e. mapping the constant sequence $(\top)_{n \in \mathbb{N}}$ to $\top$ and every other sequence to $\bot$) are continuous or computable.

We need two further hyperspaces, which both will be introduced as subspaces of $\mathcal{O}(\mathcal{O}(\mathbf{X}))$. The space $\mathcal{K}(\mathbf{X})$ of saturated compact sets identifies $A \subseteq \mathbf{X}$ with $\{U \in \mathcal{O}(\mathbf{X}) \mid A \subseteq U\} \in \mathcal{O}(\mathcal{O}(\mathbf{X}))$. Recall that a set is saturated, iff it is equal to the intersection of all open sets containing it (this makes the identification work). The saturation of A is denoted by $\uparrow A := \bigcap \{U \in \mathcal{O}(\mathbf{X}) \mid A \subseteq U\}$. Compactness of A corresponds to $\{U \in \mathcal{O}(\mathbf{X}) \mid A \subseteq U\}$ being open itself. The dual notion of compactness is *overtness*. We obtain the space $\mathcal{V}(\mathbf{X})$ of overt sets by identifying a closed set A with $\{U \in \mathcal{O}(\mathbf{X}) \mid A \cap U \neq \emptyset\} \in \mathcal{O}(\mathcal{O}(\mathbf{X}))$.

Aligned with the definition of the compact and overt subsets of a space, we can also define when a space itself is compact (respectively overt):

Definition 7. *A represented space* $\mathbf{X}$ *is (computably) compact, iff isFull :* $\mathcal{O}(\mathbf{X}) \to \mathbb{S}$ *mapping* X *to* $\top$ *and any other open set to* $\bot$ *is continuous (computable). Dually, it is (computably) overt, iff isNonEmpty :* $\mathcal{O}(\mathbf{X}) \to \mathbb{S}$ *mapping* $\emptyset$ *to* $\bot$ *and any non-empty open set to* $\top$ *is continuous (computable).*

The relevance of $\mathcal{K}(\mathbf{X})$ and $\mathcal{V}(\mathbf{X})$ is found in particular in the following characterisations, which show that compactness just makes universal quantification preserve open predicates, and dually, overtness makes existential quantification preserve open predicates.

Proposition 1 ([16, **Proposition 40 and 42**]). *The following are computable:*

1. *The map* $\exists : \mathcal{O}(\mathbf{X} \times \mathbf{Y}) \times \mathcal{V}(\mathbf{X}) \to \mathcal{O}(\mathbf{Y})$ *defined by*

$$\exists(R, A) = \{y \in Y \mid \exists x \in A \; (x, y) \in R\}.$$

2. *The map* $\forall : \mathcal{O}(\mathbf{X} \times \mathbf{Y}) \times \mathcal{K}(\mathbf{X}) \to \mathcal{O}(\mathbf{Y})$ *defined by*

$$\forall(R, A) = \{y \in Y \mid \forall x \in A \; (x, y) \in R\}.$$

The represented space $(\mathcal{V} \wedge \mathcal{K})(\mathbf{X})$ contains the sets which are both compact and overt, and codes them by providing the compact and the overt information simultaneously. Thus, both universal and existential quantification over elements of $(\mathcal{V} \wedge \mathcal{K})(\mathbf{X})$ preserve open predicates.

4   A Theory of Verified ML

Here we provide the mathematical counterpart to Sect. 2.

4.1   A Theory of Classifiers

As stated above, we consider classification tasks only. This means that a trained model will take as input some description of an object, and either outputs a class (which we take to be an integer from $\mathbf{k} = \{0, \ldots, k - 1\}$, $k > 0$), or it does not give an answer. Here, not giving an answer can happen by the algorithm failing to terminate, rather than by an explicit refusal to select a class. This is important to handle connected domains such as the reals, in light of the continuity of all computable functions. Formally, we are dealing with the represented space $\mathbf{k}_\perp$, which contains the elements $\{0, \ldots, k - 1, \perp\}$, where 0^ω is the only name for $\perp$, and any $0^m 1^\ell 0^\omega$ is a name for $\ell < k$, $m \in \mathbb{N}$.

Definition 8. *A* classifier *is a (computable/continuous) procedure that takes some $x \in \mathbf{X}$ as input, and either outputs a colour $j \in \mathbf{k}$, or diverges (which is seen as outputting $\perp$). The collection of classifiers is the space $C(\mathbf{X}, \mathbf{k}_\perp)$.*

Example 8 (Expanding Example 1). Consider the classifier we would obtain from Support Vector Machine [6]. The relevant space $\mathbf{X}$ will be $\mathbb{R}^n$ for some $n \in \mathbb{N}$. The classifier is described by a hyperplane P splitting $\mathbb{R}^n$ into two connected components C_0 and C_1. We have two colours, so the classifier is a map $p : \mathbb{R}^n \to \mathbf{2}_\perp$. If $x \in C_i$, then $p(x) = i$. If $x \in P$, then $p(x) = \perp$.

On the fundamental level, we need the *no-answer answer* $\perp$ as we will never be able to be certain that a numerical input is exactly on the separating hyperplane, even if we keep increasing the precision: equality on reals is not decidable.

Practically, computations might be performed using floating-point arithmetic, where equality is decidable. In this, the use of $\perp$ is still meaningful: If we keep track of the rounding errors encountered, we can use $\perp$ to denote that the errors have become too large to classify an input.

Example 9. Neural network classifiers compute a class score for every colour, which, when these class scores are normalised, share similar properties as a probability distribution. This translates into our framework by fixing a threshold $p \geq 0.5$, and then assigning a particular colour to an input iff its class score exceeds the threshold p. If no colour has a sufficiently high score, the output is $\perp$. As long as the function computing the class scores is computable, so is the classifier we obtain in this fashion. If our class scores can use arbitrary real numbers, we cannot assign a colour for the inputs leading to the exact threshold.

As motivated and discussed in Sect. 2, we show that we can compute the answers to the following verification questions:

Proposition 2. *The following maps are computable:*

1. existsValue : $\mathbf{k} \times \mathcal{V}(\mathbf{X}) \times \mathcal{C}(\mathbf{X}, \mathbf{k}_\perp) \to \mathbb{S}$, *which answers* true *on input* (n, A, f)
   iff $\exists x \in A\ f(x) = n$.
2. forallValue : $\mathbf{k} \times \mathcal{K}(\mathbf{X}) \times \mathcal{C}(\mathbf{X}, \mathbf{k}_\perp) \to \mathbb{S}$, *which answers* true *on input* (n, A, f)
   iff $\forall x \in A\ f(x) = n$.
3. fixedValue : $\mathbf{k} \times (\mathcal{V} \wedge \mathcal{K})(\mathbf{X}) \times \mathcal{C}(\mathbf{X}, \mathbf{k}_\perp) \to \mathbf{2}_\perp$, *which on input* (n, A, f)
   answers 1 *iff* $\forall x \in A\ f(x) = n$, *and answer* 0 *iff* $\exists x \in A\ f(x) \in \mathbf{k} \setminus \{n\}$, *and*
   $\perp$ *otherwise.*
4. constantValue : $(\mathcal{V} \wedge \mathcal{K})(\mathbf{X}) \times \mathcal{C}(\mathbf{X}, \mathbf{k}_\perp) \to \mathbf{2}_\perp$, *which on input* (A, f) *answers*
   1 *iff there is some* $n \in \mathbf{k}$ *such that* fixedValue(n, A, f) *answers* 1, *and which*
   answers 0 *iff* fixedValue(n, A, f) *answers* 0 *for all* $n \in \mathbf{k}$.

4.2   A Theory of Treating Adversarial Examples

One useful application of the map constantValue is using it on some *small* regions
that we are interested in. In ML terms, it addresses the question if there are
adversarial examples for a classifier in the vicinity of x. To characterise small
regions, we would have available a metric, and then wish to use closed balls
$\overline{B}(x, r)$ as inputs to constantValue.

To this end, we need to obtain closed balls $\overline{B}(x, r)$ as elements of $(\mathcal{V} \wedge \mathcal{K})(\mathbf{X})$.
The property that for every $x \in \mathbf{X}$ we can find an $R > 0$ such that for every
$r < R$ we can compute $\overline{B}(x, r) \in \mathcal{K}(\mathbf{X})$ is a characterization of effective local
compactness of a computable metric space $\mathbf{X}$ [17]. We generally get clB(x, r),
the closure of the open ball, as elements of $\mathcal{V}(\mathbf{X})$. For all but countably many
radii r we have that $\overline{B}(x, r) = $ clB(x, r), and we can effectively compute suitable
radii within any interval [17].

Theorem 1. *Let* $\mathbf{X}$ *be an effectively locally compact computable metric space*
with metric d *such that every closed ball is compact. The map* locallyConstant :
$\mathbf{X} \times \mathbb{R}^+ \times \mathcal{C}(\mathbf{X}, \mathbf{k}_\perp) \to \mathbf{2}_\perp$ *is computable, where* locallyConstant$(x, r, f) = 1$ *iff*
$\forall y \in \overline{B}(x, r)\ f(x) = f(y) \neq \perp$, *and* locallyConstant$(x, r, f) = 0$ *iff* $\exists y_0, y_1 \in$
$B(x, r)\ \perp \neq f(y_0) \neq f(y_1) \neq \perp$.

An adversarial example is the result of a small change or perturbation to
the original input that results in a change of classification made by, say, a DNN.
I.e. given the classifier f and an input x, an adversarial example is $f(x) \neq f(x+r)$
for $||r|| \leq \epsilon$ and $\epsilon > 0$. The question is: what do we call a 'small' perturbation,
i.e., how does one choose the parameter r?

Example 10. Assume that we want to use our classifier to classify measurement
results with some measurement errors. As an example, let us consider the use
of ML techniques to separate LIGO sensor data indicating gravitational waves
from terrestrial noise (e.g. [21]). If our measurements are only precise up to ε,
then having an adversarial example for $r = \varepsilon$ tells us that we cannot trust the
answers from our classifier. In the example, this could mean finding that the
precise values our sensors show are classified as indicating a gravitational wave,
but a negligible perturbation would lead to a 'noise'-classification.

We could use domain knowledge to select the radius r [13]. For example, in an image classification task, we could assert a priori that changing a few pixels only can never turn a picture of an elephant into a picture of a car. If we use Hamming distance as a metric on the pictures, stating what we mean with *a few pixels* gives us the value r such that any adversarial example demonstrates a fault in the classifier. Another example by [19] finds the upper and lower bounds of the input space via an optimisation procedure, following that DNNs are Lipschitz continuous functions and all values between these bounds are reachable.

So far it was the responsibility of the user to specify a numerical value for what a 'small' perturbation is in the definition of adversarial examples. As an alternative, we can try to compute the maximal value r such that on any scale smaller than r the point under consideration is not an adversarial example.

Corollary 1. *Let* $\mathbf{X}$ *be an effectively locally compact computable metric space with metric d such that all closed balls are compact. The map* OptimalRadius $:\subseteq$ $\mathbf{X} \times C(\mathbf{X}, \mathbf{k}_\perp) \to \mathbb{R}$ *defined by* $(x, f) \in$ dom(OptimalRadius) *iff* $f(x) \neq \perp$, $\exists y \perp \neq f(y) \neq f(x)$ *and* $\forall r, \varepsilon > 0 \; \exists z \in B(x, r + \varepsilon) \setminus B(x, r) \; f(z) \neq \perp$; *and by*

$$\text{OptimalRadius}(x, f) = \sup \{r \in \mathbb{R} \mid \exists i \in \mathbf{k} \; \forall y \in \overline{B}(x, r) \; f(y) = i\}$$
$$= \inf \{r \in \mathbb{R} \mid \exists y \in B(x, r) \perp \neq f(x) \neq f(y) \neq \perp\}$$

is computable.

4.3   A Theory of Learners and Their Robustness

Let us now consider the process of training the classifier. To keep matters simple, we will not adopt a dynamic view, but rather model this as a one-step process. We also only consider supervised learning, i.e., machine learning where the data set consists of labelled examples and the learning algorithm is learning a function that maps feature vectors to labels. Definition 3 formalised our conception of a learner as a map from finite sequences of labelled points to classifiers.

We do not prescribe any particular relationship between the training data and the behaviour of the resulting classifier. It could seem reasonable to ask that a learner L faithfully reproduces the training data, i.e. satisfies $L((x_i, n_i)_{i \leq \ell})(x_m) = n_m$. But such a criterion is, in general, impossible to satisfy. This is because our notion of training data does not rule out having multiple occurrences of the same sample point with different labels. It would also not match applications, as it often is desirable that a model can disregard parts of its training data as being plausibly faulty.

We can, however, ask whether a learner (e.g. CNN) when given non-contradictory training data will output a classifier faithfully reproducing it:

Proposition 3. *Let* $\mathbf{X}$ *be computably overt and computably Hausdorff. The operation*

$$\text{doesDeviate} : C((\mathbf{X} \times \mathbf{k})^*, C(\mathbf{X}, \mathbf{k}_\perp)) \to \mathbb{S}$$

returning true *on input* L *iff there is some input* $(x_i, n_i)_{i \leq \ell} \in (\mathbf{X} \times \mathbf{k})^*$ *with* $x_i \neq x_j$ *for* $i \neq j$, *and some* $m \leq \ell$ *such that* $L((x_i, n_i)_{i \leq \ell})(x_m) \in \mathbf{k} \setminus \{n_m\}$ *is computable.*

Robustness Under Additional Training Data. Generally, our goal will not be so much to algorithmically verify properties of learners for arbitrary training data, but rather be interested in the behaviour of the learner on the given training data and hypothetical small additions to it. One question here would be to ask how robust a classifier is under small additions to the training data. A basic version of this would be:

Proposition 4. *Let* $\mathbf{X}$ *be computably compact and computably overt. The map*

$$\text{robustPoint} : \mathbf{X} \times (\mathbf{X} \times \mathbf{k})^* \times \mathcal{C}((\mathbf{X} \times \mathbf{k})^*, \mathcal{C}(\mathbf{X}, \mathbf{k}_\perp)) \to \mathbf{2}_\perp$$

answering 1 on input x, $(x_i, n_i)_{i \leq \ell}$ *and* L *iff*

$$\forall x_{\ell+1} \in \mathbf{X} \; \forall n_{\ell+1} \in \mathbf{k} \quad L((x_i, n_i)_{i \leq \ell})(x) = L((x_i, n_i)_{i \leq \ell+1})(x) \in \mathbf{k}$$

and answering 0 iff

$$\exists x_{\ell+1} \in \mathbf{X} \; \exists n_{\ell+1} \in \mathbf{k} \quad \perp \neq L((x_i, n_i)_{i \leq \ell})(x) \neq L((x_i, n_i)_{i \leq \ell+1})(x) \neq \perp$$

is computable.

We can lift robustPoint to ask about all points in a given region, or even in the entire space as a corollary:

Corollary 2. *Let* $\mathbf{X}$ *be computably compact and computably overt. The map*

$$\text{robustRegion} : (\mathcal{K} \wedge \mathcal{V})(\mathbf{X}) \times (\mathbf{X} \times \mathbf{k})^* \times \mathcal{C}((\mathbf{X} \times \mathbf{k})^*, \mathcal{C}(\mathbf{X}, \mathbf{k}_\perp)) \to \mathbf{2}_\perp$$

answering 1 on input A, $(x_i, n_i)_{i \leq \ell}$ *and* L *iff* robustPoint *answers 1 for every* $x \in A$ *together with* $(x_i, n_i)_{i \leq \ell}$ *and* L, *and which answer 0 iff there exists some* $x \in A$ *such that* robustPoint *answers 0 on input* x, $(x_i, n_i)_{i \leq \ell}$ *and* L, *and which answers* $\perp$ *otherwise, is computable.*

Sparsity of Training Data. Allowing arbitrary additional training data as in the definition of robustness might not be too suitable – for example, if we add the relevant query point together with another label to the training data, it would not be particularly surprising if the new classifier follows the new data. If we bring in a metric structure, we can exclude new training data which is too close to the given point.

Definition 9. *Fix a learner* $L : (\mathbf{X} \times \mathbf{k})^* \to \mathcal{C}(\mathbf{X}, \mathbf{k}_\perp)$, *some* $N \in \mathbb{N}$ *and* $\varepsilon > 0$. *We say that* $(x_i, n_i)_{i \leq \ell}$ *is sparse at* $x \in \mathbf{X}$, *if there are* $(y_i, m_i)_{i \leq j}$ *and* $(y_i', m_i')_{i \leq j'}$ *such that* $\ell + N \geq j, j' \geq \ell$, $y_i = y_i' = x_i$ *and* $m_i = m_i' = n_i$ *for* $i \leq \ell$, *and* $d(y_i, x), d(y_i', x) > \varepsilon$ *for* $i > \ell$ *satisfying* $\perp \neq L((y_i, m_i)_{i \leq j})(x) \neq L((y_i', m_i')_{i \leq j'})(x) \neq \perp$.

We say that $(x_i, n_i)_{i \leq \ell}$ *is dense at* $x \in \mathbf{X}$ *if for all* $(y_i, m_i)_{i \leq j}$ *and* $(y_i', m_i')_{i \leq j'}$ *such that* $\ell + N \geq j, j' \geq \ell$, $y_i = y_i' = x_i$ *and* $m_i = m_i' = n_i$ *for* $i \leq \ell$, *and* $d(y_i, x), d(y_i', x) \geq \varepsilon$ *for* $i > \ell$ *it holds that* $L((y_i, m_i)_{i \leq j})(x) = L((y_i', m_i')_{i \leq j'})(x) \neq \perp$.

To put it in words: Training data is dense at a point whose label it determines, even if we add up to N additional points to the training data, which have to be at least ε away from that point. Conversely, at a sparse point, we can achieve different labels by such an augmentation of the training data. If we have chosen the parameters N and ε well, then we can conclude that based on the training data we can make reasonable assertions about the dense query points, but unless we have some additional external knowledge of the true distribution of labels, we cannot draw reliable conclusion about the sparse query points. We concede that it would make sense to include points under *sparse* where the classifiers will always output $\bot$ even if we enhance the training data, but this would destroy any hope of nice algorithmic properties.

Theorem 2. *Let* $\mathbf{X}$ *be a computably compact computable metric space. The operation*

$$\text{SprsOrDns} : \mathcal{C}((\mathbf{X} \times \mathbf{k})^*, \mathcal{C}(\mathbf{X}, \mathbf{k}_\bot)) \times \mathbb{N} \times \mathbb{R}_+ \times (\mathbf{X} \times \mathbf{k})^* \times \mathbf{X} \to \mathbf{2}_\bot$$

answering 0 *on input* $L, N, \varepsilon, (x_i, n_i)_{i \le \ell}$ *and* x *iff* $(x_i, n_i)_{i \le \ell}$ *is sparse at* x, *and answers* 1 *if* $(x_i, n_i)_{i \le \ell}$ *is dense at* x *is computable.*

5   Related Work

For Neural Networks already in 2010, Pulina and Tachella presented an approach for verifying linear arithmetic constraints on multiplayer perceptions by translating them into SAT-instances [18]. A decade later, a systematic review on testing and verification of neural networks already covered 91 articles [24]. A survey focused on verification of deep neural networks is [11]. The focus here is on the operation we call forallValue (Proposition 2) and its generalization beyond classification tasks. The computation is carried out by taking into account the specific structure of the network and the use of piecewise linear activation functions, which allows for the treatment of regions as rational polytopes. While taking these details into account enables the development of efficient algorithms, it is somewhat disappointing if using sigmoidal activation functions (as necessary for the final activation in a binary classification setup) instead requires one to modify even the theoretical framework behind the verification approach. (Such a modification has been carried out using Taylor models in place of polytopes, and the Taylor expansion of the sigmoidal activation function [8]). Our approach is model agnostic, in particular, independent of small details such as the choice of activation functions.

Again for Neural Networks, a more general approach to decidability of verification questions starts with the observation that as long as we are using piecewise linear activation functions and specifications definable in the theory of real closed fields (i.e. quantified formulas involving $+$, $\times$ and $\le$), we obtain decidability (i.e. yes/no-answers, no need for $\bot$) for free. This follows the theory of real closed fields and is decidable (albeit with infeasible complexity). This was remarked e.g. in [8]. If we want to ask questions involving a particular data set, we need to be able to define the data set in the theory of real closed fields. This seems like an awkward requirement for experimental data. In contrast, our theory is compatible with data obtained through imprecise measurements [15]. Extending the approach based on real-closed fields to sigmoidal activation functions seems to require the truth of Schanuel's conjecture [12]. Again, our approach is model agnostic.

Recently using probably approximately correct (PAC) learning theory (for background [20]), a study into the intermediate setting where learners are required to be computable but not resource-bounded has been achieved by [1]. They have developed a notion of a computable learner similar to ours. They used key concepts of a computable enumerable representable (CER) hypothesis class, along with an empirical risk minimization (ERM) learner. This allowed them to find an ERM learner that is computable on every CER class that is PAC learnable in the realizable case. However, verification questions are not considered in [1].

6 Summary and Future Work

We motivated and presented a number of questions that one might want to ask when verifying classifiers obtained by ML. These include elementary questions such as whether any point in a region gets assigned a particular colour, but also more advanced ones such as whether adversarial examples exist. Finally, we make a contribution to the phenomenon of underspecification by studying the robustness of learners. Using the framework of computable analysis we are capable of precisely formalizing these questions, and to prove them to be computable under reasonable (and necessary) assumptions.

Regarding the necessity of the assumptions, we point out that dropping conditions, or considering maps providing more information instead, will generally lead to non-computability. We leave the provision of counterexamples, as well as potentially a classification of *how* non-computable these maps are to future work. The notion of a *maximal partial algorithm* recently proposed by Neumann [14] also seems a promising approach to prove optimality of our results.

There is a trade-off between the robustness of a classifier and its 'accuracy'. It seems possible to develop a computable quantitative notion of robustness for our function locallyConstant, which could then be used as part of the training process in a learner. This could be a next step to adversarial robustness [3,5].

Rather than just asking questions about particular given classifiers or learners, we could start with a preconception regarding what classifier we would want to obtain for given training data. Natural algorithmic questions then are whether there is a learner in the first place that is guaranteed to meet our criteria for the classifiers, and whether we can compute such a learner from the criteria.

Our choice to consider classifiers as the sole entities to be learned in the present paper is meant to keep verification questions simple. Our framework allows for straight-forward extensions to any desired broader setting.

References

1. Ackerman, N., Asilis, J., Di, J., Freer, C., Tristan, J.B.: On the computable learning of continuous features. In: Presentation at CCA 2021 (2021)
2. de Brecht, M., Pauly, A.: Noetherian Quasi-Polish spaces. In: 26th EACSL Annual Conference on Computer Science Logic (CSL 2017). LIPIcs, vol. 82, pp. 16:1–16:17 (2017)
3. Carlini, N., Wagner, D.: Towards evaluating the robustness of neural networks. In: IEEE Symposium on Security and Privacy, pp. 39–57 (2017)
4. D'Amour, A., et al.: Underspecification presents challenges for credibility in modern machine learning. J. Mach. Learn. Res. **23**(226), 1–61 (2022). http://jmlr.org/papers/v23/20-1335.html
5. Goodfellow, I., Bengio, Y., Courville, A.: Deep Learning. MIT Press, Cambridge (2016)
6. Hearst, M.A., Dumais, S.T., Osuna, E., Platt, J., Scholkopf, B.: Support vector machines. IEEE Intell. Syst. Appl. **13**(4), 18–28 (1998)
7. Huang, X., Kwiatkowska, M., Wang, S., Wu, M.: Safety verification of deep neural networks. In: Majumdar, R., Kunčak, V. (eds.) CAV 2017. LNCS, vol. 10426, pp. 3–29. Springer, Cham (2017). https://doi.org/10.1007/978-3-319-63387-9_1
8. Ivanov, R., Carpenter, T.J., Weimer, J., Alur, R., Pappas, G.J., Lee, I.: Verifying the safety of autonomous systems with neural network controllers. ACM Trans. Embed. Comput. Syst. **20**(1), 1–26 (2020). https://doi.org/10.1145/3419742
9. Kwiatkowska, M.Z.: Safety verification for deep neural networks with provable guarantees (Invited Paper). In: Fokkink, W., van Glabbeek, R. (eds.) 30th International Conference on Concurrency Theory (CONCUR 2019). Leibniz International Proceedings in Informatics (LIPIcs), vol. 140, pp. 1:1–1:5. Schloss Dagstuhl-Leibniz-Zentrum fuer Informatik, Dagstuhl, Germany (2019). http://drops.dagstuhl.de/opus/volltexte/2019/10903
10. Leino, K., Wang, Z., Fredrikson, M.: Globally-robust neural networks. In: Proceedings of the 38th International Conference on Machine Learning, pp. 6212–6222. PMLR, July 2021
11. Liu, C., Arnon, T., Lazarus, C., Strong, C.A., Barrett, C.W., Kochenderfer, M.J.: Algorithms for verifying deep neural networks. Found. Trends Optim. **4**(3–4), 244–404 (2021). https://doi.org/10.1561/2400000035
12. Macintyre, A., Wilkie, A.J.: On the decidability of the real exponential field. In: Odifreddi, P. (ed.) Kreiseliana. About and Around Georg Kreisel, pp. 441–467. A K Peters (1996)
13. Morgan, J., Paiement, A., Pauly, A., Seisenberger, M.: Adaptive neighbourhoods for the discovery of adversarial examples. arXiv preprint arXiv:2101.09108 (2021)
14. Neumann, E.: Decision problems for linear recurrences involving arbitrary real numbers. Logical Methods in Computer Science (2021). https://arxiv.org/abs/2008.00583
15. Pauly, A.: Representing measurement results. J. Univ. Comput. Sci. **15**(6), 1280–1300 (2009)
16. Pauly, A.: On the topological aspects of the theory of represented spaces. Computability **5**(2), 159–180 (2016). https://doi.org/10.3233/COM-150049
17. Pauly, A.: Effective local compactness and the hyperspace of located sets. arXiv preprint arXiv:1903.05490 (2019)

18. Pulina, L., Tacchella, A.: An abstraction-refinement approach to verification of artificial neural networks. In: Touili, T., Cook, B., Jackson, P. (eds.) CAV 2010. LNCS, vol. 6174, pp. 243–257. Springer, Heidelberg (2010). https://doi.org/10.1007/978-3-642-14295-6_24

19. Ruan, W., Huang, X., Kwiatkowska, M.: Reachability analysis of deep neural networks with provable guarantees. In: Proceedings of the Twenty-Seventh International Joint Conference on Artificial Intelligence, pp. 2651–2659, July 2018

20. Shalev-Shwartz, S., Ben-David, S.: Understanding Machine Learning: From Theory to Algorithms. Cambridge University Press, Cambridge (2014)

21. Skliris, V., Norman, M.R.K., Sutton, P.J.: Real-time detection of unmodelled gravitational-wave transients using convolutional neural networks (2020). https://doi.org/10.48550/ARXIV.2009.14611

22. Szegedy, C., et al.: Intriguing Properties of Neural Networks. arXiv preprint arXiv:1312.6199 (2013)

23. Wicker, M., Huang, X., Kwiatkowska, M.: Feature-guided black-box safety testing of deep neural networks. In: Beyer, D., Huisman, M. (eds.) TACAS 2018. LNCS, vol. 10805, pp. 408–426. Springer, Cham (2018). https://doi.org/10.1007/978-3-319-89960-2_22

24. Zhang, J., Li, J.: Testing and verification of neural-network-based safety-critical control software: a systematic literature review. Inf. Softw. Technol. **123**, 106296 (2020). https://www.sciencedirect.com/science/article/pii/S0950584920300471

A Presheaf Semantics for Quantified Temporal Logics

Fabio Gadducci[✉] and Davide Trotta

Department of Computer Science, University of Pisa, Pisa, Italy
fabio.gadducci@unipi.it, trottadavide92@gmail.com

Abstract. Temporal logics encompass a family of formalisms for the verification of computational devices, and its quantified extensions allow to reason about the properties of individual components of a system. The expressiveness of these logics poses problems in identifying a semantics that exploits its features without imposing restrictions on the acceptable behaviours. We address this issue by introducing a counterpart-based semantics and we provide a categorical presentation of such semantics in terms of relational presheaves.

Keywords: Quantified temporal logics · Counterpart semantics · Relational presheaves

1 Introduction

Temporal logics encompass a widely adopted family of formalisms for the specification and verification of computational devices, ranging from standalone programs to large-scale systems, which find applications in diverse areas such as synthesis, planning and knowledge representation, see [6,33] among many others. Usually, these logics have a propositional fragment at their core, which is extended by operators predicating on the stepwise behaviour of a system. The framework proved extremely effective, and after the foundational work carried out since Pnueli's seminal paper [32], research focused on developing techniques for the verification of properties specified via such logics.

Several models for temporal logics have been developed, with the leading example being the notion of transition system, also known as Kripke frame: a set of states, each one representing a configuration of the system, and a binary relation among them, each one identifying a possible state evolution. However, one may be interested in enriching both states and transitions with more structure, for example by taking states as algebras and transitions as algebra homomorphisms. A prominent use case of these models is the one exploiting graph logics [7,8], where states are specialised as graphs and transitions are families of (partial) graph morphisms. The resulting logics allow the interaction of temporal and spatial reasoning and thus to express the possible transformations of the structure of a graph over time, see [2,23,34] for three early entries.

There are many quantified extensions of the modal/temporal logics paradigm, and in general adding quantifiers to such logics involves a number of difficulties. Consider

Research partially supported by the Italian MIUR project PRIN 2017FTXR7S "IT-MaTTerS" and by the University of Pisa project PRA_2022_99 "FM4HD".

A. Madeira and M. A. Martins (Eds.): WADT 2022, LNCS 13710, pp. 81–99, 2023.
https://doi.org/10.1007/978-3-031-43345-0_4

a model with two states s_0, s_1, a transition from s_0 to s_1 and another transition going backward, and an item i that appears in s_0 only. Is item i being destroyed and (re)created again and again? Or is it just an identifier that is reused? The issue is denoted in the literature as the *trans-world identity problem* (see [15, Sect. 16] for a survey of the related philosophical issues). An often adopted solution is to choose a set of universal items, which are used to form each state, making it immediate to refer to the same element across states. Despite their simplicity, solutions based on a fixed domain of individuals are not perfectly suited to model systems with dynamic allocation and deallocation of components. Consider again the above example. The problem is that item i belongs to the universal domain, and hence it is exactly the same after every deallocation in state s_1. But intuitively, every instance of i should instead be considered to be distinct (even if syntactically equivalent).

Am alternative solution to the fixed domain approach was advanced by Lewis [27] with the counterpart paradigm: each state identifies a local set of elements, and (possibly partial) morphisms connect them by carrying elements from one state to the other. This allows to speak formally about entities that are destroyed, duplicated, (re)created, or merged, and to adequately deal with the identity problem of individuals between worlds. Going back to graph logics, semantics based on domains relative to each state has been adopted for a μ-calculus with second-order quantifiers in [11] and, more recently, in metric temporal graph logic [19]: see [12, Sect. 6] for an overview on temporal graph logics. In fact, the paper builds on the set-theoretical description of the counterpart semantics introduced in [11], with the goal of explaining how the model admits a natural presentation in a categorical setting and how it can be adapted to offer a counterpart semantics for (linear) temporal logics with second-order quantifiers.

From a technical perspective, our starting point was the hyperdoctrine presentation of first-order logics, as originally described by Lawvere in his work on categories with equational structure [25,26]. More precisely, the direct inspiration was the presheaf model for modal logics with first-order quantifiers presented in [16]. Our work extends and generalises the latter proposal in a few directions. First of all, the focus on temporal logics, with an explicit next operator: the need to account for the single steps of evolution requires to tweak the original proposal by Ghilardi and Meloni by equipping our models with a chosen family of arrows, each one representing a basic step of the system at hand. Furthermore, the choice of a counterpart semantics forces the transition relation between worlds to be given by families of possibly partial morphisms between the algebras forming each world: this is modelled by using relational presheaves, instead of functional ones. Related to this, tackling second-order quantification requires additional effort since relational presheaves do not form a topos, due to the fact that the category of sets and relations is not a topos [30].

The paper has the following structure. Section 2 recalls basic properties of multi-sorted algebras, which describe the structure of our worlds. Section 3 presents relational presheaves, showing how they capture a generalised notion of transition system and how they support second-order operators. Section 4 introduces our logic, a monadic second-order extension of classical linear time temporal logics, and Sect. 5 finally shows how to provide it with a counterpart semantics, thanks to the categorical set-up of the previous sections. This paper is rounded up by a concluding section and by a running example, highlighting the features of the chosen logics.

Related Works. Functional presheaves can be seen as the categorical abstraction of Kripke frames [16, 17]. Building on this intuition, relational presheaves (see [30] for an analysis of the structure of the associated category) can be thought of as a categorification of *counterpart* Kripke frames in the sense of Lewis [27], see also the similar use advocated in [36]. An in-depth presentation of classical counterpart semantics is in [3, 20]. In this work we use relational presheaves to provide a categorical account of the counterpart models in [11], further specialising them to temporal logics.

As we already recalled, many authors considered quantified temporal logics and addressed decidability and complexity issues. Since our examples are motivated by applications to graph rewriting, we refer to the works surveyed in [15, Sect. 16]. Less explored is the side of categorical semantics. More precisely, we are aware of a topostheoretical description of a semantics for modal logics in [1] and a presentation in terms of Lawvere's doctrines in [5]. Moreover, for connections between the areas of coalgebra and modal logics we refer to [24], while specifically for temporal logics to [21, 22]. Note however that, as far as we are aware, currently these approaches generalise to the categorical setting the usual Kripke-style semantics, not the counterpart one.

2 Some Notions on Multi-sorted Algebras

We begin by recalling the definition of many-sorted algebras and their homomorphisms, which lies at the basis of the structure of our worlds.

Definition 1. *A **many-sorted signature** Σ is a pair (S_Σ, F_Σ) given by a set of* **sorts** *$S_\Sigma := \{\tau_1, \ldots, \tau_m\}$ and by a set $F_\Sigma := \{f_\Sigma \colon \tau_1 \times \cdots \times \tau_m \to \tau \mid \tau_i, \tau \in S_\Sigma\}$ of* **function symbols** *typed over S_Σ^*.*

In the following we fix a many-sorted signature $\Sigma := (S_\Sigma, F_\Sigma)$.

Definition 2. *A **many-sorted algebra** A with signature Σ, i.e. a Σ-algebra, is a pair (A, F_Σ^A) such that*

- *A is a set whose elements are typed over S_Σ;*
- *$F_\Sigma^A := \{f_\Sigma^A \colon A_{\tau_1} \times \cdots \times A_{\tau_m} \to A_\tau \mid f_\Sigma \in F_\Sigma \wedge f_\Sigma \colon \tau_1 \times \cdots \times \tau_m \to \tau\}$ is a set of typed functions.*

Notice that we denoted by A_τ the set $\{a \in A \mid a : \tau\}$ of elements of A with type τ.

Definition 3. *Given two Σ-algebras A and B, a (**partial**) **homomorphism** ρ is a family of (partial) functions $\rho := \{\rho_\tau \colon A_\tau \rightharpoonup B_\tau \mid \tau \in S_\Sigma\}$ typed over S_Σ such that for every function symbol $f_\Sigma \colon \tau_1 \times \cdots \times \tau_m \to \tau$ and for every list of elements $(a_1, \ldots, a_m)$, if ρ_{τ_i} is defined for the element a_i of type τ_i, then ρ_τ is defined for the element $f_\Sigma^A(a_1, \ldots, a_m)$ and $\rho_\tau(f_\Sigma^A(a_1, \ldots, a_m)) = f_\Sigma^B(\rho_{\tau_1}(a_1), \ldots, \rho_{\tau_m}(a_m))$.*

Example 1. Let us consider the signature $\Sigma_{Gr} := (S_{Gr}, F_{Gr})$ for directed graphs. The set S_{Gr} consists of the sorts of nodes τ_N and edges τ_E, while the set F_{Gr} is composed by the function symbols $s, t \colon \tau_E \to \tau_N$, which determine, respectively, the source and the target node of an edge. In this case, a Σ_{Gr}-algebra G is a directed graph and a homomorphism of Σ_{Gr}-algebras is exactly a (partial) morphism of directed graphs. In Fig. 1 we find the visual representations for three graphs G_0, G_1 and G_2.

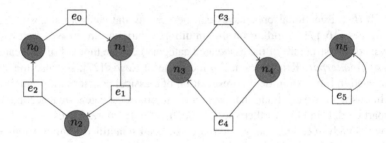

Fig. 1. Three graphs: G_0 (left), G_1 (middle) and G_2 (right)

Let Σ be a many-sorted signature, and let us fix disjoint sets X_τ of variables for each sort symbol of S_Σ. In order to introduce the notion of term, we take into account signatures of the kind $\Sigma_X := (S_\Sigma, F_\Sigma \uplus X)$, i.e. obtained by extending a many-sorted signature Σ with a denumerable set $X = \bigcup_\tau X_\tau$ of variables typed over S_Σ.

Definition 4. *Let Σ_X be a many-sorted signature. The many-sorted set $T(\Sigma_X)$ of* **terms** *obtained from Σ_X is the smallest such that*

$$\frac{x \in X_\tau}{x : \tau \in T(\Sigma_X)}$$

$$\frac{f_\Sigma : \tau_1 \times \cdots \times \tau_m \to \tau \in F_\Sigma \qquad t_i : \tau_i \in T(\Sigma_X)}{f_\Sigma(t_1, \ldots, t_m) : \tau \in T(\Sigma_X)}$$

Finally, we recall the notion of *context* and *term-in-context* over a signature Σ_X.

Definition 5. *Let Σ_X be a many-sorted signature. A* **context** *Γ over Σ_X is a finite list $[x_1 : \tau_1, \ldots, x_n : \tau_n]$ of (variable, sort)-pairs, subject to the condition that $x_1, \ldots, x_n$ are distinct.*

A *term-in-context* takes the form $t : \tau \; [\Gamma]$ where t is a term, τ is a sort, and Γ is a context over the given signature Σ_X. The well-formed terms-in-context are inductively generated by the two rules

$$\overline{x : \tau \; [\Gamma', x : \tau, \Gamma]}$$

$$\frac{t_1 : \tau_1 \; [\Gamma] \cdots t_m : \tau_m \; [\Gamma]}{f_\Sigma(t_1, \ldots, t_m) : \tau \; [\Gamma]}$$

where $f_\Sigma : \tau_1 \times \cdots \times \tau_m \to \tau$ is a function symbol of F_Σ.

Definition 6. *Let Σ_X be a many-sorted signature. The* **syntactic category** *or category of contexts $\mathrm{Con}(\Sigma)$ of Σ_X is defined as follows*

– *its objects are α-equivalence class of contexts;*

- *a morphism* $\gamma\colon \Gamma \to \Gamma'$, *where* $\Gamma' = [y_1 : \tau_1, \ldots, y_m : \tau_m]$, *is specified by an equivalence class of lists of the form* $\gamma = [t_1, \ldots, t_m]$ *of terms over* Σ_X *such that* $t_i : \tau_i\ [\Gamma]$ *holds for* $i = 1, \ldots, m$.

The composition of two morphisms is formed by making substitutions.

Recall that two contexts are α-equivalent if they differ only in their variables; in other words, the list of sorts occurring in each context are equal (and in particular, the contexts are of equal length). Requiring the objects of the syntactic category to be α-equivalence classes of contexts ensures that the category $\mathsf{Con}(\Sigma)$ has finite products, given by the concatenations of contexts. As for morphisms, the equivalence relation we consider is the one identifying two terms if they are equal up to substitution.

3 A Categorical View of Counterpart Models

We start this section recalling the notion of *Kripke frame*, largely used in the analysis of modal languages [4], and its development into counterpart semantics.

Definition 7. *A **Kripke frame** is a triple* $\langle W, R, D \rangle$ *such that* W *is a non-empty set,* R *is a binary relation on* W, *and* D *is a function assigning to every* $w \in W$ *a non-empty set* $D(w)$ *such that if* wRw' *then* $D(w) \subseteq D(w')$.

The set W is the domain of *possible worlds*, whereas R is the *accessibility relation* among worlds. The elements of each *domain* $D(w)$ represent *individuals* existing in w.

Kripke frames are assumed to satisfy the *increasing domain condition*, i.e. for all $w, w' \in W$, if wRw' then $D(w) \subseteq D(w')$, but this condition represents a strong constraint, philosophically and from the point of view of applications. Over the years, this condition has been at the heart of several discussions and controversies. In particular, Lewis denied the possibility of identifying the same individual across worlds, and he substituted the notion of trans-world identity with a *counterpart relation* C among the worlds [27]. In order to assign a meaning to terms *necessary* and *possible* according to Lewis' theory, Kripke frames are enriched by a function C such that for all $w, w \in W$, $C_{w,w'}$ is a subset of $D(w) \times D(w')$, interpreted as the counterpart relation.

Definition 8. *A **counterpart frame** is a 4-tuple* $\langle W, R, D, C \rangle$ *such that* W, R, *and* D *are as for Kripke frames (but* D *may not satisfy the increasing domain condition) and* C *is a function assigning to every pair* $\langle w, w' \rangle$ *a subset of* $D(w) \times D(w')$.

As anticipated, Kripke-like solutions are not perfectly suited to model systems with *dynamic allocation and deallocation* of components. This will be clearer later, when we present Example 9. Alternative solutions based on counterpart relations are e.g. introduced in [11], where the authors propose a novel approach to the semantics of quantified μ-calculi, considering a sort of labeled transition systems as semantic domain (called counterpart models), where states are algebras and transitions are defined by counterpart relations (a family of partial homomorphisms) between states.

We conclude this section recalling the notion of counterpart model from [11].

Definition 9. *Let Σ be a many-sorted signature and $\mathcal{A}$ the set of algebras over Σ. A* **counterpart model** *is a triple $\mathfrak{M} := \langle W, \rightsquigarrow, d \rangle$ such that W is a set of worlds, $d \colon W \to \mathcal{A}$ is a function assigning to every $\omega \in W$ a Σ-algebra, and $\rightsquigarrow \subseteq (W \times (\mathcal{A} \rightharpoonup \mathcal{A}) \times W)$ is the* accessibility relation *over W enriched with (partial) homomorphisms between the algebras of the connected worlds.*

In other words, for every element $(w_1, cr, w_2) \in \rightsquigarrow$ we have a (partial) homomorphism $cr : d(w_1) \rightharpoonup d(w_2)$, which explicitly defines the counterparts in (the algebra assigned to) the target world of (the algebra assigned to) the source world. The intuition is that we are considering a transition system labeled with morphisms between algebras, as a generalisation of graph transition systems. The counterpart relations allow us to avoid the trans-world identity problem, i.e. the implicit identification of elements of (the algebras of) different worlds sharing the same name. As a consequence, the name of the elements has a meaning that is local to the world they belong to. As we will see, this is the reason allowing to the counterpart relations the creation, deletion, renaming, and merging of elements in a type-respecting way.

3.1 Relational Presheaves Models

The main goal of this section is to explain how the counterpart model introduced in [11] admits a natural generalisation in a categorical setting. To fix the notation, and to provide the intuition behind our models, we briefly recall from [16] a presheaf presentation of the notions of *world*, *process*, and *individuals* arising from modal logic.

Given a small category $\mathcal{W}$, its objects $\sigma, \omega, \rho, \ldots$ can be considered as *worlds* or *instants of time*, and its arrows $f \colon \sigma \to \omega$ thus represent possible *temporal developments*. In the usual notion of Kripke-frame the accessibility relation is simply required to be a binary relation on the set of worlds, and this means that there is *at most one way to evolve from a given world to another*. This is a constraint we want to avoid, reflecting e.g. the many ways a source graph may evolve preserving different sets of nodes and edges, yet reaching the same target graph. To this end, the immediate generalisation of a set of worlds W and a relation R is given by a category $\mathcal{W}$.

From this perspective, a presheaf $D \colon \mathcal{W}^{\mathrm{op}} \to \mathbf{Set}$ assigns to every world ω the set $D_\omega := D(\omega)$ of its *individuals*, and to a temporal development $f \colon \sigma \to \omega$ a function $D_f \colon D_\omega \to D_\sigma$ between the individuals living in the worlds ω and σ. Therefore, if we consider two elements $a \in D_\omega$ and $b \in D_\sigma$, the equality $b = D_f(a)$ can be read as *a is a future development of b with respect to f*. In other words, *the notion of presheaf represents the natural categorification of the notion of counterpart frame whose counterpart relation is functional*. In particular, it is direct to check that, given a presheaf $D \colon \mathcal{W}^{\mathrm{op}} \to \mathbf{Set}$, one can define a counterpart frame $\langle W, R, D, C \rangle$ where

- W is given by the objects of the category $\mathcal{W}$,
- $\omega R \sigma$ if and only if there exists at least an arrow $\omega \to \sigma$ of $\mathcal{W}$,
- D is given by the action of $D \colon \mathcal{W}^{\mathrm{op}} \to \mathbf{Set}$ on the objects of $\mathcal{W}$,
- C assigns to every pair $\langle \omega, \omega' \rangle$ the subset of $D(\omega) \times D(\omega')$ whose elements are pairs $\langle a, a' \rangle$ such that there exists an arrow $f \colon \omega \to \omega'$ such that $a = D_f(a')$.

Thus, we have seen that the choice of presheaves for the counterpart semantics is quite natural, but it comes with some restrictions: one of the main reasons why such semantics has been introduced is not only to avoid the increasing domain condition, but more generally to avoid the constraint that every individual of a world w has to admit a counterpart in every world connected to w. Presheaves are not subject to the increasing domain condition but if we consider a temporal development $f: \omega \rightarrow \sigma$, and being D_f a total function, we have that for every individual of D_σ there exists a counterpart in D_ω. This forces that an individual t living of the world σ *necessarily has a counterpart in the world ω* with respect to the development $f: \omega \rightarrow \sigma$. To fully abstract the idea of counterpart semantics in categorical logic and the notion of counterpart frame, we have to consider the case in which $D_f: D_\sigma \rightleftharpoons D_\tau$ is an arbitrary relation. Therefore, in this context an element $\langle a, b \rangle \in D_f$ can be read as *a is the future counterpart of b with respect the development f*. We recall now the notion of *relational presheaf* [18,35].

Definition 10. *A **relational presheaf** is a functor $V: C^{\mathrm{op}} \rightarrow \mathbf{Rel}$ for $\mathbf{Rel}$ the category of sets and relations.*

The generality of relational presheaves allows to deal with *partial functions*, thus avoiding the difficult situations we previously described. Indeed, as observed in [16], relational presheaves form a category with finite limits if as morphisms we consider the families of set functions $\psi := \{f_\sigma: V_\sigma \rightarrow U_\sigma\}_{\sigma \in C}$ such that for every $g: \sigma \rightarrow \rho$ of the base category, if $\langle t, s \rangle \in V_g$ then $\langle f_\rho(t), f_\sigma(s) \rangle \in U_g$ where $s \in V_\sigma$ and $t \in V_\rho$. Such a choice for morphisms of relational presheaves has become standard, and we refer to [16,29,36] or to [35, Definition 3.3.3], where this kind of morphisms are called generalised rp-morphisms. Here we simply call them **relational morphisms**, and we denote by $[\mathcal{W}^{\mathrm{op}}, \mathbf{Rel}]$ the category of relational presheaves and relational morphisms, again following the notation used in [16]. Having seen the link between counterpart frames and relational presheaves, we now introduce the new notion of counterpart $\mathcal{W}$-model and we explain how this is a categorification of the counterpart models in [11].

Definition 11. *Let Σ be a many-sorted signature. A **counterpart $\mathcal{W}$-model** is a triple $\mathfrak{T} = (\mathcal{W}, \mathfrak{S}_\Sigma, \mathfrak{F}_\Sigma)$ such that $\mathcal{W}$ is a category of worlds, $\mathfrak{S}_\Sigma := \{|\tau|^{\mathfrak{T}}: \mathcal{W}^{\mathrm{op}} \rightarrow \mathbf{Rel}\}_{\tau \in S_\Sigma}$ is a set of relational presheaves on $\mathcal{W}$, and $\mathfrak{F}_\Sigma := \{\mathcal{I}(f_\Sigma): |\tau_1|^{\mathfrak{T}} \times \cdots \times |\tau_m|^{\mathfrak{T}} \rightarrow |\tau|^{\mathfrak{T}}\}_{f_\Sigma \in F_\Sigma}$ is a set of relational morphisms.*

Definition 12. *Let Σ be a many-sorted signature and $\mathcal{W}$ a category. We define the **category of counterpart $\mathcal{W}$-models**, denoted by $\mathrm{count}\text{-}\mathcal{W}\text{-}\mathrm{model}(\Sigma)$, as the category whose objects are counterpart $\mathcal{W}$-models $\mathfrak{T}$ and whose morphisms $F: \mathfrak{T} \rightarrow \mathfrak{T}'$ are families of morphisms $F := \{F_\tau: |\tau|^{\mathfrak{T}} \rightarrow |\tau|^{\mathfrak{T}'}\}_{\tau \in S_\Sigma}$ of relational presheaves, commuting with the relational morphisms of $\mathfrak{F}_\Sigma$ and $\mathfrak{F}'_\Sigma$, i.e. $F_\tau \circ \mathcal{I}(f_\Sigma) = \mathcal{I}'(f_\Sigma) \circ (F_{\tau_1} \times \cdots \times F_{\tau_m})$ for every function symbols $f_\Sigma: \tau_1 \times \cdots \times \tau_m \rightarrow \tau \in F_\Sigma$ of the signature.*

The notion of counterpart $\mathcal{W}$-model admits a clear interpretation from the categorical perspective of functorial semantics. Observe that, by definition, a counterpart $\mathcal{W}$-model $\mathfrak{T} = (\mathcal{W}, \mathfrak{S}_\Sigma, \mathfrak{F}_\Sigma)$ assigns to a sort τ of the signature Σ a relational presheaf $|\tau|^{\mathfrak{T}}: \mathcal{W}^{\mathrm{op}} \rightarrow \mathbf{Rel}$ and to a function symbol f_Σ a relational morphism $\mathcal{I}(f_\Sigma): |\tau_1|^{\mathfrak{T}} \times \cdots \times |\tau_m|^{\mathfrak{T}} \rightarrow |\tau|^{\mathfrak{T}}$. Thus a counterpart $\mathcal{W}$-model can be represented as a functor $F_W\colon \mathsf{Con}(\Sigma) \to [\mathcal{W}^{\mathrm{op}}, \mathbf{Rel}]$ preserving finite products from the syntactic category $\mathsf{Con}(\Sigma)$, see Definition 6, into the category of $\mathcal{W}$-presheaves.

Similarly, every such functor $F_W\colon \mathsf{Con}(\Sigma) \to [\mathcal{W}^{\mathrm{op}}, \mathbf{Rel}]$ induces a counterpart $\mathcal{W}$-model. It is thus straightforward to check that the following result holds.

Theorem 1. *Let $\mathcal{W}$ be a category. The category of counterpart $\mathcal{W}$-models is equivalent to the category* $\mathsf{FP}(\mathsf{Con}(\Sigma), [\mathcal{W}^{\mathrm{op}}, \mathbf{Rel}])$ *of finite product preserving functors and natural transformations from the syntactic category* $\mathsf{Con}(\Sigma)$ *over Σ to the category* $[\mathcal{W}^{\mathrm{op}}, \mathbf{Rel}]$ *of relational presheaves over $\mathcal{W}$.*

Note that if we want to recover in our framework the original idea behind the notion of counterpart models introduced in [11], i.e., that every world is sent to a Σ-algebra, we just need to consider counterpart $\mathcal{W}$-models $\mathfrak{T} = (\mathcal{W}, \mathfrak{S}_\Sigma, \mathfrak{F}_\Sigma)$ where every relational presheaf of $\mathfrak{S}_\Sigma$ sends a morphism $f\colon \omega \to \sigma$ of the category $\mathcal{W}$ to a relation $|\tau|_f^{\mathfrak{T}}\colon |\tau|_\sigma^{\mathfrak{T}} \rightleftharpoons |\tau|_\omega^{\mathfrak{T}}$ whose converse relation $(|\tau|_f^{\mathfrak{T}})^\dagger\colon |\tau|_\omega^{\mathfrak{T}} \rightleftharpoons |\tau|_\sigma^{\mathfrak{T}}$ is a partial function. In particular, the following two results provide the link between counterpart models in the sense of [11] (see Definition 9) and counterpart $\mathcal{W}$-models.

Proposition 1. *Let $\mathfrak{T} := (\mathcal{W}, \mathfrak{S}_\Sigma, \mathfrak{F}_\Sigma)$ be a counterpart $\mathcal{W}$-model. If every relational presheaf of $\mathfrak{S}_\Sigma$ sends an arrow $f\colon \omega \to \sigma$ of $\mathcal{W}$ to a relation $|\tau|_f^{\mathfrak{T}}\colon |\tau|_\sigma^{\mathfrak{T}} \rightleftharpoons |\tau|_\omega^{\mathfrak{T}}$ whose converse relation $(|\tau|_f^{\mathfrak{T}})^\dagger\colon |\tau|_\omega^{\mathfrak{T}} \rightleftharpoons |\tau|_\sigma^{\mathfrak{T}}$ is a partial function, then the triple $\mathfrak{M}_\mathfrak{T} := \langle W_\mathfrak{T}, \rightsquigarrow_\mathfrak{T}, d_\mathfrak{T}\rangle$ is a counterpart model, where*

- *the set of worlds is given by the objects of the category $\mathcal{W}$, i.e. $W_\mathfrak{T} = \mathrm{ob}(\mathcal{W})$,*
- *$d_\mathfrak{T}\colon W_\mathfrak{T} \to \mathcal{A}$ is a function assigning to every $\omega \in W_\mathfrak{T}$ the Σ-algebra $d_\mathfrak{T}(\omega) := (A_\omega, F_\Sigma^{A_\omega})$ with $A_\omega := \bigcup_{\tau \in S_\Sigma}\{|\tau|_\omega^{\mathfrak{T}}\}$ and $F_\Sigma^{A_\omega} := \bigcup_{f_\Sigma \in F_\Sigma}\{\mathcal{I}(f_\Sigma)_\omega\}$,*
- *for every $f\colon \omega \to \sigma$ of $\mathcal{W}$ we have $(\omega, cr_f, \sigma) \in\rightsquigarrow_\mathfrak{T}$ with the function $cr_f : d_\mathfrak{T}(\omega) \rightharpoonup d_\mathfrak{T}(\sigma)$ defined on $a \in |\tau|_\sigma^{\mathfrak{T}}$ as $cr_f(a) := (|\tau|_f^{\mathfrak{T}})^\dagger(a)$.*

Notice that in the previous proposition the only property to check is that every cr_f is a partial homomorphism of Σ-algebras, which follows from each $\mathcal{I}(f_\Sigma)$ being a relational morphism. Similarly, one can directly check the dual result.

Proposition 2. *Let Σ be a many-sorted signature and $\mathfrak{M} := \langle W, \rightsquigarrow, d\rangle$ a counterpart model. Then the triple $\mathfrak{T}_\mathfrak{M} = (\mathcal{W}, \mathfrak{S}_\Sigma, \mathfrak{F}_\Sigma)$ is a counterpart $\mathcal{W}$-model, where*

- *the category $\mathcal{W}$ has the worlds of W as objects and as arrows those obtained by defining for every $(\omega_1, cr, \omega_2) \in\rightsquigarrow$ a generating arrow $cr\colon \omega_1 \to \omega_2$,*
- *for every sort τ of S_Σ we define the relational presheaf $|\tau|^{\mathfrak{T}_\mathfrak{M}}\colon \mathcal{W}^{\mathrm{op}} \to \mathbf{Rel}$ by the assignment $|\tau|_\omega^{\mathfrak{T}_\mathfrak{M}} := d(\omega)_\tau$ and for every generating $cr\colon \omega_1 \to \omega_2$ of $\mathcal{W}$ by $|\tau|_\omega^{\mathfrak{T}_\mathfrak{M}} := (cr)_\tau^\dagger$,*
- *for every function $f_\Sigma\colon \tau_1 \times \cdots \times \tau_m \to \tau$ of F_Σ we define the relational morphism $\mathcal{I}(f_\Sigma)\colon |\tau_1|^{\mathfrak{T}_\mathfrak{M}} \times \cdots \times |\tau_m|^{\mathfrak{T}_\mathfrak{M}} \to |\tau|^{\mathfrak{T}_\mathfrak{M}}$ by the assignment $\mathcal{I}(f_\Sigma)_\omega := f_\Sigma^{d(\omega)}$.*

Remark 1. Let Σ be a many-sorted signature and $\mathfrak{M} := \langle W, \rightsquigarrow, d\rangle$ a counterpart model. Note that if we first construct the counterpart $\mathcal{W}$-model $\mathfrak{T}_\mathfrak{M}$ employing Proposition 2, and then the counterpart model $\mathfrak{M}_{(\mathfrak{T}_\mathfrak{M})}$ employing Proposition 1, we have that the counterpart model $\mathfrak{M}_{(\mathfrak{T}_\mathfrak{M})}$ may be different from $\mathfrak{M}$. As it will be shown in Theorem 2, when considering *temporal* structures such a difference will be irrelevant, from a semantic point of view.

Example 2. Let us consider the signature $\Sigma_{Gr} := (S_{Gr}, F_{Gr})$ for directed graphs from Example 1. Recall that the set S_{Gr} consists of the sorts of nodes τ_N and edges τ_E, while the set F_{Gr} consists of the function symbols $s, t : \tau_E \to \tau_N$, which determine, respectively, the source and the target node of an edge. In this case, a Σ_{Gr}-algebra G is a directed graph and a homomorphism of Σ_{Gr}-algebras is exactly a (partial) morphism of directed graphs. The notion of counterpart $\mathcal{W}$-model allows us to provide a categorical presentation of the semantics in [11]. In this case, a counterpart $\mathcal{W}$-model $\mathfrak{T}_{Gr} = (\mathcal{W}, \mathfrak{S}_{\Sigma_{Gr}}, \mathfrak{F}_{\Sigma_{Gr}})$ consists of

- a category of worlds $\mathcal{W}$,
- $\mathfrak{S}_{\Sigma_{Gr}} = \{|\tau_N|^{\mathfrak{T}}, |\tau_E|^{\mathfrak{T}}\}$, where $|\tau_N|^{\mathfrak{T}}$ and $|\tau_E|^{\mathfrak{T}}$ are relational presheaves on the category $\mathcal{W}$ of worlds such that $(|\tau_N|^{\mathfrak{T}}_f)^\dagger$ and $(|\tau_E|^{\mathfrak{T}}_f)^\dagger$ are partial functions for every $f : \omega \to \sigma$ of $\mathcal{W}$,
- $\mathfrak{F}_{\Sigma_{Gr}} = \{\mathcal{I}(s), \mathcal{I}(t)\}$, where $\mathcal{I}(s) : |\tau_E|^{\mathfrak{T}} \to |\tau_N|^{\mathfrak{T}}$ and $\mathcal{I}(t) : |\tau_E|^{\mathfrak{T}} \to |\tau_N|^{\mathfrak{T}}$ are morphisms of relational presheaves.

As anticipated in Proposition 1, this recasts the notion of counterpart model in [11]. Thus, given the model $\mathfrak{T}_{Gr}$, we have again that every ω is mapped to a directed graph $d(\omega) := (|\tau_N|^{\mathfrak{T}}_\omega, |\tau_E|^{\mathfrak{T}}_\omega, \mathcal{I}(s)_\omega, \mathcal{I}(t)_\omega)$ identified by the set of nodes $|\tau_N|^{\mathfrak{T}}_\omega$, the set of arcs $|\tau_E|^{\mathfrak{T}}_\omega$, and the functions $\mathcal{I}(s)_\omega, \mathcal{I}(t)_\omega : |\tau_E|^{\mathfrak{T}}_\omega \to |\tau_N|^{\mathfrak{T}}_\omega$. Moreover, every morphism $f : \omega \to \sigma$ of the category $\mathcal{W}$ induces a *partial homomorphism* of directed graphs $cr_f : d(\omega) \rightharpoonup d(\sigma)$ given by $cr_f := ((|\tau_N|^{\mathfrak{T}}_f)^\dagger, (|\tau_E|^{\mathfrak{T}}_f)^\dagger)$.

Example 3. Let us consider again the signature $\Sigma_{Gr} := (S_{Gr}, F_{Gr})$ for directed graphs, and consider the three graphs depicted in Fig. 1. In this case we consider a category $\mathcal{W}$ whose objects are three worlds ω_0, ω_1, and ω_2 and the morphisms are generated by the compositions of four arrows

$$\omega_0 \xrightarrow{f_0} \omega_1 \underset{f_2}{\overset{f_1}{\rightrightarrows}} \omega_2 \xrightarrow{f_3} \omega_2.$$

The relational presheaves of nodes and edges are given by the assignment

- $|\tau_N|^{\mathfrak{T}}_{\omega_i} := N_{\mathbf{G}_i}$, where $N_{\mathbf{G}_i}$ is the set of nodes of the graph $\mathbf{G}_i$;
- $|\tau_N|^{\mathfrak{T}}_{f_0} := \{(n_3, n_0), (n_4, n_1), (n_3, n_2)\} \subseteq N_{\mathbf{G}_1} \times N_{\mathbf{G}_0}$;
- $|\tau_N|^{\mathfrak{T}}_{f_1} := \{(n_5, n_3), (n_5, n_4)\} \subseteq N_{\mathbf{G}_2} \times N_{\mathbf{G}_1}$;
- $|\tau_N|^{\mathfrak{T}}_{f_2} := \{(n_5, n_3), (n_5, n_4)\} \subseteq N_{\mathbf{G}_2} \times N_{\mathbf{G}_1}$;
- $|\tau_N|^{\mathfrak{T}}_{f_3} := \{(n_5, n_5)\} \subseteq N_{\mathbf{G}_2} \times N_{\mathbf{G}_2}$.
- $|\tau_E|^{\mathfrak{T}}_{\omega_i} := E_{\mathbf{G}_i}$, where $E_{\mathbf{G}_i}$ is the set of edges of the graph $\mathbf{G}_i$;
- $|\tau_E|^{\mathfrak{T}}_{f_0} := \{(e_3, e_0), (e_4, e_1)\} \subseteq E_{\mathbf{G}_1} \times E_{\mathbf{G}_0}$;
- $|\tau_E|^{\mathfrak{T}}_{f_1} := \{(e_5, e_3)\} \subseteq E_{\mathbf{G}_2} \times E_{\mathbf{G}_1}$;
- $|\tau_E|^{\mathfrak{T}}_{f_2} := \{(e_5, e_4)\} \subseteq E_{\mathbf{G}_2} \times E_{\mathbf{G}_1}$;
- $|\tau_E|^{\mathfrak{T}}_{f_3} := \{(e_5, e_5)\} \subseteq E_{\mathbf{G}_2} \times E_{\mathbf{G}_2}$.

Natural transformations $\mathcal{I}(s)$ and $\mathcal{I}(t)$ are the domain and codomain maps. Note that $(|\tau_N|^{\mathfrak{T}}_{f_i})^\dagger$ and $(|\tau_E|^{\mathfrak{T}}_{f_i})^\dagger$ are partial functions for $i = 0 \dots 3$, hence we are under the hypotheses of Proposition 1. Thus, following the assignment of Example 2, a counterpart model $\langle W, \leadsto, d \rangle$ corresponds to the counterpart $\mathcal{W}$-model, and we have that $d(\omega_i) = \mathbf{G}_i$, and cr_{f_i} can be represented graphically as

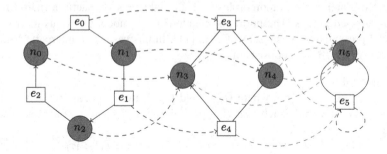

Fig. 2. A counterpart model with three sequential worlds

The counterpart model in Fig. 2 illustrates two executions for our running example. They illustrate the main features of our logic, as presented in the next sections. The counterpart relations (drawn with dotted lines and colours to distinguish cr_{f_1} from cr_{f_2}) indicates that at each transition one edge is discarded and its source and target nodes are merged. For example, the transition $cr_{f_0} := ((\lvert \tau_N \rvert_{f_0}^{\mathfrak{T}})^\dagger, (\lvert \tau_E \rvert_{f_0}^{\mathfrak{T}})^\dagger)$ deletes edge e_2 and merges nodes n_0 and n_2 into n_3. Similarly for cr_{f_1} and cr_{f_2}, while cr_{f_3} is a cycle preserving both e_5 and n_5, denoting that the system is idle, yet alive.

3.2 Relational Power-Set Presheaf

The category of presheaves is a topos, and hence it is rich enough to deal with higher-order features, since it admits *power objects*, which are generalisation of standard power sets to an arbitrary category with finite limits. Unfortunately, relational presheaves rarely have such a structure [30]. Indeed, the category **Set** is a topos while the category of sets and relations **Rel** is just an *allegory* [10], and, as the slogan says, *allegories are to binary relations between sets as categories are to functions between sets*.

However, one could employ relational presheaves for higher-order features using the structure of *power allegory* of the category of relations. For the formal definition and the proof that **Rel** is a power allegory we refer the reader to [10, Proposition 2.414], while now we briefly discuss how one can define the *power-set relational presheaf* $P(V) \colon \mathcal{C}^{\text{op}} \to \mathbf{Rel}$ of a given presheaf $V \colon \mathcal{C}^{\text{op}} \to \mathbf{Rel}$.

To this aim we employ the equivalence between relations and Galois connections (or maps) on power-sets [14], i.e. the equivalence between **Rel** and $\mathrm{Map}(\mathbf{Pow})$, where the latter category is that whose objects are power-sets and whose morphisms are maps. Recall from [14, Example 2] that once we have a relation $R \colon A \rightleftharpoons B$, we can define a function $P_R \colon P(B) \to P(A)$ (preserving arbitrary unions) by assigning $P_R(S) := \{a \in A \mid \exists b \in S : aRb\}$ to every subset $S \subseteq B$. Moreover, given the equivalence $\mathbf{Rel} \equiv \mathrm{Map}(\mathbf{Pow})$, and using the fact that $\mathbf{Pow} = (\mathbf{Pow}^{\text{op}})^{\text{op}}$, we can conclude that the assignment $R \mapsto P_R$ preserves compositions and identities.

Definition 13. *Let* $V : \mathcal{C}^{\mathrm{op}} \to \mathbf{Rel}$ *be a relational presheaf. The* **relational power-set presheaf** $\mathrm{P}(V) : \mathcal{C}^{\mathrm{op}} \to \mathbf{Rel}$ *is the functor defined as*

- *for every object* $\sigma \in \mathcal{C}$, $\mathrm{P}(V)(\sigma)$ *is the power-set of* V_σ,
- *for every arrow* $f : \sigma \to \omega$ *of* $\mathcal{C}$ *the relation* $\mathrm{P}(V)_f : \mathrm{P}(V)_\omega \rightleftharpoons \mathrm{P}(V)_\sigma$ *is defined as* $\mathrm{P}(V)_f := P_{V_f}$.

The relational presheaf $\mathrm{P}(V) : \mathcal{C}^{\mathrm{op}} \to \mathbf{Rel}$ is thus an ordinary presheaf over **Set**. Finally, given a relational presheaf $V : \mathcal{C}^{\mathrm{op}} \to \mathbf{Rel}$ we define the *epsiloff relational presheaf* $\in_V : \mathcal{C}^{\mathrm{op}} \to \mathbf{Rel}$.

Definition 14. *Let* $V : \mathcal{C}^{\mathrm{op}} \to \mathbf{Rel}$ *be a relational presheaf. The* **epsiloff relational presheaf** *is the functor* $\in_V : \mathcal{C}^{\mathrm{op}} \to \mathbf{Rel}$ *defined as*

- *for every* $\sigma \in \mathcal{C}$, $\in_V (\sigma) := \{(a, A) \in V_\sigma \times \mathrm{P}(V)_\sigma \mid a \in A\}$,
- *for every* $f : \sigma \to \omega$, $(\in_V)_f$ *is the relation given by* $\langle (b, B), (a, A) \rangle \in (\in_V)_f$ *if* $\langle b, a \rangle \in V_f$ *and* $\mathrm{P}(V)_f(B) = A$ *where* $B \subseteq V_\omega$ *and* $A \subseteq V_\sigma$.

We now have in place all the pieces that are needed for the semantics of our logic.

4 Syntax of Quantified Temporal Logic

Before presenting the syntax of our logic, we consider a set of second-order variables $\chi \in \mathcal{X}$, where a variable χ_τ with sort $\tau \in S_\Sigma$ ranges over sets of elements of sort τ. We introduce our syntax employing a sort of *positive normal form*. It is a standard presentation for linear temporal logics: it includes derived operators to have negation applied only to atomic propositions, thus allowing to capture negation in terms of set complements. As we will see, to properly tackle existential quantification, we will also require a non-standard *not-next* operator.

Definition 15. *Let* Σ *be a many-sorted signature,* X *a set of first-order variables, and* $\mathcal{X}$ *a set of second-order variables, both typed over* S_Σ. *The set* $\mathcal{F}_\Sigma$ *of formulae of our temporal logic is generated by the rules*

$$\phi := \mathsf{tt} \mid \varepsilon \in_\tau \chi \mid \neg\phi,$$

$$\psi := \phi \mid \psi \vee \psi \mid \psi \wedge \psi \mid \exists_\tau x.\phi \mid \exists_\tau \chi.\psi \mid \forall_\tau x.\phi \mid \forall_\tau \chi.\psi \mid \mathsf{O}\psi \mid \mathsf{nO}\psi \mid \psi_1 \mathsf{U}\psi_2 \mid \psi_1 \mathsf{W}\psi_2.$$

Note that $\in_\tau$ is a family of membership predicates typed over S_Σ indicating that the evaluation of a term ε with sort τ belongs to the evaluation of a second-order variable χ with the same sort τ. The *next* operator O provides a way of asserting that something has to be true after every step, i.e. $\mathsf{O}\phi$ means that ϕ has to hold at the next state. The *not-next* operator nO provides a way of asserting that something has to be false at every next step of length one, i.e. $\mathsf{nO}\phi$ means that ϕ does not hold at the next state. The *until* operator U is explained as follows: $\phi_1 \mathsf{U}\phi_2$ means that ϕ_1 has to hold at least until ϕ_2 becomes true, which must hold at the current or a future position. The operator $\psi_1 \mathsf{W}\psi_2$ denotes the *weak until operator*, meaning that ψ_2 may never hold true.

We will often use ff for $\neg$tt. The *sometimes* modality $\Diamond$ is obtained as $\Diamond\phi := $ ttUϕ and the *always* modality $\Box$ as $\Box\psi := \psi$Wff. The typed equality $\varepsilon_1 =_\tau \varepsilon_2$ can be derived as $\forall_\tau\chi.(\varepsilon_1 \in_\tau \chi \leftrightarrow \varepsilon_2 \in_\tau \chi)$, and we write $x \neq_\tau y$ for $\exists_\tau\chi.(x \in_\tau \chi \wedge y \notin_\tau \chi)$.

As usual, we consider formulae in context, defined as $[\Gamma, \Delta]\ \phi$, where ϕ is a formula of $\mathcal{F}_\Sigma$, Γ is a first-order context and Δ is a second-order context.

Example 4. Consider again the graph signature, the counterpart model of Fig. 2, and the predicates $\mathbf{present}_\tau(x) := \exists_\tau y.x =_\tau y$ regarding the presence of an entity with sort τ in a world (the typing is usually omitted). Combining this with the next operator, we can for example speak about elements that are present at the given world and that will be present at the next step, i.e. $\mathbf{present}_\tau(x) \wedge \mathsf{O}(\mathbf{present}_\tau(x))$. Similarly, we can speak about elements that are present at a given world, but that are always deleted at very next step, i.e. $\mathbf{present}_\tau(x) \wedge \mathsf{nO}(\mathbf{present}_\tau(x))$. The formula $\Box(\mathbf{present}_{\tau_E}(x))$ means that for all the evolutions of our systems there exists at least an edge. The formula $\exists_{\tau_N} x.(((x \neq y) \wedge \mathsf{O}(x = y))$ means that given a node y there exists another different node that will be identified with y at the next step. Finally, the formula $\Box(\exists_{\tau_E} e.s(e) = x \wedge t(e) = y)$ means that the nodes x and y will always be connected by an edge.

5   Temporal Structures and Semantics

The notion of *hyperdoctrine* was introduced by Lawvere in a series of seminal papers [25, 26] to provide a categorical framework for first order logic. In recent years, this notion has been generalised in several settings, for example introducing elementary and existential doctrines [28, 37] and modal hyperdoctrines [5]. In particular, in [17, 18] modal hyperdoctrines are introduced employing the notion of *attribute* associated to a presheaf as a categorification of the modal semantics. We start recalling the notion of set of classical attributes, and then we show how by simply fixing a class of morphisms of the base category of a presheaf, we can construct the main temporal operators.

Definition 16. *Let* $V: \mathcal{W}^{\mathrm{op}} \to \mathbf{Rel}$ *be a relational presheaf. We define the set* $T(V) := \{\{A_\omega\}_{\omega\in\mathcal{W}} \mid A_\omega \subseteq V_\omega\}$ *whose objects are called* **classical attributes**.

The set of classical attributes has the structure of a complete boolean algebra with respect to inclusion. Moreover, a morphism $f: V \to U$ of relational presheaves induces a morphism of boolean algebras $f^*: T(U) \to T(V)$ between sets of classical attributes. This action is given by pulling back world-by-world, i.e. for $A \in T(U)$ computing the pullback for every ω and defining $f^*(A) := \{f^*_\omega(A_\omega)\}_{\omega\in\mathcal{W}} \in T(V)$ for each $A \in T(U)$.

Given a relational presheaf $V: \mathcal{W}^{\mathrm{op}} \to \mathbf{Rel}$, a classical attribute $A = \{A_\omega\}_{\omega\in\mathcal{W}}$ of $T(V)$, and an element $s \in V_\omega$, we use the validity notation $s \vDash^V_\omega A$ to mean that $s \in A_\omega$. Therefore, writing $s \vDash^V_\omega A$ means that at the world or instant ω, an individual s of V_ω satisfies the property A.

Definition 17. *A* **temporal structure** *on a category* $\mathcal{W}$ *is a class* T *of arrows of* $\mathcal{W}$.

Given a relational presheaf $V\colon \mathcal{W}^{\mathrm{op}} \to \mathbf{Rel}$, the idea is that the class T represents the *atomic processes* or the *indecomposable operations* of $\mathcal{W}$. Each of them represent a single evolution step of the system at heand, and as such they are used for the encoding of the next step operator.

Definition 18. *Let* T *be a temporal structure on a category* $\mathcal{W}$ *and* ω *an object of* T. *We denote by* $\mathrm{path}(\mathrm{T}, \omega)$ *the class of sequences* $t := (t_1, t_2, t_3, \dots)$ *of arrows such that* $t_n \in T$ *for every* $n \geq 1$ *and such that* $\mathrm{dom}(t_1) = \omega$ *and* $\mathrm{cod}(t_i) = \mathrm{dom}(t_{i+1})$ *for every* $i \geq 1$.

Definition 19. *Let* T *be a temporal structure on a category* $\mathcal{W}$, $V\colon \mathcal{W}^{\mathrm{op}} \to \mathbf{Rel}$ *a relational presheaf,* $s \in V_\omega$ *and* $t\colon \omega \to \sigma$ *an arrow of* $\mathcal{W}$. *We denote by* $\mathrm{count}_t^\sigma(s) :=$ $\{z \in V_\sigma \mid \langle z, s \rangle \in V_t\}$ *the set of **counterparts** of* s *at* σ *with respect to* t.

Given a sequence $t := (t_1, t_2, t_3, \dots)$ we denote by $t_{\leq i}$ the arrow $t_i t_{i-1} \cdots t_1$. Moreover we denote $\omega_i := \mathrm{cod}(t_i)$. The intuition is that the arrows in $\mathrm{path}(\mathrm{T}, \omega)$ represents the T-*evolutions of* the state ω. The choice of the name *temporal structure* recalls that by simply fixing a class T, we can define operators O, nO, U, and W on the complete boolean algebra $\mathcal{T}(V)$ of classical attributes.

Definition 20. *Let* T *be a temporal structure on a category* $\mathcal{W}$ *and* $V\colon \mathcal{W}^{\mathrm{op}} \to \mathbf{Rel}$ *a relational presheaf. Then for every* $s \in V_\omega$ *and* $A := \{A_\omega\}_{\omega \in \mathcal{W}}$ *of* $\mathcal{T}(V)$ *we define*

- $s \vDash_\omega^V O(A)$ *if for every arrow* $t\colon \omega \to \sigma$ *of* T, *the set* $\mathrm{count}_t(s)$ *is non-empty and for every* $z \in \mathrm{count}_t^\sigma(s)$ *we have* $z \vDash_\sigma^V A$;
- $s \vDash_\omega^V nO(A)$ *if for every arrow* $t\colon \omega \to \sigma$ *of* T, *the set* $\mathrm{count}_t(s)$ *is empty or for every* $z \in \mathrm{count}_t^\sigma(s)$ *we have* $z \vDash_\sigma^V X \setminus A$, *where* $V \setminus A := \{V_\omega \setminus A_\omega\}_{\omega \in \mathcal{W}}$ *is the attribute given by the set-theoretical complements of* A *in* V.
- $s \vDash_\omega^V A \mathrm{U} B$ *if for every* $t \in \mathrm{path}(T, \omega)$ *there exists* $\bar{n}$ *such that for every* $i < \bar{n}$ *the set counterparts* $\mathrm{count}_{t_{\leq i}}^{\omega_i}(s)$ *is non-empty and for every* $z \in \mathrm{count}_{t_{\leq i}}^{\omega_i}(s)$ *we have* $z \vDash_{\omega_i}^V A$. *Moreover, the set* $\mathrm{count}_{t_{\leq \bar{n}}}^{\omega_{\bar{n}}}(s)$ *is non-empty and for every* $\bar{z} \in \mathrm{count}_{t_{\leq \bar{n}}}^{\omega_{\bar{n}}}(s)$ *we have* $\bar{z} \vDash_{\omega_{\bar{n}}}^V B$.
- $s \vDash_\omega^V A \mathrm{W} B$ *if for every* $t \in \mathrm{path}(T, \omega)$, *we have that for every* i *the set* $\mathrm{count}_{t_{\leq i}}^{\omega_i}(s)$ *is non-empty and for every* $z \in \mathrm{count}_{t_{\leq i}}^{\omega_i}(s)$ $z \vDash_{\omega_i}^V A$ *or there exists* $\bar{n}$ *such that for every* $i < \bar{n}$ *the set counterparts* $\mathrm{count}_{t_{\leq i}}^{\omega_i}(s)$ *is non-empty, for every* $z \in \mathrm{count}_{t_{\leq i}}^{\omega_i}(s)$ *we have* $z \vDash_{\omega_i}^V A$ *and the set* $\mathrm{count}_{t_{\leq \bar{n}}}^{\omega_{\bar{n}}}(s)$ *is non-empty and for every* $\bar{z} \in \mathrm{count}_{t_{\leq \bar{n}}}^{\omega_{\bar{n}}}(s)$ *we have* $\bar{z} \vDash_{\omega_{\bar{n}}}^V B$.

Recall that given a relational presheaf $V\colon \mathcal{W}^{\mathrm{op}} \to \mathbf{Rel}$, the top element of $\mathcal{T}(V)$ is given by the attributes $\top = \{V_\omega\}_{\omega \in \mathcal{W}}$ and bottom element by $\bot = \{\emptyset_\omega\}_{\omega \in \mathcal{W}}$ since the order of $\mathcal{T}(V)$ is given by the inclusion of sets. Thus, employing the previous notions, we can define the operators $\Diamond A$ and $\Box A$ as $\Diamond A := \top \mathrm{U} A$ and $\Box A := A \mathrm{W} \bot$.

Example 5. We already noted that a counterpart model, as defined in Definition 9, is an instance of a labelled transition system (LTS), i.e. a triple $(S, L, \to)$, where S is a non-empty set of *states*, L is the set of *labels*, and $\to \subseteq S \times L \times S$ is a relation, which is total in the first component, i.e. for every $s \in S$ there exists a label $l \in L$ and a state s' such that $(s, l, s') \in \rightarrow$. Therefore, another meaningful choice for the category of worlds and the temporal structure is considering an LTS $(S, L, \rightarrow)$ and the free category $\mathcal{W}(S)$ on it: a temporal structure is given by the set T_S of arrows of the relation $\rightarrow$, where the next time operator O has exactly the meaning of *it holds after every step of length one*.

5.1 Semantics via Temporal Structures

In this section we show how relational presheaves and temporal structures can be employed to obtain models for our quantified temporal logic. Recall that in the semantics of worlds, providing the interpretation of a formula means providing an interpretation of such a formula in every world.

Definition 21. *Let Σ be a many-sorted signature. A* **temporal counterpart $\mathcal{W}$-model** *is a 4-tuple $\mathfrak{T} := (\mathcal{W}, T, \mathfrak{S}_\Sigma, \mathfrak{F}_\Sigma)$ such that the triple $(\mathcal{W}, \mathfrak{S}_\Sigma, \mathfrak{F}_\Sigma)$ is a counterpart $\mathcal{W}$-model and T is a temporal structure on $\mathcal{W}$.*

Now, the presence of a temporal structure in the definition of temporal counterpart model allows us to refine Proposition 1 and Proposition 2 in the context of temporal $\mathcal{W}$-counterpart models. We then to obtain the following correspondence with counterpart models in the sense of [11].

Theorem 2. *There is a bijective correspondence between counterpart models $\langle \mathcal{W}, \rightsquigarrow , d \rangle$ and temporal $\mathcal{W}$-counterpart models $(\mathcal{W}, T, \mathfrak{S}_\Sigma, \mathfrak{F}_\Sigma)$ where $\mathcal{W}$ is freely generated by the set of objects $\mathrm{ob}(\mathcal{W})$ and the arrows in T and a relational presheaf in $\mathfrak{S}_\Sigma$ sends a morphism $f \colon \omega \to \sigma$ of $\mathcal{W}$ to a relation $|\tau|_f^\mathfrak{T} \colon |\tau|_\sigma^\mathfrak{T} \rightleftharpoons |\tau|_\omega^\mathfrak{T}$ whose converse $(|\tau|_f^\mathfrak{T})^\dagger \colon |\tau|_\omega^\mathfrak{T} \rightleftharpoons |\tau|_\sigma^\mathfrak{T}$ is a partial function.*

Proof. The construction of a temporal $\mathcal{W}$-counterpart model from a counterpart model is given exactly as in Proposition 2 with the obvious choice of the temporal structure. What changes is only the definition of a counterpart model from a temporal $\mathcal{W}$-counterpart model. In fact, while in Proposition 1 every arrow $f \colon \omega_1 \to \omega_2$ of the base category induces an element $(\omega_1, cr_f, \omega_2) \in \rightsquigarrow$, if we start from a temporal $\mathcal{W}$-counterpart model as in Theorem 2, we define an elements $(\omega_1, cr_f, \omega_2) \in \rightsquigarrow$ only for those arrows $f \in T$ of the temporal structure. It is direct to check that these two constructions provide a bijective correspondence.

Theorem 2 highlights the role of arrows in T: they are precisely those arrows of $\mathcal{W}$ that are actually relevant. This intuition is going to be made explicit below in the presentation of the semantics.

Now we show how terms-in-context and formulae-in-context are interpreted, noting that by definition of temporal $\mathcal{W}$-counterpart model, the interpretation of sorts, function and relation symbols is fixed. Thus, for the rest of this section we fix a temporal $\mathcal{W}$-counterpart model $\mathfrak{T} = (\mathcal{W}, T, \mathfrak{S}_\Sigma, \mathfrak{F}_\Sigma)$.

First of all, given a first-order context $\Gamma = [x_1 : \tau_1, \ldots, x_n : \tau_n]$, we denote by

$$|\Gamma|^{\mathfrak{T}} := |\tau_1|^{\mathfrak{T}} \times \cdots \times |\tau_n|^{\mathfrak{T}}$$

the relational presheaf associated to context Γ via the counterpart $\mathcal{W}$-model $(\mathcal{W}, \mathfrak{S}_\Sigma, \mathfrak{F}_\Sigma)$. Then, given a second-order context $\Delta = [\chi_1 : \tau_1, \ldots, \chi_m : \tau_m]$, we denote by

$$|\Delta|^{\mathfrak{T}} := \mathrm{P}(|\tau_1|^{\mathfrak{T}}) \times \cdots \times \mathrm{P}(|\tau_m|^{\mathfrak{T}})$$

where $\mathrm{P}(|\tau_i|^{\mathfrak{T}})$ denotes the relational power-set presheaf of $|\tau_i|^{\mathfrak{T}}$, see Definition 13. Thus we define the interpretation $|\Gamma, \Delta|^{\mathfrak{T}} := |\Gamma|^{\mathfrak{T}} \times |\Delta|^{\mathfrak{T}}$.

A term in a context $[\Gamma, \Delta]\ t : \tau$ is interpreted as a morphism of relational presheaves

- if $t = x_i$, then $|t|^{\mathfrak{T}}$ is the projection $\pi_i \colon |\Gamma, \Delta|^{\mathfrak{T}} \to |\tau|^{\mathfrak{T}}$;
- if $t = f(t_1, \ldots, t_k)$, then $|t|^{\mathfrak{T}}$ is $\mathcal{I}(f) \circ \langle |t_1|^{\mathfrak{T}}, \ldots, |t_k|^{\mathfrak{T}} \rangle \colon |\Gamma, \Delta|^{\mathfrak{T}} \to |\tau|^{\mathfrak{T}}$.

The interpretation of a given formula ϕ in a context $[\Gamma]$ has to be defined for each world, in line with the usual Kripke-style semantics. Therefore, the interpretation of $[\Gamma]\ \phi$ is given as a classical attribute

$$[[\Gamma]\ \phi]^{\mathfrak{T}} := \{[[\Gamma]\ \phi]_\omega^{\mathfrak{T}}\}_{\omega \in W}$$

of the relational presheaf $[\Gamma]^{\mathfrak{T}}$, where every $[[\Gamma]\ \phi]_\omega^{\mathfrak{T}}$ is a subset of $|\Gamma|_\omega^{\mathfrak{T}}$. Recall that the notation $|\Gamma|_\omega^{\mathfrak{T}}$ indicates the set given by the evaluation $|\Gamma|^{\mathfrak{T}}$ at ω.

Moreover, we start defining the interpretation of a formula at a given fixed world, and we use induction on the structure on ϕ as usual.

The interpretation of standard formulae at a world ω is given as follows

- $[[\Gamma, \Delta]\ \mathsf{tt}]_\omega^{\mathfrak{T}} := |\Gamma, \Delta|_\omega^{\mathfrak{T}}$;
- $[[\Gamma, \Delta]\ \varepsilon \in_\tau \chi]_\omega^{\mathfrak{T}} := \langle \pi_\varepsilon, \pi_\chi \rangle_\omega^*(\in_{|\tau|^{\mathfrak{T}}}(\omega))$ where $\langle \pi_\varepsilon, \pi_\chi \rangle \colon |[\Gamma, \Delta]|^{\mathfrak{T}} \to |[\varepsilon : \tau, \chi : \tau]|^{\mathfrak{T}}$ are the opportune projections;
- for every ϕ, then $[[\Gamma, \Delta]\ \neg\phi]_\omega^{\mathfrak{T}} := \overline{[\Gamma, \Delta]\ \phi}_\omega^{\mathfrak{T}}$ where $\overline{(-)}$ denotes the set-theoretical complements, i.e. we have $[[\Gamma, \Delta]\ \neg\phi]_\omega^{\mathfrak{T}} := |\Gamma, \Delta|_\omega^{\mathfrak{T}} \setminus [\Gamma, \Delta]\ \phi|_\omega^{\mathfrak{T}}$.

We also have that

- $[[\Gamma, \Delta]\ \psi \vee \psi]_\omega^{\mathfrak{T}} := [[\Gamma, \Delta]\ \psi]_\omega^{\mathfrak{T}} \cup [[\Gamma, \Delta]\ \psi]_\omega^{\mathfrak{T}}$;
- $[[\Gamma, \Delta]\ \psi \wedge \psi]_\omega^{\mathfrak{T}} := [[\Gamma, \Delta]\ \psi]_\omega^{\mathfrak{T}} \cap [[\Gamma, \Delta]\ \psi]_\omega^{\mathfrak{T}}$;
- $[[\Gamma, \Delta]\ \forall_\tau y.\psi]_\omega^{\mathfrak{T}} := \{a \in |\Gamma, \Delta|^{\mathfrak{T}}(\omega)\ |\forall b \in |\tau|_\omega^{\mathfrak{T}}$ we have $(a, b) \in [[\Gamma, y : \tau, \Delta]\ \psi]_\omega^{\mathfrak{T}}\}$;
- $[[\Gamma, \Delta]\ \forall_\tau \chi.\psi]_\omega^{\mathfrak{T}} := \{a \in |\Gamma, \Delta|^{\mathfrak{T}}(\omega)\ |\forall b \in \mathrm{P}(|\tau|^{\mathfrak{T}})(\omega)$ we have $(a, b) \in [[\Gamma, \Delta, \chi : \tau]\ \psi]_\omega^{\mathfrak{T}}\}$;
- $[[\Gamma, \Delta]\ \exists_\tau y.\psi]_\omega^{\mathfrak{T}} := \{a \in |\Gamma, \Delta|^{\mathfrak{T}}(\omega)\ |\exists b \in |\tau|_\omega^{\mathfrak{T}}$ such that $(a, b) \in [[\Gamma, y : \tau, \Delta]\ \psi]_\omega^{\mathfrak{T}}\}$;
- $[[\Gamma, \Delta]\ \exists_\tau \chi.\psi]_\omega^{\mathfrak{T}} := \{a \in |\Gamma, \Delta|^{\mathfrak{T}}(\omega)\ |\exists b \in \mathrm{P}(|\tau|^{\mathfrak{T}})(\omega)$ such that $(a, b) \in [[\Gamma, \Delta, \chi : \tau]\ \psi]_\omega^{\mathfrak{T}}\}$.

Finally, we have the interpretation of formulae in which temporal operators occur

- $[[\Gamma, \Delta]\ \bigcirc\psi]_\omega^{\mathfrak{T}} := \bigcirc[[\Gamma, \Delta]\ \psi]_\omega^{\mathfrak{T}}$;

- $[[\Gamma, \Delta] \ nO\psi|^{\mathfrak{T}}_{\omega} := nO[[\Gamma, \Delta] \ \psi|^{\mathfrak{T}}_{\omega};$
- $[[\Gamma, \Delta] \ \psi U\psi|^{\mathfrak{T}}_{\omega} := [[\Gamma, \Delta] \ \psi|^{\mathfrak{T}}_{\omega} U[[\Gamma, \Delta] \ \psi|^{\mathfrak{T}}_{\omega};$
- $[[\Gamma, \Delta] \ \psi W\psi|^{\mathfrak{T}}_{\omega} := [[\Gamma, \Delta] \ \psi|^{\mathfrak{T}}_{\omega} W[[\Gamma, \Delta] \ \psi|^{\mathfrak{T}}_{\omega};$

where O, nO, U, and W are the operators induced by the temporal structure T.

In particular, We now conclude by employing the correspondence in Theorem 2 to prove that the semantics introduced in [11] and the one we present for temporal counterpart models are equivalent.

Theorem 3. *A formula is satisfied by a counterpart model if and only if it is satisfied by the corresponding temporal W-counterpart model.*

Finally, notice that Theorem 3 holds also in a stronger form, where the satisfiability is required to hold world by world, i.e. a formula is satisfied at a given world by a counterpart model if and only if it is satisfied by the corresponding temporal W-counterpart model at the corresponding world.

Example 6. Temporal W-counterpart models allow us to obtain as an instance the semantics for standard LTL by considering as temporal structure the free category generated by a tree order. In particular, the interpretation of the classical temporal operators O, U, and W coincide with the usual one of LTL.

Example 7. Let us consider our running example of Fig. 2 and the temporal structure given by the morphism $T := \{f_0, f_1, f_2, f_3\}$. Now let us consider the property $[y : \tau_N] \exists_{\tau_N} x.(((x \neq y) \wedge O(x = y))$ presented in Example 4: we have that

- $[[y : \tau_N] \exists_{\tau_N} x.((x \neq y) \wedge O(x = y))|^{\mathfrak{T}}_{\omega_0} = \{n_0, n_2\}$ is the set of nodes of the graph $\mathbf{G}_0$ that will be identified at the next step, i.e. at the world ω_1;
- $[[y : \tau_N] \exists_{\tau_N} x.((x \neq y) \wedge O(x = y))|^{\mathfrak{T}}_{\omega_1} = \{n_3, n_4\}$ is the set of nodes of the graph $\mathbf{G}_1$ that will be identified at the next step, i.e. at the world ω_2;
- $[[y : \tau_N] \exists_{\tau_N} x.((x \neq y) \wedge O(x = y))|^{\mathfrak{T}}_{\omega_2} = \emptyset$ is the set of nodes of the graph $\mathbf{G}_2$ that will be identified at the next step.

Example 8. Recall the toy example presented in the introduction, i.e. the model with two states s_0 and s_1. In order to describe it, consider a one-sorted signature $\Sigma = \{\tau\}$ with no function symbols, and the free category S generated by two arrows $\{f_0: s_0 \rightarrow s_1, f_1: s_1 \rightarrow s_0\}$ and the relational presheaf $D: S^{\mathrm{op}} \rightarrow \mathbf{Rel}$ such that $D_{s_0} = \{i\}$, $D_{s_1} = \emptyset$, and both D_{f_0} and D_{f_1} are the empty relation. Then consider the counterpart model given by $(S, T := \{f_0, f_1\}, D, \emptyset)$. One of the main advantages of the counterpart semantics is the possibility to deal with processes *destroying elements*. In this setting an interesting formula is $[x : \tau] \mathbf{present}(x) \wedge O(O\mathbf{present}(x))$, i.e. meaning that there exists an entity at a given world that has a counterpart after two steps. If we consider its interpretation at world s_0 in the model $(S, \{f_0, f_1\}, D, \emptyset)$, it is direct to check that

$$[[x : \tau] \mathbf{present}(x) \wedge O(O\mathbf{present}(x))|^{\mathfrak{T}}_{s_0} = \emptyset.$$

This is exactly what we expected, since it essentially means that entity i has no counterpart at the world s_0 after two steps, even if it belongs to the world relative to s_0.

Example 9. The creation and destruction of entities has attracted the interest of various authors (see e.g. [9,38]) as a means for reasoning about the allocation and deallocation of resources or processes. Our logic does not offer an explicit mechanism for this purpose. Nevertheless, as we have shown in Example 4, we can easily derive a predicate regarding the presence of an entity in a certain world as $\mathbf{present}_\tau(x)$. Using this predicate together with the next-time modalities O and nO, we can reason about the preservation and deallocation of some entities after one step of evolution of the system as $\mathbf{nextStepPreserved}(x) := \mathbf{present}_\tau(x) \wedge \mathrm{O}(\mathbf{present}_\tau(x))$ and $\mathbf{nextStepDeallocated}(x) := \mathbf{present}_\tau(x) \wedge \mathrm{nO}(\mathbf{present}_\tau(x))$.

Now we provide an interpretation of these two formulae for our running example in Fig. 2 and the temporal structure given by the morphism $\mathrm{T} := \{f_0, f_1, f_2, f_3\}$. Then

- $[\![x : \tau_E]\!]\,\mathbf{nextStepPreserved}(x)|_{\omega_0}^{\mathfrak{T}} = \{e_0, e_1\}$ is the set of edges of $\mathbf{G}_0$ surviving next steps;
- $[\![x : \tau_E]\!]\,\mathbf{nextStepPreserved}(x)|_{\omega_1}^{\mathfrak{T}} = \emptyset$ is the set of edges of $\mathbf{G}_1$ surviving next steps;
- $[\![x : \tau_E]\!]\,\mathbf{nextStepPreserved}(x)|_{\omega_2}^{\mathfrak{T}} = \{e_5\}$ is the set of edges of $\mathbf{G}_2$ surviving next steps.

Notice that $[\![x : \tau_E]\!]\,\mathbf{nextstepPreserved}(x)|_{\omega_1}^{\mathfrak{T}} = \emptyset$ because we have that $d(f_1)$ forgets the arrow e_4, while $d(f_2)$ forgets the arrow e_3. This follows from our definition of the next operator, where we require that a given property has to hold for *every step of length one*. Then, we conclude considering the case of next-step deallocation

- $[\![x : \tau_E]\!]\,\mathbf{nextstepDeallocated}(x)|_{\omega_0}^{\mathfrak{T}} = \{e_2\}$ is the set of edges of $\mathbf{G}_0$ that are deallocated at the next steps;
- $[\![x : \tau_E]\!]\,\mathbf{nextStepDeallocated}(x))|_{\omega_1}^{\mathfrak{T}} = \emptyset$ is the set of edges of $\mathbf{G}_1$ that are deallocated at the next steps;
- $[\![x : \tau_E]\!]\,\mathbf{nextStepDeallocated}(x)|_{\omega_2}^{\mathfrak{T}} = \emptyset$ is the set of edges of $\mathbf{G}_2$ that are deallocated at the next steps.

6   Conclusions and Future Works

In the paper we presented a counterpart semantics for quantified temporal logics that is based on relational presheaves. Starting points were previous works on modal logics, namely the set-theoretical counterpart semantics in [11] and the functional presheaves model for Kripke frames in [16], and indeed they are both recovered in our framework.

Counterpart semantics offers a solution to the trans-world identity problem The use of presheaves allows us to recover it, as well as to model second-order quantification.

The choice of temporal logics asked for some ingenuity in the way to model the next operator, with the introduction of what we called temporal structures, as well as in the treatment of negation, which required the use of a restricted syntax and an operator *not-next*. Our presheaf framework may as well recover the semantics of other temporal logics, and in fact we believe that it is general enough that it could be adapted to many different formalisms: indeed, with respect to our focus on partial ones, relational presheaves allows for a very general notion of morphism between worlds, which could be pivotal for formalisms where non-determinism plays a central role.

From a categorical perspective, our results open two challenging lines for future works. The first one regards deduction systems, which we overlooked since our aims lie more on the verification side [13]: see e.g. [31] for a recent take with respect to counterpart-based semantics for quantified modal logics. Using relational presheaves makes this task tricky to pursue, but it deserves future investigations. The second regards the study of formal criteria for the semantics of quantified temporal logic in the spirit of categorical logic, where models are thought of as opportune morphisms. A possible solution could be presenting temporal models as morphisms of suitable Lawvere doctrines. This is also a non-trivial problem that we will deal with in future work.

References

1. Awodey, S., Kishida, K., Kotzsch, H.: Topos semantics for higher-order temporal modal logic. Logique et Analyse **57**(228), 591–636 (2014)
2. Baldan, P., Corradini, A., König, B., Lluch Lafuente, A.: A temporal graph logic for verification of graph transformation systems. In: Fiadeiro, J.L., Schobbens, P.-Y. (eds.) WADT 2006. LNCS, vol. 4409, pp. 1–20. Springer, Heidelberg (2007). https://doi.org/10.1007/978-3-540-71998-4_1
3. Belardinelli, F.: Quantified Modal Logic and the Ontology of Physical Objects. Ph.D. thesis, Scuola Normale Superiore of Pisa (2006)
4. Blackburn, P., van Benthem, J., Wolter, F. (eds.): Handbook of Modal Logic, North-Holland, vol. 3 (2007)
5. Braüner, T., Ghilardi, S.: First-order modal logic. In: Blackburn et al. [4], pp. 549–620 (2007)
6. Cardelli, L., Gardner, P., Ghelli, G.: A spatial logic for querying graphs. In: Widmayer, P., Eidenbenz, S., Triguero, F., Morales, R., Conejo, R., Hennessy, M. (eds.) ICALP 2002. LNCS, vol. 2380, pp. 597–610. Springer, Heidelberg (2002). https://doi.org/10.1007/3-540-45465-9_51
7. Courcelle, B.: The monadic second-order logic of graphs. I. Recognizable sets of finite graphs. Inf. Comput. **85**(1), 12–75 (1990)
8. Dawar, A., Gardner, P., Ghelli, G.: Expressiveness and complexity of graph logic. Inf. Comput. **205**(3), 263–310 (2007)
9. Distefano, D., Rensink, A., Katoen, J.: Model checking birth and death. In: Baeza-Yates, R., Montanari, U., Santoro, N. (eds.) IFIP TCS 2002. IFIP Conference Proceedings, vol. 223, pp. 435–447. Kluwer (2002)
10. Freyd, P., Scedrov, A.: Categories, Allegories. Elsevier, Amsterdam (1990)
11. Gadducci, F., Lluch Lafuente, A., Vandin, A.: Counterpart semantics for a second-order μ-calculus. Fundamenta Informaticae **118**(1–2), 177–205 (2012)
12. Gadducci, F., Laretto, A., Trotta, D.: Specification and verification of a linear-time temporal logic for graph transformation. In: Poskitt, C.M., Fernandez, M. (eds.) ICGT 2023. LNCS, vol. 13961, pp. 22–42. Springer, Heidelberg (2023). https://doi.org/10.1007/978-3-031-36709-0_2
13. Gadducci, F., Lluch Lafuente, A., Vandin, A.: Exploiting over- and under-approximations for infinite-state counterpart models. In: Ehrig, H., Engels, G., Kreowski, H.-J., Rozenberg, G. (eds.) ICGT 2012. LNCS, vol. 7562, pp. 51–65. Springer, Heidelberg (2012). https://doi.org/10.1007/978-3-642-33654-6_4
14. Gardiner, P., Martin, C., de Moor, O.: An algebraic construction of predicate transformers. Sci. Comput. Program. **22**(1), 21–44 (1994)
15. Garson, J.: Modal logic. In: Zalta, E.N., Nodelman, U. (eds.) The Stanford Encyclopedia of Philosophy. Metaphysics Research Lab, Stanford University, Spring 2023 edn. (2023)

16. Ghilardi, S., Meloni, G.C.: Modal and tense predicate logic: models in presheaves and categorical conceptualization. In: Borceux, F. (ed.) Categorical Algebra and its Applications. LNM, vol. 1348, pp. 130–142. Springer, Heidelberg (1988). https://doi.org/10.1007/BFb0081355

17. Ghilardi, S., Meloni, G.: Relational and topological semantics for temporal and modal predicative logic. In: Corsi, G., Sambin, G. (eds.) Nuovi problemi della logica e della scienza II, pp. 59–77. CLUEB (1990)

18. Ghilardi, S., Meloni, G.: Relational and partial variable sets and basic predicate logic. J. Symb. Logic **61**(3), 843–872 (1996)

19. Giese, H., Maximova, M., Sakizloglou, L., Schneider, S.: Metric temporal graph logic over typed attributed graphs. In: Hähnle, R., van der Aalst, W. (eds.) FASE 2019. LNCS, vol. 11424, pp. 282–298. Springer, Cham (2019). https://doi.org/10.1007/978-3-030-16722-6_16

20. Hazen, A.: Counterpart-theoretic semantics for modal logic. J. Phil. **76**(6), 319–338 (1979)

21. Jacobs, B.: Many-sorted coalgebraic modal logic: a model-theoretic study. RAIRO-Theor. Inf. Appl. **35**, 31–59 (2001)

22. Jacobs, B.: The temporal logic of coalgebras via Galois algebras. Math. Struct. Comput. Sci. **12**(6), 875–903 (2002)

23. Kastenberg, H., Rensink, A.: Model checking dynamic states in GROOVE. In: Valmari, A. (ed.) SPIN 2006. LNCS, vol. 3925, pp. 299–305. Springer, Heidelberg (2006). https://doi.org/10.1007/11691617_19

24. Kupke, C., Pattinson, D.: Coalgebraic semantics of modal logics: an overview. Theor. Comput. Sci. **412**(38), 5070–5094 (2011)

25. Lawvere, F.: Adjointness in foundations. Dialectica **23**, 281–296 (1969)

26. Lawvere, F.W.: Diagonal arguments and cartesian closed categories. In: Category Theory, Homology Theory and their Applications II. LNM, vol. 92, pp. 134–145. Springer, Heidelberg (1969). https://doi.org/10.1007/BFb0080769

27. Lewis, D.: Counterpart theory and quantified modal logic. J. Phil. **65**(5), 113–126 (1968)

28. Maietti, M., Rosolini, G.: Quotient completion for the foundation of constructive mathematics. Logica Universalis **7**(3), 371–402 (2013)

29. Niefield, S.: Change of base for relational variable sets. Theory Appl. Categories **12**(7), 248–261 (2004)

30. Niefield, S.: Lax presheaves and exponentiability. Theory Appl. Categories **24**(12), 288–301 (2010)

31. Orlandelli, E.: Labelled sequent calculi for indexed modal logics. CLEUB (2023)

32. Pnueli, A.: The temporal logic of programs. In: FOCS 1977, pp. 46–57. IEEE Computer Society (1977)

33. Reif, J., Sistla, A.: A multiprocess network logic with temporal and spatial modalities. J. Comput. Syst. Sci. **30**(1), 41–53 (1985)

34. Rensink, A.: Model checking quantified computation tree logic. In: Baier, C., Hermanns, H. (eds.) CONCUR 2006. LNCS, vol. 4137, pp. 110–125. Springer, Heidelberg (2006). https://doi.org/10.1007/11817949_8

35. Rosenthal, K.: Quantales and Their Applications. Longman, London (1990)

36. Sobocinski, P.: Relational presheaves, change of base and weak simulation. J. Comput. Syst. Sci. **81**(5), 901–910 (2015)

37. Trotta, D.: The existential completion. Theory Appl. Categories **35**, 1576–1607 (2020)

38. Yahav, E., Reps, T., Sagiv, M., Wilhelm, R.: Verifying temporal heap properties specified via evolution logic. Logic J. IGPL **14**(5), 755–783 (2006)

Shades of Iteration: From Elgot to Kleene

Sergey Goncharov[✉]

Friedrich-Alexander-Universität Erlangen-Nürnberg, Erlangen, Germany
sergey.goncharov@fau.de

Abstract. Notions of iteration range from the arguably most general *Elgot iteration* to a very specific *Kleene iteration*. The fundamental nature of Elgot iteration has been extensively explored by Bloom and Esik in the form of *iteration theories*, while *Kleene iteration* became extremely popular as an integral part of (untyped) formalisms, such as automata theory, regular expressions and Kleene algebra. Here, we establish a formal connection between Elgot iteration and Kleene iteration in the form of Elgot monads and Kleene monads, respectively. We also introduce a novel class of *while-monads*, which like Kleene monads admit a relatively simple description in algebraic terms. Like Elgot monads, while-monads cover a large variety of models that meaningfully support while-loops, but may fail the Kleene algebra laws, or even fail to support a Kleen iteration operator altogether.

1 Introduction

Iteration is fundamental in many areas of computer science, such as semantics, verification, theorem proving, automata theory, formal languages, computability theory, compiler optimisation, etc. An early effort to identifying a generic notion of iteration is due to Elgot [7], who proposed to consider an *algebraic theory* induced by a notion of abstract machine (motivated by *Turing machines*, and their variants) and regard iteration as an operator over this algebraic theory.

Roughly speaking, an algebraic theory carries composable spaces of morphisms $L(n, m)$, indexed by natural numbers n and m and including all functions from n to m^1, called *base morphisms*. For example, following Elgot, one can consider as $L(n, m)$ the space of all functions $n \times S \to m \times S$ representing transitions from a machine state ranging over n to a machine state ranging over m, and updating the background store over S (e.g. with S being the Turing machine's tape) in the meanwhile. In modern speech, $L(n, m)$ is essentially the space of Kleisli morphisms $n \to Tm$ of the *state monad* $T = (- \times S)^S$. Then a machine over m halting states and n non-halting states is represented by a morphism in $L(n, m + n)$, and the iteration operator is meant to compute a morphism in $L(n, m)$, representing a run of the machine, obtained by feedbacking all non-halting states. This perspective has been extensively elaborated by Bloom and Esik [4] who identified the ultimate equational theory of Elgot iteration together

---

[1] Here we identify numbers $n \in \mathbb{N}$ with finite ordinals $\{0, \dots, n - 1\}$.

© Springer Nature Switzerland AG 2023
A. Madeira and M. A. Martins (Eds.): WADT 2022, LNCS 13710, pp. 100–120, 2023.
https://doi.org/10.1007/978-3-031-43345-0_5

with plenty other examples of algebraic theories induced by existing semantic models, for which the theory turned out to be sound and complete.

By replacing natural numbers with arbitrary objects of a category with finite coproducts and by moving from purely equational to a closely related and practically appealing quasi-equational theory of iteration, one arrives at *(complete) Elgot monads* [2,15], which are monads T, equipped with an iteration operator

$$\frac{f\colon X \to T(Y + X)}{f^\dagger\colon X \to TY} \tag{$\dagger$}$$

In view of the connection between computational effects and monads, pioneered by Moggi [32], Elgot monads provide arguably the most general model of iteration w.r.t. functions carrying computational effects, such as mutable store, non-determinism, probability, exceptional and abnormal termination, input-output actions of process algebra. The standard way of semantics via *domain theory* yields a general (least) fixpoint operator, which sidelines Elgot iteration and overshadows its fundamental role. This role becomes material again when it comes to the cases when the standard scenario cannot be applied or is difficult to apply, e.g. in constructive setting [12], for deterministic hybrid system semantics [13], and infinite trace semantics [30].

In contrast to Elgot iteration, *Kleene iteration*, manifested by *Kleene algebra*, is rooted in logic and automata theory [22], and crucially relies on non-determinism. The laws of Kleene algebra are from the outset determined by a rather conservative observation model, describing discrete events, coming one after another in linear order and in finite quantities. Nevertheless, Kleene algebra and thus Kleene iteration proved to be extremely successful (especially after the celebrated complete algebraic axiomatization of Kleene algebra by Kozen [25]) and have been accommodated in various formalizations and verification frameworks from those for concurrency [18] to those for modelling hybrid systems [34]. A significant competitive advantage of Kleene iteration is that it needs no (even very rudimental) type grammar for governing well-definedness of syntactic constructs, although this cannot be avoided when extending Kleene algebra with standard programming features [1,26,27]. Semantically, just as Elgot iteration, Kleene iteration can be reconciled with computational effects, leading to *Kleene monads* [11], which postulate Kleene iteration with the type profile:

$$\frac{f\colon X \to TX}{f^*\colon X \to TX} \tag{$*$}$$

Given f, f^* self-composes it non-deterministically indefinitely many times. In contrast to Elgot monads, the stock of computational effects modelled by Kleene monads is rather limited, which is due to the fact that many computational effects are subject to laws, which contradict the Kleene algebra laws. For a simple example, consider the computational effect of exception raising, constrained by the law, stating that postcomposing an exception raising program by another program is ineffective. Together with the Kleene algebra laws, we obtain a havoc:

$$\mathsf{raise}\, e_1 = \mathsf{raise}\, e_1;\ \bot = \bot = \mathsf{raise}\, e_2;\ \bot = \mathsf{raise}\, e_2,$$

where $\bot$ is the unit of non-deterministic choice. This and similar issues led to a number of proposals to weaken Kleene algebra laws [9,10,31,33] (potentially leading to other classes of monads, somewhere between Elgot and Kleene), although not attempting to identify the weakest set of such laws from the foundational perspective. At the same time, it seems undebatable that Kleene iteration and the Kleene algebra laws yield the most restricted notion of iteration.

We thus obtain a spectrum of potential notions of iteration between Elgot monads and Kleene monads. The goal of the present work is, on the one hand to explore this spectrum, and on the other hand to contribute into closing the conceptual gap between Kleene iteration and Elgot iteration. To that end, we introduce *while-monads*, which capture iteration in the conventional form of while-loops. Somewhat surprisingly, despite extensive work on axiomatizing iteration in terms of (†), a corresponding generic axiomatization in terms of "while" did not seem to be available. We highlight the following main technical contributions of the present work:

- We provide a novel axiomatization of Kleene iteration laws, which is effective both for Kleene algebras and Kleene monads (Proposition 4);
- We show that the existing axiomatization of Elgot monads is minimal (Proposition 12);
- We establish a connection between Elgot monads and while-monads (Theorem 18);
- We render Kleene monads as Elgot monads with additional properties (Theorem 22).

Additional proof details can be found in the full version of this paper: https://arxiv.org/abs/2301.06202.

2   Preliminaries

We rely on rudimentary notions and facts of category theory, as used in semantics, most notably *monads* [3]. For a (locally small) category $\mathbf{C}$ we denote by $|\mathbf{C}|$ the class of its objects and by $\mathbf{C}(X, Y)$ the set of morphisms from $X \in |\mathbf{C}|$ to $Y \in |\mathbf{C}|$. We often omit indices at components of natural transformations to avoid clutter. **Set** will denote the category of classical sets and functions, i.e. sets and functions formalized in a classical logic with the law of excluded middle (we will make no use of the axiom of choice). By $\langle f, g \rangle \colon X \to Y \times Z$ we will denote the *pairing* of two morphisms $f \colon X \to Y$ and $g \colon X \to Z$ (in a category with binary products), and dually, by $[f, g] \colon X + Y \to Z$ we will denote the *copairing* of $f \colon X \to Z$ and $g \colon Y \to Z$ (in a category with binary coproducts). By $! \colon X \to 1$ we will denote terminal morphisms (if 1 is an terminal object).

An $(F\text{-})$algebra for an endofunctor $F \colon \mathbf{C} \to \mathbf{C}$ is a pair $(A, a \colon FA \to A)$. Algebras form a category under the following notion of morphism: $f \colon A \to B$ if a morphism from (A, a) to (B, b) if $bf = (Ff)a$. The *initial algebra* is an initial object of this category (which may or may not exit). We denote this object $(\mu F, \mathsf{in})$. $(F\text{-})$coalgebras are defined dually as pairs of the form

$(A, a: A \to FA)$. The final coalgebra will be denoted $(\nu F, \text{out})$. By Lambek's Lemma [29], both in and out are isomorphisms, and we commonly make use of their inverses in^{-1} and out^{-1}.

3   Monads for Computation

We work with monads represented by *Kleisli triples* $(T, \eta, (-)^{\sharp})$ where T is a map $|\mathbf{C}| \to |\mathbf{C}|$, η is the family $(\eta_X: X \to TX)_{X \in |\mathbf{C}|}$ and $(-)^{\sharp}$ sends $f: X \to TY$ to $f^{\sharp}: TX \to TY$ in such a way that the standard *monad laws*

$$\eta^{\sharp} = \text{id}, \qquad\qquad f^{\sharp}\eta = f, \qquad\qquad (f^{\sharp}g)^{\sharp} = f^{\sharp}g^{\sharp}$$

hold true. It is then provable that T extends to a functor with $Tf = (\eta f)^{\sharp}$ and η to a *unit* natural transformation. Additionally, we can define the *multiplication* natural transformation $\mu: TT \to T$ with $\mu_X = \text{id}^{\sharp}$ (thus extending T to a monoid in the category of endufunctors). We preferably use bold letters, e.g. $\mathbf{T}$, for monads, to contrast with the underlying functor T. The axioms of monads entail that the morphisms of the form $X \to TY$ determine a category, called *Kleisli category*, and denoted $\mathbf{C_T}$, under *Kleisli composition* $f \cdot g = f^{\sharp}g$ with η as the identity morphism. Intuitively, Kleisli category is the category of (generalized) effectful programs w.r.t. $\mathbf{C}$ as the category of "pure", or effectless, programs. More precisely, we will call *pure* those morphisms in $\mathbf{C_T}$ that are of the form ηf. We thus use diagrammatic composition $g; f$ alongside and equivalently to functional composition $f \cdot g$, as the former fits with the sequential composition operators of traditional programming languages.

A monad $\mathbf{T}$ is *strong* if it comes with a natural transformation $\tau_{X,Y}: X \times TY \to T(X \times Y)$ called *strength* and satisfying a number of coherence conditions [32]. Any monad on **Set** is canonically strong [23].

Example 1 (Monads). Recall some computationally relevant monads on **Set** (all monads on **Set** are strong [32]).

1. *Maybe-monad:* $TX = X + 1$, $\eta(x) = \text{inl}\,x$, $f^{\sharp}(\text{inl}\,x) = f(x)$, $f^{\sharp}(\text{inr}\,\star) = \text{inr}\,\star$.
2. *Powerset monad:* $TX = \mathcal{P}X$, $\eta(x) = \{x\}$, $f^{\sharp}(S \subseteq X) = \{y \in f(x) \mid x \in S\}$.
3. $TX = \{S \mid S \in \mathcal{P}^{+}(X + 1), \text{if } S \text{ is infinite then } \text{inr}\,\star \in S\}$ where $\mathcal{P}^{+}$ is the non-empty powerset functor, $\eta(x) = \{\text{inl}\,x\}$, $f^{\sharp}(S \subseteq X) = \{y \in f(x) \mid \text{inl}\,x \in S\} \cup (\{\text{inr}\,\star\} \cap S)$.
4. *Exception monad:* $TX = X + E$ where E is a fixed (unstructured) non-empty set of exceptions, $\eta(x) = \text{inl}\,x$, $f^{\sharp}(\text{inl}\,x) = f(x)$, $f^{\sharp}(\text{inr}\,e) = \text{inr}\,e$.
5. *Non-deterministic writer monad:* $TX = \mathcal{P}(M \times X)$ where $(M, \epsilon, \bullet)$ is any monoid, $\eta(x) = \{(e, x)\}$, $f^{\sharp}(S \subseteq M \times X) = \{(n \bullet m, y) \mid (m, x) \in S, (n, y) \in f(x)\}$.
6. *Discrete sub-distribution monad:* $TX = \{d: [0, 1] \to X \mid \sum_{x \in X} d(x) \leq 1\}$ (the *supports* of d, $\{x \in X \mid d(x) > 0\}$ are necessarily countable – otherwise the sum $\sum_{x \in X} d(x)$ would diverge), $\eta(x)$ is the *Dirac distribution* δ_x, centred in x, i.e. $\delta_x(y) = 1$ if $x = y$, $\delta_x(y) = 0$ otherwise, $(f: X \to DY)^{\sharp}(d)(y) = \sum_{x \in X} f(x)(y) \cdot d(x)$.

7. *Partial state monad:* $TX = (X \times S + 1)^S$, where S is a fixed set of global states, $\eta(x)(s) = \text{inl}(x, s)$, $f^\sharp(g \colon S \to X \times S + 1)(s) = \text{inr} \star$ if $g(s) = \text{inr} \star$ and $f^\sharp(g \colon S \to Y \times S + 1)(s) = f(x)(s')$ if $g(s) = \text{inl}(x, s')$.
8. *Partial interactive input:* $TX = \nu\gamma. ((X + \gamma^I) + 1)$, where I is a set of input values, $\eta(x) = \text{out}^{-1}(\text{inl inl } x)$, $(f \colon X \to TY)^\sharp$ is the unique such morphism $f^\sharp \colon TX \to TY$ that (eliding the isomorphisms $T \cong (-+T^I) + 1$)

$$f^\sharp(\text{inl inl } x) = f(x), \quad f^\sharp(\text{inl inr } h) = \text{inl inr}(f^\sharp h), \quad f^\sharp(\text{inr} \star) = \text{inr} \star .$$

Intuitively, $p \in TX$ is a computation that either finishes and gives a result in X, or takes an input from I and continues recursively, or (unproductively) diverges.

9. *Partial interactive output:* $TX = \nu\gamma. ((X + \gamma \times O) + 1)$, where O is a set of output values, $\eta(x) = \text{out}^{-1}(\text{inl inl } x)$, $(f \colon X \to TY)^\sharp$ is the unique such morphism $f^\sharp \colon TX \to TY$ that (eliding the isomorphisms $T \cong (-+T \times O) + 1)$

$$f^\sharp(\text{inl inl } x) = f(x), \quad f^\sharp(\text{inl inr}(p, o)) = \text{inl inr}(f^\sharp(p), o), \quad f^\sharp(\text{inr} \star) = \text{inr} \star .$$

The behaviour of $p \in TX$ is as in the previous case, except that it outputs to O instead of expecting an input from I in the relevant branch.

Kleisli categories are often equivalent to categories with more familiar independent descriptions. For example, the Kleisli category of the maybe-monad is equivalent to the category of partial functions and the Kleisli category of the powerset monad is equivalent to the category of relations. Under the monads-as-effects metaphor, partial functions can thus be regarded as possibly non-terminating functions and relations as non-deterministic functions.

The above examples can often be combined. E.g. non-deterministic stateful computations are obtained as $TA = S \to \mathcal{P}(A \times S)$. The Java monad of [20],

$$TX = S \to (X \times S + E \times S) + 1$$

with S the set of states and E the set of exceptions.

4   Kleene Monads

A Kleene algebra can be concisely defined as an idempotent semiring $(S, \bot, \eta, \vee, ;)$ equipped with an operator $(-)^* \colon S \to S$, such that

- $g; f^*$ is the least (pre-)fixpoint of $g \vee (-); f$,
- $f^*; h$ is the least fixpoint of $h \vee f; (-)$,

where the order is induced by $\vee$: $f \leq g$ if $f \vee g = g$. We assume here and henceforth that sequential composition ; binds stronger than $\vee$.

More concretely, a Kleene algebra $(S, \bot, \eta, \vee, ; , (-)^*)$ is an algebraic structure, satisfying the laws in Fig. 1. A categorical version of Kleene algebra emerges as a class of monads, called *Kleene monads* [14], which can be used for interpreting effectful languages with iteration and non-determinism.

Idempotent semiring laws:

idempotence:	$f \vee f = f$
commutativity:	$f \vee g = g \vee f$
neutrality of $\bot$:	$f \vee \bot = f$
associativity of $\vee$:	$f \vee (g \vee h) = (f \vee g) \vee h$
associativity of $;$:	$f; (g; h) = (f; g); h$
right strictness:	$f; \bot = \bot$
right neutrality of η:	$f; \eta = f$
right distributivity:	$(f \vee g); h = f; h \vee g; h$
left strictness:	$\bot; f = \bot$
left neutrality of η:	$\eta; f = f$
left distributivity:	$f; (g \vee h) = f; g \vee f; h$

Iteration laws:

right unfolding:	$f^* = \eta \vee f; f^*$
right induction:	$f; g \leqslant f \implies f; g^* \leqslant f$
left unfolding:	$f^* = \eta \vee f^*; f$
left induction:	$f; g \leqslant g \implies f^*; g \leqslant g$

Fig. 1. Axioms Kleene algebras/monads.

Definition 2 (Kleene-Kozen Category/Kleene Monad). We say that a category **C** is a *Kleene-Kozen category* if **C** is enriched over bounded (i.e. possessing a least element) join-semilattices and strict join-preserving morphisms, and there is *Kleene iteration* operator

$$(-)^* \colon \mathbf{C}(X, X) \to \mathbf{C}(X, X),$$

such that, given $f\colon Y \to Y$, $g\colon Y \to Z$ and $h\colon X \to Y$, $g f^*$ is the least (pre-)fixpoint of $g \vee (-) f$ and $f^* h$ is the least (pre-)fixpoint of $h \vee f (-)$.

A monad **T** is a *Kleene monad* if $\mathbf{C_T}$ is a Kleene-Kozen category.

Recall that a monoid is nothing but a single-object category, whose morphisms are identified with monoid elements, and whose identity morphisms and morphism composition are identified with monoidal unit and composition. This suggests a connection between Kleene-Kozen categories and Kleene algebras.

Proposition 3. *A Kleene algebra is precisely a Kleene-Kozen category with one object.*

We record the following characterization of Kleene-Kozen categories (hence, also of Kleene algebras by Proposition 3).

Proposition 4. *A category* **C** *is a Kleene-Kozen category iff*

- **C** *is enriched over bounded join-semilattices and strict join-preserving morphisms;*
- *there is an operator* $(-)^*\colon \mathbf{C}(X,X) \to \mathbf{C}(X,X)$, *such that*
  1. $f^* = \mathrm{id} \vee f^* f$;
  2. $\mathrm{id}^* = \mathrm{id}$;
  3. $f^* = (f \vee \mathrm{id})^*$;
  4. $h f = f g$ *implies* $h^* f = f g^*$.

Proof. Let us show *necessity*.

1. The law $f^* = \mathrm{id} \vee f^* f$ holds by assumption.
2. Since $\mathrm{id} = \mathrm{id} \vee \mathrm{id}\,\mathrm{id}$, id is a fixpoint of $f \mapsto \mathrm{id} \vee f\,\mathrm{id}$, and thus $\mathrm{id}^* \leq \mathrm{id}$. Also $\mathrm{id}^* = \mathrm{id} \vee \mathrm{id}^*\,\mathrm{id} \geq \mathrm{id}$. Hence $\mathrm{id} = \mathrm{id}^*$ by mutual inequality.
3. To show that $(f \vee \mathrm{id})^* \leq f^*$, note that $f^* = \mathrm{id} \vee f^* f = \mathrm{id} \vee f^* f \vee f^* = \mathrm{id} \vee f^* (f \vee \mathrm{id})$, and use the fact that $(f \vee \mathrm{id})^*$ is the least fixpoint. The opposite inequality is shown analogously, by exploiting the fact that f^* is a least fixpoint.
4. Suppose that $h f = f g$, and show that $h^* f = f g^*$. Note that

$$f \vee (h^* f) g = f \vee h^* f g = f \vee h^* h f = h^* f,$$

i.e. $h^* f$ satisfies the fixpoint equation for $f g^*$, and therefore $h^* f \geq f g^*$. By a symmetric argument, $h^* f \leq f g^*$, hence $h^* f = f g^*$.

We proceed with *sufficiency*. Suppose that $(-)^*$ is as described in the second clause of the present proposition. Observe that by combining assumptions 1 and 4 we immediately obtain the dual version of 1, which is $f^* = \mathrm{id} \vee f f^*$. Now, fix $f\colon Y \to TY$ and $g\colon Y \to TZ$, and show that $f^* g$ is the least fixpoint of $g \vee f\,(-)$ – we omit proving the dual property, since it follows by a dual argument. From $f^* = \mathrm{id} \vee f^* f$ we obtain $f^* g = g \vee f\,(f^* g)$, i.e. $f^* g$ is a fixpoint. We are left to show that it is the least one. Suppose that $h = g \vee f h$ for some h, which entails

$$(\mathrm{id} \vee f)\, h = h \vee f h = g \vee f h \vee f h = h = h\,\mathrm{id}.$$

Since $g \leq h$, using assumptions 2, 3 and 4, we obtain

$$f^* g \leq (\mathrm{id} \vee f)^* g \leq (\mathrm{id} \vee f)^* h = h\,\mathrm{id}^* = h,$$

as desired.   □

The axioms of Kleene monads do not in fact need a monad, and can be interpreted in any category. We focus on Kleisli categories for two reasons: (i) in practice, Kleene-Kozen categories are often realized as Kleisli categories, and monads provide a compositional mechanism for constructing more Kleene-Kozen categories by generalities; (ii) we will relate Kleene monads and Elgot monads, and the latter are defined by axioms, which do involve both general Kleisli morphisms and the morphisms of the base category.

Example 5. Let us revisit Example 1. Many monads therein fail to be Kleene simply because they fail to support binary non-determinism. Example 1.6 is an interesting case, since we can define the operation of probabilistic choice $+_p$: $\mathbf{C}(X, TY) \times \mathbf{C}(X, TY) \to \mathbf{C}(X, TY)$ indexed by $p \in [0, 1]$, meaning that $x +_p y$ is resolved to x with probability p and to y with probability $1 - p$. For every $x \in X$, $f(x) +_p g(x)$ is a *convex sum* of the distributions $f(x)$ and $g(x)$. This operation satisfies the axioms of *barycentric algebras* (or, *abstract convex sets* [36]), which are somewhat similar to those of a monoid, but with the multiplication operator indexed over $[0, 1]$. To get rid of this indexing, one can remove the requirement that probabilities sum up to at most 1 and thus obtain spaces of *valuations* [37] instead of probability distributions. Valuations can be conveniently added pointwise, and thus defined addition satisfies monoidal laws, but fails idempotence, hence still does not yield a Kleene monad. Given two valuations v and w, we also can define $v \vee w$ as the pointwise maximum. This satisfies the axioms of semilattices, but fails both distributivity laws.

Example 1.3 is the **Set**-reduct or *Plotkin powerdomain* [35] over a flat domain. It supports proper non-deterministic choice, but the only candidate for $\bot$ is not a unit for it.

Kleene monads of Example 1 are only 2 and 5. The non-deterministic state monad over $TX = (\mathcal{P}(X \times S))^S$ obtained by adapting Example 1.7 in the obvious way is also Kleene.

Except for the powerset monad, our examples of Kleene monads are in fact obtained by generic patterns.

Proposition 6. *Let* **T** *be a Kleene monad. Then so are*

1. *the state monad transformer* $(T(- \times S))^S$ *for every* S;
2. *the writer monad transformer* $T(M \times -)$ *for every monoid* $(M, \epsilon, \bullet)$ *if* **T** *is strong and strength* $\tau_{X,Y}$: $X \times TX \to T(X \times Y)$ *respects the Kleene monad structure, as follows:*

$$\tau\,(\mathsf{id} \times \bot) = \bot, \qquad \tau\,(\mathsf{id} \times f^*) = (\tau\,(\mathsf{id} \times f))^*,$$
$$\tau\,(\mathsf{id} \times (f \vee g)) = \tau\,(\mathsf{id} \times f) \vee \tau\,(\mathsf{id} \times g). \tag{1}$$

Example 7. Note that the powerset monad $\mathcal{P}$ is a Kleene monad with f^* calculated as a least fixpoint of $\eta \vee (-) \cdot f$.

1. By Proposition 6.1, $(\mathcal{P}(- \times S))^S$ is a Kleene monad.
2. By applying Proposition 6.2, to the free monoid A^* of finite strings over an alphabet A we obtain that $\mathcal{P}(A^* \times -)$.

It is easy to see that for every Kleene monad **T**, $\mathrm{Hom}(1, T1)$ is a Kleene algebra. By applying this to the above clauses we obtain correspondingly the standard *relational* and *language-theoretic* models of Kleene algebra [28].

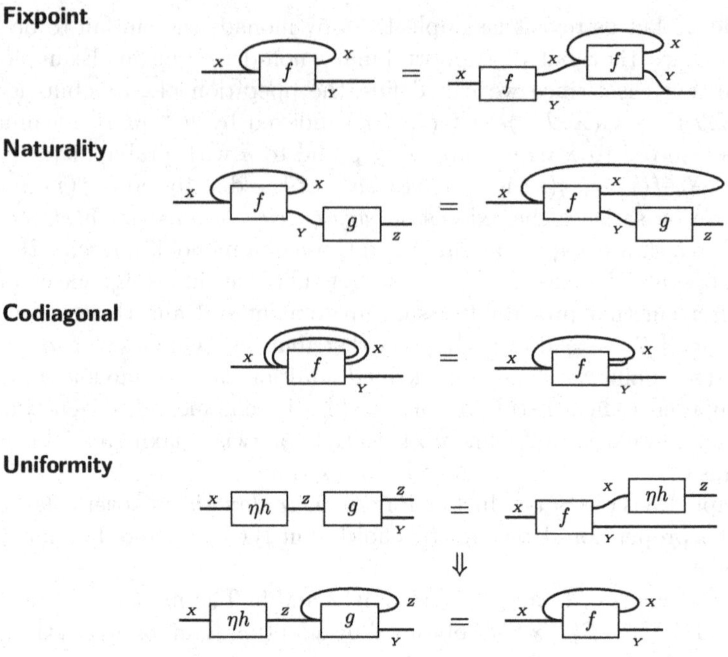

Fixpoint

Naturality

Codiagonal

Uniformity

Fig. 2. Axioms of Elgot monads.

5   Elgot Monads

A general approach to monad-based iteration is provided by Elgot monads. We continue under the assumption that $\mathbf{C}$ supports finite coproducts. This, in particular, yields an if-the-else operator sending $b \in \mathbf{C}(X, X + X)$ and $f, g \in \mathbf{C}(X, Y)$ to if b then p else $q = [q, p] \cdot b \in \mathbf{C}(X, Y)$. Note that for any monad $\mathbf{T}$ on $\mathbf{C}$, $\mathbf{C_T}$ inherits finite coproducts.

Definition 8 (Elgot monad). An *Elgot monad* in a category with binary coproducts is a monad $\mathbf{T}$ equipped with an *Elgot iteration* operator

$$(\text{-})^\dagger \colon \mathbf{C}(X, T(Y + X)) \to \mathbf{C}(X, TY),$$

subject to the following principles:

Fixpoint : $[\eta, f^\dagger] \cdot f = f^\dagger$ $(f \colon X \to T(Y + X))$

Naturality : $g \cdot f^\dagger = ([\eta \, \mathsf{inl} \cdot g, \eta \, \mathsf{inr}] \cdot f)^\dagger$ $(g \colon Y \to TZ, f \colon X \to T(Y + X))$

Codiagonal : $f^{\dagger\dagger} = ([\eta, \eta \, \mathsf{inr}] \cdot f)^\dagger$ $(f \colon X \to T((Y + X) + X))$

Uniformity : $\dfrac{g \cdot \eta h = \eta(\mathsf{id} + h) \cdot f}{g^\dagger \cdot \eta h = f^\dagger}$ $(h \colon X \to Z, g \colon Z \to T(Y + Z),$

$f \colon X \to T(Y + X))$

These laws are easier to grasp by depicting them graphically (Fig. 2), more precisely speaking, as *string diagrams* (cf. [17,21] for a rigorous treatment in terms of monoidal categories). Iterating f is depicted as a feedback loop. It is then easy to see that while **Fixpoint** expresses the basic fixpoint property of iteration, **Naturality** and **Codiagonal** are essentially rearrangements of wires. The **Uniformity** law is a form of induction: the premise states that ηh can be pushed over g, so that at the same time g is replaced by f, and the conclusion is essentially the result of closing this transformation under iteration. **Uniformity** is therefore the only law, which alludes to pure morphisms. Intuitively, the morphisms f and g can be seen as programs operating correspondingly on X and Y as their state spaces, and $h: X \to Y$ is a map between these state spaces. **Uniformity** thus ensures that the behaviour of iteration does not depend on the shape of the state space. It is critical for this view that h is pure, i.e. does not trigger any side-effects.

Remark 9 (Divergence). Every Elgot monad comes together with the definable (unproductive) divergence constant $\delta = (\eta\ \text{inr})^\dagger$. Graphically, $\delta: X \to T\emptyset$ will be depicted as ──o , symmetrically to the depiction of the initial morphism $!: \emptyset \to TX$ as ●── .

Example 10 (Elgot Monads). Clauses 1–9 of Example 1 all define Elgot monads. A standard way of introducing Elgot iteration is enriching the Kleisli category over pointed complete partial orders and defining $(f: X \to T(Y + X))^\dagger$ as a least fixpoint of the map $[\eta, -] \cdot f: \mathbf{C}(X, TY) \to \mathbf{C}(X, TY)$ by the *Kleene fixpoint theorem*. This scenario covers 1.–7. In all these cases, we inherit complete partial order structures on $\mathbf{Set}(X, TY)$ by extending canonical complete partial order structures from TY pointwise. In particular, in 4, we need to chose the divergence element $\delta \in E$. This choice induces a *flat domain* structure on $X + E: x \sqsubseteq y$ if $x = y$ or $x = \delta$. The induced divergence constant in the sense of Remark 9 then coincides with δ, and hence there are at least as many distinct Elgot monad structures on the exception monad as exceptions.

Clauses 8 and 9 fit a different pattern. For every Elgot monad $\mathbf{T}$ and every endofunctor H, if all final coalgebras $T_H X = \nu\gamma. T(X + H\gamma)$ exist then T_H extends to an Elgot monad [13], called the *coalgebraic generalized resumption transform* of $\mathbf{T}$. This yields 8 and 9 by taking $\mathbf{T}$ to be the maybe-monad in both cases and $HX = X^I$ and $HX = O \times X$ respectively.

Remark 11 (Dinaturality). A classical law of iteration, which is not included in Definition 8, is the **Dinaturality** law, which has the following graphical representation:

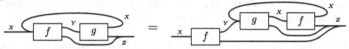

This law has been used in one of the equivalent axiomatization of iteration theories [4] (under the name *"composition identity"*) and thus was initially inherited in the definition of Elgot monads [2,15]. However, Ésik and Goncharov [8] latter discovered that **Dinaturality** is derivable in presence of **Uniformity**.

Remark 11 poses the question, if the present axiomatization of Elgot monads possibly contains further derivable laws. Here, we resolve it in the negative.

Proposition 12. *The axiomatization in Definition 8 is minimal.*

Proof. For every axiom, we construct a separating example that fails that axiom, but satisfies the other three. Every example is a monad on **Set**.

- **Fixpoint**: For any monad **T**, equipped with a natural transformation $p: 1 \to TX$, we can define $f^\dagger = [\eta, p\,!] \cdot f$ for a given $f: X \to T(Y + X)$. It is easy to see that **Naturality**, **Codiagonal** and **Uniformity** are satisfied, but **Fixpoint** need not to, e.g. with **T** being the non-deterministic writer monad (Example 1.5) over the additive monoid of natural numbers $\mathbb{N}$.
- **Naturality**: Let $\mathbf{T} = \mathcal{P}$ and let $f^\dagger(x) = Y$ for every $f: X \to T(Y + X)$ and every $x \in X$. Note that every $f: X \to T(Y + Z)$ is equivalent to a pair $(f_1: X \to TY, f_2: X \to TZ)$ and $[g, h] \cdot f = g \cdot f_1 \cup h \cdot f_2$ for any $g: Y \to TV$, $h: Z \to TV$. This helps one to see that all the axioms, except **Naturality** hold true, e.g. $([\eta, f^\dagger] \cdot f)(x) = f_1(x) \cup Y = Y = f^\dagger(x)$. **Naturality** fails, because $g \cdot \delta = g \cdot (\eta\ \mathrm{inr})^\dagger \neq ([\eta\ \mathrm{inl} \cdot g, \eta\ \mathrm{inr}] \cdot \eta\ \mathrm{inr})^\dagger = \delta$, since the image of $\delta: X \to TY$ is $\{Y\}$, while the image of $g \cdot \delta$, aka the image of g, need not be $\{Y\}$.
- **Codiagonal**: Consider the exception monad transform $TX = \mathcal{P}(2^\star \times X \cup 2^\omega)$ of the non-deterministic writer monad over the free monoid $2^\star$. This is canonically an Elgot monad, and let us denote by $(-)^\ddagger$ the corresponding iteration operator. Every $f: X \to T(Y + X)$, using the isomorphism $T(Y + X) \cong \mathcal{P}(2^\star \times Y \cup 2^\omega) \times \mathcal{P}(2^\star \times X)$, induces a map $\hat{f}: X \to \mathcal{P}(2^\star \times X)$. Let $f^\dagger: X \to TY$ be as follows: $f^\dagger(x)$ is the union of $f^\ddagger(x)$ and the set

$$\{w \in 2^\omega \mid \exists u \in 2^\star.\ uw = w_1 w_2 \ldots, (w_1, x_1) \in \hat{f}(x), (w_2, x_2) \in \hat{f}(x_1), \ldots\}.$$

That $(-)^\dagger$ satisfies **Fixpoint**, **Naturality** and **Uniformity** follows essentially from the fact that so does $(-)^\ddagger$. To show that $(-)^\dagger$ fails**Codiagonal**, consider $g: 1 \to \mathcal{P}((2^\star + 2^\star) \cup 2^\omega)$, with $g(\star) = \{\mathrm{inl}\,0,\ \mathrm{inr}\,1\}$. Let f be the composition of g with the obvious isomorphism $\mathcal{P}((2^\star + 2^\star) \cup 2^\omega) \cong T((0 + 1) + 1)$. Now $([\eta, \eta\ \mathrm{inr}] \cdot f)^\dagger(\star) = 2^\omega \neq \{0^\omega, 1^\omega\} = f^{\dagger\dagger}(\star)$.
- **Uniformity**: Consider the exception monad on $TX = X + \{0, 1\}$. This can be made into an Elgot monad in two ways: by regarding either 0 or 1 as the divergence element. Given $f: X \to T(Y + X)$, we let $f^\dagger$ be computed as a least fixpoint according to the first choice if X is a singleton and according to the second choice otherwise. The axioms except **Uniformity** are clearly satisfied. To show that **Uniformity** fails, let $|X| > 2$, $|Z| = 1$, $g = \eta\ \mathrm{inr}$, $f = \eta\ \mathrm{inr}$, $h = !$. The premise of **Uniformity** is thus satisfied, while the conclusion is not, since $f^\dagger$ is constantly 1 and $g^\dagger$ is constantly 0.   □

Although we cannot lift any of the Elgot monad laws, **Naturality** can be significantly restricted.

Proposition 13. *In the definition of Elgot monad, **Naturality** can be equivalently replaced by its instance with g of the form $\eta\ \mathrm{inr}: Y \to T(Y' + Y)$.*

6   While-Monads

We proceed to develop a novel alternative characterization of Elgot monads in more conventional for computer science terms of while-loops.

Definition 14 (Decisions). Given a monad $\mathbf{T}$ on $\mathbf{C}$, we call any family $(\mathbf{C_T^d}(X) \subseteq \mathbf{C}(X, T(X+X)))_{X \in |\mathbf{C}|}$, a family of *decisions* if every $\mathbf{C_T^d}(X)$ contains η inl, η inr, and is closed under if-then-else.

We encode logical operations on decisions as follows:

$$\text{ff} = \eta \text{ inl}, \qquad b \text{ \&\& } c = \text{if } b \text{ then } c \text{ else ff}, \qquad \overline{b} = \text{if } b \text{ then ff else tt},$$
$$\text{tt} = \eta \text{ inr}, \qquad b \parallel c = \text{if } b \text{ then tt else } c.$$

By definition, decisions can range from the smallest family with $\mathbf{C_T^d}(X) = \{\text{ff}, \text{tt}\}$, to the greatest one with $\mathbf{C_T^d}(X) = \mathbf{C}(X, T(X+X))$.

Remark 15. Our notion of decision is maximally simple and general. An alternative are morphisms of the form $b \colon X \to T2$, from which we can obtain $X \xrightarrow{\langle \text{id}, b \rangle} X \times T2 \xrightarrow{\tau} T(X \times 2) \cong T(X+X)$ if $\mathbf{T}$ is strong, with τ being the strength. The resulting decision d would satisfy many properties we are not assuming generally, e.g. if d then tt else ff $= \eta$. Both morphisms of the form $X \to T2$ and $X \to T(X+X)$ are relevant in semantics as decision making abstractions – this is explained in detail from the perspective of categorical logic by Jacobs [19], who uses the names *predicates* and *instruments* correspondingly (alluding to physical, in particular, quantum experiments).

Elgot monads are essentially the semantic gadgets for effectful while-languages. In fact, we can introduce a semantic while-operator and express it via Elgot iteration. Given $b \in \mathbf{C_T^d}(X)$ and $p \in \mathbf{C}(X, TX)$, let

$$\text{while } b \; p = (\text{if } b \text{ then } p; \text{tt else ff})^\dagger, \qquad (2)$$

or diagrammatically, while b p is expressed as

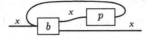

It is much less obvious that, conversely, Elgot iteration can be defined via while, and moreover that the entire class of Elgot monads can be rebased on while. We dub the corresponding class of monad *while-monads*.

Definition 16 (While-Monad). A *while-monad* is a monad $\mathbf{T}$, equipped with an operator

$$\text{while} \colon \mathbf{C_T^d}(X) \times \mathbf{C}(X, TX) \to \mathbf{C}(X, TX),$$

such that the following axioms are satisfied

W-Fix while b $p =$ if b then p; (while b p) else η

W-Or while $(b \parallel c)$ $p =$ (while b p); while c $(p;$ while b $p)$

W-And
$$\frac{\eta h; b = \eta u; \text{ff}}{\text{while}\,(b\, \&\&\, (c \parallel \eta u; \text{ff}))\ p = \text{while } b\ (\text{if } c \text{ then } p \text{ else } \eta h)}$$

W-Uni
$$\frac{\eta h; b = \text{if } c \text{ then } \eta h'; \text{tt else } \eta u; \text{ff} \qquad \eta h'; p = q; \eta h}{\eta h; \text{while } b\ p = (\text{while } c\ q); \eta u}$$

The laws of while-monads roughly correspond to **Fixpoint**, **Codiagonal**, **Naturality** and **Uniformity**. This correspondence is somewhat allusive for **W-And**, which under $u =$ id instantiates to the nicer looking

$$\frac{\eta h; b = \text{ff}}{\text{while}\,(b\, \&\&\, c)\ p = \text{while } b\ (\text{if } c \text{ then } p \text{ else } \eta h)}$$

However, this instance generally seems to be insufficient. Let us still consider it in more detail. The while-loop while $(b\, \&\&\, c)$ p repeats p as long as both b and c are satisfied, and while b (if c then p else ηh) repeats (if c then p else ηh) as long as b is satisfied, but the latter program still checks c before running p and triggers ηh only if c fails. The equality in the conclusion of the rule is thus due to the premise, which ensures that once ηh is triggered, the loop is exited at the beginning of the next iteration.

Note that using the following equations

$$\text{do } p \text{ while } b = p; \text{while } b\ p \tag{3}$$

$$\text{while } b\ p = \text{if } b \text{ then (do } p \text{ while } b) \text{ else } \eta \tag{4}$$

we can define (do p while b) from (while b p) and conversely obtain the latter from the former. Unsurprisingly, while-monads can be equivalently defined in terms of do-while.

Lemma 17. *Giving a while-monad structure on* **T** *is equivalent to equipping* **T** *with an operator, sending every $b \in \mathbf{C}_\mathbf{T}^{\mathsf{d}}(X)$ and every $p \in \mathbf{C}(X, TX)$ to* (do p while b) $\in \mathbf{C}(X, TX)$, *such that the following principles hold true:*

DW-Fix do p while $b = p$; if b then (do p while b) else η

DW-Or do p while $(b \parallel c) =$ do (do p while b) while c

DW-And
$$\frac{\eta h; b = \eta u; \text{ff}}{\text{if } c \text{ then do } p \text{ while }(b\, \&\&\, (c \parallel \eta u; \text{ff})) \text{ else } \eta u}$$
$$= \text{do (if } c \text{ then } p \text{ else } \eta h) \text{ while } b$$

DW-Uni
$$\frac{\eta h; p = q; \eta h' \qquad \eta h'; b = \text{if } c \text{ then } \eta h; \text{tt else } \eta u; \text{ff}}{\eta h; \text{do } p \text{ while } b = (\text{do } q \text{ while } c); \eta u}$$

The relevant equivalence is witnessed by the Eq. (3) and (4).

Finally, we can prove the equivalence of while-monads and Elgot monads, under an expressivity assumption, stating that sets of decisions $\mathbf{C}_\mathsf{T}^\mathsf{d}$ are sufficiently non-trivial. Such an assumption is clearly necessary, for, as we indicated above, the smallest family of decisions is the one with $\mathbf{C}_\mathsf{T}^\mathsf{d}(X) = \{\mathsf{ff}, \mathsf{tt}\}$, and it is not enough to express meaningful while-loops.

Theorem 18. *Suppose that for all $X, Y \in |\mathbf{C}|$, $\eta(inl+inr) \in \mathbf{C}_\mathsf{T}^\mathsf{d}(X+Y)$. Then $\mathbf{T}$ is and Elgot monad iff it is a while-monad w.r.t. $\mathbf{C}_\mathsf{T}^\mathsf{d}$. The equivalence is witnessed by mutual translations: (2) and*

$$f^\dagger = \eta \; inr; (\mathsf{while} \; \eta(inl + inr) \; [\eta \; inl, f]); [\eta, \delta]. \tag{5}$$

Diagrammatically, $f^\dagger$ is expressed as

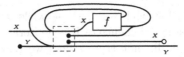

for $f: X \to T(Y + X)$.

Proof (Sketch). Note that (5) is equivalent to

$$f^\dagger = \eta \; inr; (\mathsf{do} \; [\eta \; inl, f] \; \mathsf{while} \; \eta(inl + inr)); [\eta, \delta]. \tag{6}$$

The proof consists of four parts:

(i) The composite translation $(-)^\dagger \to \mathsf{while} \to (-)^\dagger$ yields an identity w.r.t. the Elgot monad laws, i.e.

$$\eta \; inr; (\mathsf{if} \; (inl + inr) \; \mathsf{then} \; [\eta \; inl, f]; \eta \; inr \; \mathsf{else} \; \eta \; inl)^\dagger; [\eta, \delta] = f^\dagger.$$

for every $f: X \to T(Y + X)$.

(ii) The composite translation $\mathsf{while} \to (-)^\dagger \to \mathsf{while}$ yields an identity w.r.t. the while-monad laws, i.e.

$$\eta \; inr; (\mathsf{while} \; \eta(inl + inr) \; [\eta \; inl, \mathsf{if} \; b \; \mathsf{then} \; p; \mathsf{tt} \; \mathsf{else} \; \mathsf{ff}]); [\eta, \delta] = \mathsf{while} \; b \; p.$$

for every $p: X \to TX$ and $b \in \mathbf{C}_\mathsf{T}^\mathsf{d}(X)$.

(iii) The laws of Elgot monads follow from those of while-monads. Thanks to Proposition 13, it suffices to prove only a restricted version of **Naturality**. The verification of **Codiagonal** is facilitated by using (6) instead of (5).

(iv) The laws of while-monads follow from those of Elgot monads. This is done by verifying the equivalent characterization from Lemma 17, after proving that the identity $\mathsf{do} \; p \; \mathsf{while} \; b = (b \cdot p)^\dagger$ follows from (2).

7   Kleene Monads as Elgot Monads

If hom-sets of the Kleisli category of a while-monad $\mathbf{T}$ are equipped with a semilattice structure and every $\mathbf{C}_\mathbf{T}^d(X)$ is closed under that structure, we can define Kleene iteration as follows:

$$p^* = \mathsf{while}\,(\mathsf{ff} \vee \mathsf{tt})\; p.$$

That is, at each iteration we non-deterministically decide to finish or to continue.

Given a decision $b \in \mathbf{C}_\mathbf{T}^d(X)$, let $b? = (\mathsf{if}\ b\ \mathsf{then}\ \eta\ \mathsf{else}\ \delta) \in \mathbf{C}(X, TX)$. The standard way to express while-loops via Kleene iteration is as follows:

$$\mathsf{while}\ b\ p = (b?;p)^*;(\sim b)?$$

If the composite translation $\mathsf{while} \to (-)^* \to \mathsf{while}$ was a provable identity, this would essentially mean equivalence of Kleene iteration and while with non-determinism. This is generally not true, unless we postulate more properties that connect while and nondeterminism. We leave for future work the problem of establishing a minimal set of such laws. Here, we only establish the equivalence for the case when the induced Kleene iteration satisfies Kleene monad laws. To start off, we note an alternative to **Uniformity**, obtained by replacing the reference to pure morphisms with the reference to a larger class consisting of those h, for which $\delta \cdot h = \delta$. We need this preparatory step to relate Elgot iteration and Kleene iteration, since the latter does not hinge on a postulated class of pure morphisms, while the former does.

Definition 19 (Strong Uniformity). Given an Elgot monad $\mathbf{T}$, the *strong uniformity* law is as follows:

$$\mathbf{Uniformity^\star} : \qquad \frac{\delta \cdot h = \delta \qquad g \cdot h = [\eta\ \mathsf{inl}, \eta\ \mathsf{inr} \cdot h] \cdot f}{g^\dagger \cdot h = f^\dagger}$$

where $h\colon X \to TZ$, $g\colon Z \to T(Y + Z)$, and $f\colon X \to T(Y + X)$.

Clearly, **Uniformity** is an instance of **Uniformity***.

Example 20. An example of Elgot monad that fails **Uniformity*** can be constructed as follows. Let $\mathbf{S}$ be the reader monad transform of the maybe-monad on **Set**: $SX = (X + 1)^2$, which is an Elgot monad, since the maybe-monad is so and Elgotness is preserved by the reader monad transformer. Let $TX = X \times (X + 1) + 1$ and note that T is a retract of S under

$$\rho\colon (X + 1) \times (X + 1) \cong X \times (X + 1) + (X + 1) \xrightarrow{\ \mathsf{id}+!\ } X \times (X + 1) + 1.$$

It is easy to check that ρ is a congruence w.r.t. the Elgot monad structure, and it thus induces an Elgot monad structure on $\mathbf{T}$ [16, Theorem 20].

Now, let $T_E = T(-+E)$ for some non-empty E. The Elgot monad structure of $\mathbf{T}$ induces an Elgot monad structure on $\mathbf{T}_E$. However, $\mathbf{T}_E$ fails **Uniformity***.

Indeed, let $h\colon X \to (X+E) \times ((X+E)+1)+1$ and $f\colon X \to ((1+X)+E) \times (((1+X)+E)+1)+1$ be as follows:

$$h(x) = \mathsf{inl}(\mathsf{inl}\,x,\ \mathsf{inl}\,\mathsf{inr}\,e) \qquad\qquad f(x) = \mathsf{inl}(\mathsf{inr}\,e,\ \mathsf{inl}\,\mathsf{inl}\,\mathsf{inr}\,x)$$

where $e \in E$. Then $h \cdot \delta = \delta$, $f^\dagger(x) = \mathsf{inl}(\mathsf{inr}\,e,\ \mathsf{inr}\,\star)$, and $f \cdot h = [\eta\,\mathsf{inl}, \eta\,\mathsf{inr} \cdot h] \cdot f$, but $(f^\dagger \cdot h)(x) = \mathsf{inl}(\mathsf{inr}\,e,\ \mathsf{inl}\,\mathsf{inr}\,e) \neq \mathsf{inl}(\mathsf{inr}\,e,\ \mathsf{inr}\,\star) = f^\dagger(x)$.

Remark 21. Example 20 indicates that it is hard to come up with a general and robust notion of Elgot iteration, which would confine to a single category, without referring to another category of "well-behaved" (e.g. pure) morphisms. While the class of Elgot monads is closed under various monad transformers, the example shows that Elgot monads with strong uniformity are not even closed under the exception monad transformer.

We are in a position to relate Kleene monads and Elgot monads.

Theorem 22. *A monad* **T** *is a Kleene monad iff*

1. **T** *is an Elgot monad;*
2. *the Kleisli category of* **T** *is enriched over join-semilattices (without least elements) and join-preserving morphisms;*
3. **T** *satisfies* $(\eta\ \mathsf{inl} \vee \eta\ \mathsf{inr})^\dagger = \eta$;
4. **T** *satisfies* **Uniformity***.

To prove the theorem, we need to mutually encode Kleene iteration and Elgot iteration. These encodings go back to Căzănescu and Ştefănescu [5]. Observe the following easily provable property.

Lemma 23. *For any monad* **T**, *whose Kleisli category is enriched over join-semilattices and join-preserving morphisms,* $[f_1, g_1] \vee [f_2, g_2] = [f_1 \vee f_2, g_1 \vee g_2]$ *where* $f_1, f_2\colon X \to TZ$, $g_1, g_2\colon Y \to TZ$.

Proof (of Theorem 22). We modify the claim slightly by replacing Clause 2. with the stronger

2'. The Kleisli category of **T** is enriched over bounded join-semilattices and strict join-preserving morphisms, and $\delta = (\eta\ \mathsf{inr})^\dagger\colon X \to TY$ is the least element of $\mathbf{C}(X, TY)$.

Let us show that 1.–4. entail 2'.

- *Right strictness of Kleisli composition:* $f \cdot \delta = \delta$. Using naturality, $f \cdot \delta = f \cdot (\eta\ \mathsf{inr})^\dagger = ([\eta\ \mathsf{inl} \cdot f, \eta\ \mathsf{inr}] \cdot \eta\ \mathsf{inr})^\dagger = (\eta\ \mathsf{inr})^\dagger = \delta$.
- *Left strictness of Kleisli composition:* $\delta \cdot f = \delta$. Since $\eta\ \mathsf{inr} \cdot f = [\eta\ \mathsf{inl}, \eta\ \mathsf{inr} \cdot f] \cdot \eta\ \mathsf{inr}$, by strong uniformity, $\delta \cdot f = (\eta\ \mathsf{inr})^\dagger \cdot f = (\eta\ \mathsf{inr})^\dagger = \delta$.
- δ *is the least element,* equivalently, $f \vee \delta = f$ for all suitably typed f. It suffices to consider the special case $f = \eta$, for then $f \vee \delta = f \cdot (\eta \vee \delta) = f \cdot \eta = f$ for a general f.
  Note that $(\eta\ \mathsf{inl} \vee \eta\ \mathsf{inr}) \cdot (\eta \vee \delta) = [\eta\ \mathsf{inl}, \eta\ \mathsf{inr} \cdot (\eta \vee \delta)] \cdot (\eta\ \mathsf{inl} \vee \eta\ \mathsf{inr})$, which by 3. and 4. entails $\eta \vee \delta = (\eta\ \mathsf{inl} \vee \eta\ \mathsf{inr})^\dagger \cdot (\eta \vee \delta) = (\eta\ \mathsf{inl} \vee \eta\ \mathsf{inr})^\dagger = \eta$.

Now, given $(-)^\dagger$ of an Elgot monad, whose Kleisli category is enriched over join-semilattices, let

$$(f\colon X \to TX)^* = \left(\eta \text{ inl} \vee \eta \text{ inr} \cdot f\colon X \to T(X+X)\right)^\dagger.$$

Conversely, given $(-)^*$ of a Kleene monad, let

$$(f\colon X \to T(Y+X))^\dagger = ([\eta,\delta] \cdot f) \cdot ([\delta,\eta] \cdot f\colon X \to TX)^*.$$

We are left to check that these transformations are mutually inverse and that the expected properties of defined operators are satisfied.

(i) $(-)^\dagger \to (-)^* \to (-)^\dagger$: Given $f\colon X \to T(Y+X)$, we need to show that

$$([\eta,\delta] \cdot f) \cdot (\eta \text{ inl} \vee \eta \text{ inr} \cdot [\delta,\eta] \cdot f)^\dagger = f^\dagger.$$

Indeed,

$$
\begin{aligned}
([\eta,\delta]\cdot f) &\cdot (\eta \text{ inl} \vee \eta \text{ inr} \cdot [\delta,\eta] \cdot f)^\dagger \\
&= \left([\eta \text{ inl} \cdot [\eta,\delta] \cdot f, \eta \text{ inr}]^{\#} (\eta \text{ inl} \vee \eta \text{ inr} \cdot [\delta,\eta] \cdot f)\right)^\dagger && /\!/ \text{ \textbf{Naturality}} \\
&= ([\eta \text{ inl}, \delta] \cdot f \vee [\delta, \eta \text{ inr}] \cdot f)^\dagger \\
&= ([\eta \text{ inl} \vee \delta, \delta \vee \eta \text{ inr}] \cdot f)^\dagger && /\!/ \text{ Lemma 23} \\
&= ([\eta \text{ inl}, \eta \text{ inr}] \cdot f)^\dagger \\
&= f^\dagger.
\end{aligned}
$$

(ii) $(-)^* \to (-)^\dagger \to (-)^*$: Given $f\colon X \to TX$, we need to show that

$$([\eta,\delta] \cdot (\eta \text{ inl} \vee \eta \text{ inr} \cdot f)) \cdot ([\delta,\eta] \cdot (\eta \text{ inl} \vee \eta \text{ inr} \cdot f))^* = f^*.$$

Indeed, $[\eta,\delta]\cdot(\eta \text{ inl} \vee \eta \text{ inr}\cdot f) = \eta \vee \delta = \eta$, and $[\delta,\eta]\cdot(\eta \text{ inl} \vee \eta \text{ inr}\cdot f) = \delta \vee \eta \cdot f = f$, and therefore the right-hand side reduces to $\eta \cdot f^* = f^*$.

The rest of the proof amount to (iii) deriving Kleene iteration axioms from those of Elgot iteration (using Proposition 4), and to (iv) deriving Elgot iteration axioms from those of Kleene iteration.

In presence of assumptions 1.–3., the distinction between **Uniformity** and **Uniformity*** becomes very subtle.

Example 24 (Filter Monad). There is an Elgot monad **T**, whose Kleisli category is enriched over bounded semilattices, $(\eta \text{ inl} \vee \eta \text{ inr})^\dagger = \eta$, but **T** fails strong uniformity. We prove it by adapting Kozen's separating example for left-handed and right-handed Kleene algebras [24, Proposition 7].

Recall that the *filter monad* [6] sends every X to the set of all filters on X, equivalently to those maps $h\colon (X \to 2) \to 2$, which preserve $\top$ and $\wedge$: $h(\top) = \top$, $h(f \wedge g) = h(f) \wedge h(g)$ where $\top$ and $\wedge$ on $X \to 2$ are computed pointwise. For us, it will be more convenient to use the equivalent formulation, obtained by flipping the order on 2 (so, the resulting monad **T** could be actually called the *ideal monad*). Every TX is then the set of those $h\colon \mathcal{P}X \to 2$, for which

$$f(\emptyset) = \bot, \qquad\qquad f(s \cup t) = f(s) \vee f(t).$$

1. Note that Kleisli category $\mathbf{Set_T}$ is dually isomorphic to a category $\mathbf{C}$, for which every $\mathbf{C}(X, Y)$ consists of functions $\mathcal{P}X \to \mathcal{P}Y$, preserving finite joins (in particular, monotone). This category has finite products: $\mathcal{P}\emptyset$ is the terminal object and $\mathcal{P}X \times \mathcal{P}Y = \mathcal{P}(X + Y)$, by definition.
2. Under this dual isomorphism, every morphism $f \colon X \to T(Y + X)$ corresponds to a morphism $\hat{f} \colon \mathcal{P}Y \times \mathcal{P}X \to \mathcal{P}X$ in $\mathbf{C}$ where we compute a fixpoint $\mathcal{P}Y \to \mathcal{P}X$ using the *Knaster-Tarski theorem*, and transfer it back to $\mathbf{C}$ as $f^\dagger \colon X \to TY$.
3. The construction of $f^\dagger$ entails both $(\eta \ \mathsf{inl} \vee \eta \ \mathsf{inr})^\dagger \leq \eta$ and $(\eta \ \mathsf{inl} \vee \eta \ \mathsf{inr})^\dagger \geq \eta$, hence $(\eta \ \mathsf{inl} \vee \eta \ \mathsf{inr})^\dagger = \eta$.
4. Enrichment in semilattices is obvious in view of the dual isomorphism of $\mathbf{Set_T}$ and $\mathbf{C}$.
5. The **Fixpoint** law follows by construction. The remaining Elgot monad laws follow by *transfinite induction*.
6. If $\mathbf{T}$ was a Kleene monad, any $\mathbf{C}(X, X)$ would be a Kleene algebra, but Kozen showed that it is not, hence $\mathbf{T}$ is not a Kleene monad.
7. By Theorem 22, $\mathbf{T}$ fails **Uniformity***.

8   Conclusions

When it comes to modelling and semantics, many issues can be framed and treated in terms of universal algebra and coalgebra. However, certain phenomena, such as recursion, partiality, extensionality, require additional structures, often imported from the theory of complete partial orders, by enriching categories and functors, and devising suitable structures, such as recursion and more specifically iteration. In many settings though, iteration is sufficient, and can be treated as a self-contained ingredient whose properties matter, while a particular construction behind it does not. From this perspective, Elgot monads present a base fundamental building block in semantics.

We formally compared Elgot monads with Kleene monads, which are a modest generalization of Kleene algebras. In contrast to inherently categorical Elgot monads, Kleene algebra is a simple notion, couched in traditional algebraic terms. The price of this simplicity is a tight pack of laws, which must be accepted altogether, but which are well-known to be conflicting with many models of iteration. We proposed a novel notion of *while-monad*, which in the categorical context are essentially equivalent to Elgot monads, and yet while-monads are morally a three-sorted algebra over (Boolean) decisions, programs and certain well-behaved programs (figuring in the so-called uniformity principle). This is somewhat similar to the extension of Kleene algebra with *tests* [28]. The resulting *Kleene algebra with tests* is two-sorted, with tests being a subsort of programs, and forming a Boolean algebra. Our *decisions* unlike tests do not form a subsort of programs, but they do support operations of Boolean algebra, without however complying with all the Boolean algebra laws. We have then related Elgot monads (and while-monads) with Kleene monads, and as a side-effect produced a novel axiomatization of Kleene algebra (Proposition 4), based on a version of the uniformity principle. We regard the present work as a step towards bringing the gap between Elgot iteration and Kleene iteration, not only in technical sense, but also in the sense of concrete usage scenarios. We plan to further explore algebraic axiomatizations of iteration, based on the current axiomatization of while-monads.

References

1. Aboul-Hosn, K., Kozen, D.: Relational semantics for higher-order programs. In: Uustalu, T. (ed.) MPC 2006. LNCS, vol. 4014, pp. 29–48. Springer, Heidelberg (2006). https://doi.org/10.1007/11783596_5
2. Adámek, J., Milius, S., Velebil, J.: Equational properties of iterative monads. Inf. Comput. **208**(12), 1306–1348 (2010)
3. Awodey, S.: Category Theory, 2nd edn. Oxford University Press Inc, Oxford (2010)
4. Bloom, S., Ésik, Z.: Iteration Theories: The Equational Logic of Iterative Processes. Springer, Cham (1993). https://doi.org/10.1007/978-3-642-78034-9
5. Căzănescu, V.E., Gheorghe, S.: Feedback, iteration, and repetition. In: Gheorghe, P. (ed.) Mathematical Aspects of Natural and Formal Languages, Volume 43 of World Scientific Series in Computer Science, pp. 43–61. World Scientific (1994)
6. Day, A.: Filter monads, continuous lattices and closure systems. Can. J. Math. **27**(1), 50–59 (1975)
7. Elgot, C.: Monadic computation and iterative algebraic theories. In: Rose, H.E., Shepherdson, J.C. (eds.) Logic Colloquium 1973, Volume 80 of Studies in Logic and the Foundations of Mathematics, pp. 175–230. Elsevier (1975)
8. Ésik, Z., Goncharov, S.: Some remarks on Conway and iteration theories. CoRR, abs/1603.00838 (2016)
9. Fokkink, W.J., Zantema, H.: Basic process algebra with iteration: completeness of its equational axioms. Comput. J. **37**(4), 259–268 (1994)
10. Gomes, L., Madeira, A., Barbosa, L.S.: On Kleene algebras for weighted computation. In: Cavalheiro, S., Fiadeiro, J. (eds.) SBMF 2017. LNCS, vol. 10623, pp. 271–286. Springer, Cham (2017). https://doi.org/10.1007/978-3-319-70848-5_17
11. Goncharov, S.: Kleene monads. PhD thesis, Universität Bremen (2010)
12. Goncharov, S.: Uniform Elgot iteration in foundations. In: 48th International Colloquium on Automata, Languages, and Programming, ICALP 2021, Volume 198 of LIPIcs, pp. 131:1–131:16. Schloss Dagstuhl - Leibniz-Zentrum für Informatik (2021)
13. Goncharov, S., Jakob, J., Neves, R.: A semantics for hybrid iteration. In: Schewe, S., Zhang, L. (eds.) 29th International Conference on Concurrency Theory, CONCUR 2018, Volume 118 of LIPIcs, pp. 22:1–22:17. Schloss Dagstuhl - Leibniz-Zentrum für Informatik (2018)
14. Goncharov, S., Schröder, L., Mossakowski, T.: Kleene monads: handling iteration in a framework of generic effects. In: Kurz, A., Lenisa, M., Tarlecki, A. (eds.) CALCO 2009. LNCS, vol. 5728, pp. 18–33. Springer, Heidelberg (2009). https://doi.org/10.1007/978-3-642-03741-2_3
15. Goncharov, S., Schröder, L., Rauch, C., Jakob, J.: Unguarded recursion on coinductive resumptions. Log. Methods Comput. Sci **14**(3) (2018)
16. Goncharov, S., Schröder, L., Rauch, C., Piróg, M.: Unifying guarded and unguarded iteration. In: Esparza, J., Murawski, A.S. (eds.) FoSSaCS 2017. LNCS, vol. 10203, pp. 517–533. Springer, Heidelberg (2017). https://doi.org/10.1007/978-3-662-54458-7_30

17. Hasegawa, M.: The uniformity principle on traced monoidal categories. In: Category Theory and Computer Science, CTCS 2002, Volume 69 of ENTCS, pp. 137–155 (2003)
18. Hoare, C.A.R.T., Möller, B., Struth, G., Wehrman, I.: Concurrent Kleene algebra. In: Bravetti, M., Zavattaro, G. (eds.) CONCUR 2009. LNCS, vol. 5710, pp. 399–414. Springer, Heidelberg (2009). https://doi.org/10.1007/978-3-642-04081-8_27
19. Jacobs, B.: Affine monads and side-effect-freeness. In: Hasuo, I. (ed.) CMCS 2016. LNCS, vol. 9608, pp. 53–72. Springer, Cham (2016). https://doi.org/10.1007/978-3-319-40370-0_5
20. Jacobs, B., Poll, E.: Coalgebras and monads in the semantics of java. Theoret. Comput. Sci. **291**, 329–349 (2003)
21. Joyal, A., Street, R., Verity, D.: Traced monoidal categories. In: Mathematical Proceedings of the Cambridge Philosophical Society, vol. 119, pp. 447–468 (1996)
22. Kleene, S.C.: Representation of events in nerve nets and finite automata. In: Shannon, C., McCarthy, J. (eds.) Automata Studies, pp. 3–41. Princeton University Press (1956)
23. Kock, A.: Strong functors and monoidal monads. Arch. Math. **23**(1), 113–120 (1972)
24. Kozen, D.: On Kleene algebras and closed semirings. In: Rovan, B. (ed.) MFCS 1990. LNCS, vol. 452, pp. 26–47. Springer, Heidelberg (1990). https://doi.org/10.1007/BFb0029594
25. Kozen, D.: A completeness theorem for Kleene algebras and the algebra of regular events. Inf. Comput. **110**(2), 366–390 (1994)
26. Kozen, D.: On the complexity of reasoning in Kleene algebra. Inf. Comput. **179**, 152–162 (2002)
27. Kozen, D., Mamouras, K.: Kleene algebra with products and iteration theories. In: Ronchi, S., Rocca, D. (eds.) Proceedings Computer Science Logic 2013, CSL 2013, Volume 23 of LIPIcs, pp. 415–431. Schloss Dagstuhl - Leibniz-Zentrum für Informatik (2013)
28. Kozen, D., Smith, F.: Kleene algebra with tests: completeness and decidability. In: van Dalen, D., Bezem, M. (eds.) CSL 1996. LNCS, vol. 1258, pp. 244–259. Springer, Heidelberg (1997). https://doi.org/10.1007/3-540-63172-0_43
29. Lambek, J.: A fixpoint theorem for complete categories. Math. Z. **103**, 151–161 (1968)
30. Levy, P.B., Goncharov, S.: Coinductive resumption monads: guarded iterative and guarded Elgot. In: Proceedings 8rd International Conference on Algebra and Coalgebra in Computer Science, CALCO 2019, LIPIcs. Schloss Dagstuhl - Leibniz-Zentrum für Informatik (2019)
31. McIver, A., Rabehaja, T.M., Struth, G.: On probabilistic Kleene algebras, automata and simulations. In: de Swart, H. (ed.) RAMICS 2011. LNCS, vol. 6663, pp. 264–279. Springer, Heidelberg (2011). https://doi.org/10.1007/978-3-642-21070-9_20
32. Moggi, E.: A modular approach to denotational semantics. In: Pitt, D.H., Curien, P.-L., Abramsky, S., Pitts, A.M., Poigné, A., Rydeheard, D.E. (eds.) CTCS 1991. LNCS, vol. 530, pp. 138–139. Springer, Heidelberg (1991). https://doi.org/10.1007/BFb0013462
33. Möller, B.: Kleene getting lazy. Sci. Comput. Programm. **65**(2), 195–214 (2007). Special Issue Dedicated to Selected Papers from the Conference of Program Construction 2004, MPC 2004
34. Platzer, A.: Differential dynamic logic for hybrid systems. J. Autom. Reasoning **41**(2), 143–189 (2008)

35. Plotkin, G.D.: A powerdomain construction. SIAM J. Comput. **5**(3), 452–487 (1976)
36. Stone, M.: Postulates for the barycentric calculus. Ann. Mat. Pura Appl. **29**(1), 25–30 (1949)
37. Varacca, D., Winskel, G.: Distributing probability over non-determinism. Math. Struct. Comput. Sci. **16**(1), 87–113 (2006)

Automated QoS-Aware Service Selection Based on Soft Constraints

Elias Keis[1,2,3] , Carlos Gustavo Lopez Pombo[4] ,
Agustín Eloy Martinez Suñé[5(✉)] , and Alexander Knapp[1]

¹ Universität Augsburg, Augsburg, Germany
`elias.keis@tum.de`, `alexander.knapp@uni-a.de`
² Technische Universität München, Munich, Germany
³ Ludwig-Maximilians-Universität München, Munich, Germany
⁴ Universidad Nacional de Río Negro and CONICET, San Carlos de Bariloche, Argentina
`cglopezpombo@unrn.edu.ar`
⁵ Universidad de Buenos Aires and CONICET, Buenos Aires, Argentina
`aemartinez@dc.uba.ar`

Abstract. QoS attributes are one of the key factors taken into account when selecting services for a composite application. While there are systems for automated service selection based on QoS constraints, most of them are very limited in the preferences the user can state. In this paper we present: a) a simple, yet versatile, language for describing composite applications, b) a rich set of notations for stating complex preferences over the QoS attributes, including checkpoints and invariants, and c) an automatic tool for optimal global QoS-aware service selection based on MiniBrass, a state-of-the-art soft-constraint solver. We provide a running example accompanying the definitions and a preliminary performance analysis showing the practical usefulness of the tools.

Keywords: Service selection · Soft-constraint solving · Quality of service · Service-oriented computing

1 Introduction

In software-as-a-service paradigms such as service-oriented computing, software systems are no longer monolithic chunks of code executing within the boundaries of an organization. As stated in [21], the vision is to assemble "application components into a network of services that can be loosely coupled to create flexible, dynamic business processes and agile applications that span organizations and computing platforms".

Services are "autonomous, platform-independent entities that can be described, published, discovered, and loosely coupled in novel ways" [21, p. 38]. When several services are combined to achieve a particular goal, it is called *Service Composition* [4, p. 55]. While there are several disciplines of Service

ⓒ Springer Nature Switzerland AG 2023
A. Madeira and M. A. Martins (Eds.): WADT 2022, LNCS 13710, pp. 121–140, 2023.
https://doi.org/10.1007/978-3-031-43345-0_6

Composition, we focus on Service Orchestration, i.e., creating new services "by combining several existing services in a process flow" [4, p. 57].

When composing or using existing services, we hopefully have multiple services fulfilling the functional requirements of our tasks. Beyond that, they typically stand out against each other in several non-functional attributes. While the price is an important aspect, they usually also differ in their *Quality of Service* (QoS) attributes, for example, latency or availability [16]. Therefore, an essential aspect of the Service Selection Problem [6, pt. II] is determining whether the QoS profile of a service satisfies the QoS requirements of a client.

Our approach is based on Constraint Programming (CP) [23] leaning on soft constraint solving to automate the process of selecting adequate services based on their QoS properties. Adding hard constraints to reduce the number of matching services is simple but might lead to either a still too extensive range of services or not a single one left if we overconstrain the problem. Soft constraints come in handy as the solver can omit them if the Constraint Satisfaction Problem (CSP) [11] would be overconstrained otherwise.

We present a tool, named QosAgg, for solving the service selection problem for composite services in a soft way. We leverage on MiniBrass, a tool presented in [26] that extends the MiniZinc [20] constraint modeling language and tool, providing various options to model and solve soft CSPs based on the unifying algebraic theory of Partial Valuation Structures (PVSs) [27]. Specifically, our approach provides the means for: 1) describing a service workflow over which the service selection has to be performed, 2) expressing QoS profiles associated with concrete services as values of its QoS attributes, 3) expressing QoS requirements as soft constraints over the aggregated value of QoS attributes along the execution of the workflow, 4) automatically finding the best (if any) assignment of services to tasks given the above set up.

In Sect. 2, we present our approach to the problem of selecting services to optimize global QoS requirements of a workflow. In Sect. 3 we introduce the MiniBrass modelling language. In Sect. 4 we show how to model and solve QoS aware service selection in MiniBrass. In Sect. 5 we perform preliminary performance experiments. Finally, in Sect. 6 we draw some conclusions and point out possible future lines of research.

Related Work. Our work consists of QoS-aware service selection for workflows, based on soft constraint solving. While optimization-based techniques can be separated into locally and globally optimizing ones, we focus on global optimization-based service selection, where the QoS of each service is considered pre-determined. In most cases, global optimization means that QoS has to be aggregated, Sakellariou and Yarmolenko [24] discuss how this can be done for several attributes.

There are knapsack and graph-path-finding-based approaches for modelling and solving the optimization problem [30]. Zheng, Luo, and Song [32] propose a colony-based selection algorithm applicable to multi-agent service composition [29]. We will delegate the solving of the problem to dedicated solvers but use a multidimensional, multiple-choice knapsack problem for modelling as well.

In most of the works that apply Constraint Programming for service selection, such as [14], only hard constraints are used. When soft constraints are used, the way to express preferences over solutions is quite limited. For example, [22] supports softness by assigning importance levels to constraints. Deng et al. [8] use constraint solving but concentrate on the domain of mobile cloud computing and therefore put emphasis on temporal constraints. Arbab et al. are working with (Soft) Constraint Automata [1,2,9] and use them for service discovery [3, 25]. However, Soft Constraint Automata turn out to be representable by soft constraint satisfaction problems (SCSPs) [2, sec. 6.1], and they concentrate on local optimization only.

Rosenberg et al. [22] provide an implementation as part of their VRESCo project [18] that also supports soft constraints [17], but only weighted ones as well. A more general formalization for soft constraints is c-semirings (Constraint Semirings) [5] that can also be used for service selection, as Zemni, Benbernou, and Carro [31] show, but without an implementation. We will fill this gap and provide flexible soft constraints for service selection in an easy-to-use manner for users with basic knowledge of constraint programming.

2   Service Selection for Composite Services

Composite services can often be described as workflows [4]. A workflow consists of one or multiple abstract services. An abstract service is a task that needs to be done. Each abstract service can be instantiated by any of a class of concrete ones that can fulfil the task. To avoid confusion, we refer to abstract services as *tasks* and to concrete services merely as *services*. The tasks in a workflow can be composed sequentially, in parallel, be subject to a choice and put within a loop.

The selection of services to fulfil the tasks in a workflow can be done in many ways. In our case, workflows are converted to execution plans defining the paths traversing the workflow. This allows the selection of adequate services for every task instance in the path, even admitting the selection of different services for performing different instances of the same task if it has to be executed more than once, e.g., in loops.

We'll start with a simple example workflow inspired by [19, Fig. 13.1].

Imagine a workflow with an initialization task A that can be done by two provisioning services a_1 and a_2 and a finalization task E with two eligible services e_1, e_2. In between, there are two possible paths: either task B is done, which has three provisions b_1 to b_3; or instead, task C with the same provisions is executed but then succeeded by task D that is done by the only available service d_1.

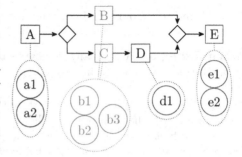

Definition 1. Workflow graphs *are defined by the following grammar:*

$$\langle\,Task\rangle ::= Task\ name$$
$$\langle G\rangle ::= Null\ \mid\ \langle\,Task\rangle\ \mid\ \langle G\rangle \to \langle G\rangle\ \mid\ \langle G\rangle|\langle G\rangle\ \mid\ \langle G\rangle + \langle G\rangle$$
$$Additionally,\ \langle G\rangle^n\ serves\ as\ syntactic\ sugar\ (n \in \mathbb{Z}_{>0}).$$

where A $\to$ B *(or short:* A B*) denotes sequential composition,* A | B *parallel composition,* A + B *choice, and* A^n *a loop with a fixed number of iterations n. The graph shown above looks like this:* A $\to$ (B + C D) $\to$ E.

As it is clear from the previous definition, we assume that iterations in a workflow graph are bounded, so every execution plan is finite and the procedure of service selection is safe from the pothole posed by the termination problem of unbounded iterations.

Definition 2 (Provisioning service description). *A service description consists of: 1) a service name, 2) a set of tasks it can be assigned to, and 3) a set of QoS attribute names associated with the specific values the service guarantees.*

For instance, recalling the previous example, provision b3 can be assigned to tasks B, C, and have the following QoS attributes: cost = 9, responsetime = 2, availability = 98, accuracy = 99.5, etc.

Since we aim at performing a global selection we should be able to define preferences about the overall QoS of the composition. Therefore, we need a way to aggregate the QoS attributes of the individual services in a workflow configuration. For the QoS attributes that should be aggregated over the whole workflow, there needs to be information on how to aggregate them.

Definition 3 (Aggregation operator). *Each QoS attribute has two associated aggregation operators:*

– $\mathrm{agg}_{\to}$, *a binary operator for aggregating it over sequential composition, and*
– $\mathrm{agg}_{\parallel}$, *a binary operator for aggregating it over parallel composition.*

Next we introduce our running example.

Running Example: A company dedicated to manufacture skateboards rents two workstations in a co-working workshop.

Workflow. The company needs to rent storage for the wheels, boards, and the finished skateboards that it produces. The co-working workshop offers two rental models. In the first model, one can rent storage for precisely 10 or 15 items. In the second, one also has to decide in advance how many items to store but can rent storage for between 10 and 15 items. The second rental model is a bit more expensive on a per-item basis and takes a bit longer to set up.

Once the storage is rented, the company can start producing the boards. The work is organized in iterations. In each iteration, each workstation can work individually: one crafts wheels, the other one boards. Alternatively, work can be done together to assemble four wheels and one board to a skateboard. When assembling, one can decide to assemble three boards at once, which is a bit faster. Also, when crafting boards, you either can craft a single board or craft three boards of a different kind in a single iteration, which is a bit more time and cost-efficient, and the boards are a bit more pliable but also heavier. Regarding the wheels, we always create four wheels in a single iteration, but we can choose from four different kinds of wheels that differ in durability, friction, and cost.

When one workstation is done with the own task of an iteration, it waits for the other one to finish, too. After ten iterations, we pack

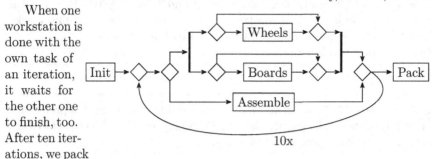

the finished skateboards either not at all, using cardboard or in a wooden box. Cardboard—and wood even more—provides better protection but is more expensive and time-consuming.

Attributes. We care about the following global attributes that affect the overall outcome or the dependencies between tasks: cost, time, storage, number of produced boards, number of produced wheels, number of finished products.

3 Soft Constraint Solving with MiniBrass

MiniZinc [20] is a solver-independent constraint modeling language for describing CSPs and constraint optimization problems (COPs) and an associated tool which translates MiniZinc specifications into the lower-level solver input language FlatZinc, supported by numerous constraint solvers. MiniZinc is also used as a frontend for invoking the user-defined specific solver; which, in our case, will be Gurobi[1], a state-of-the-art commercial optimization solver. In contrast to traditional programming, where the programmer states what the program should do in order to compute the result, in constraint programming, the modeller only states what the solution must satisfy; then, a solver is responsible for coming up with potential solutions, checking them against the constraints in the model, and then returning any, or the best, solution.

MiniZinc differentiates between decision and parameter variables. While parameter variables are compile-time constant, i.e., their value is known even before the solver starts working, decision variables are the ones that the solver

---
[1] Available at https://www.gurobi.com.

can variate to come up with new solutions. MiniZinc supports a lot more capabilities, like arrays, quantifiers, or optimization, to name a few[2].

Example 1 demonstrates the usage of MiniZinc by showing a toy specification, together with its output and some considerations.

Example 1. MiniZinc specification:

```
1    set of int: DOM = 1..2; % DOM = {1, 2}
2    var DOM: x; var DOM: y; % x, y in DOM
3    constraint x!=y;
4    solve satisfy;
```

Line 1 defines a set DOM containing the integers 1 and 2, line 2 defines two decision variables x and y in DOM, line 3 constrains them to be different, and line 4 asks MiniZinc to solve the problem and return any satisfying solution.

MiniZinc's output after running:

```
x = 2;
y = 1;
```

Obviously, $(x, y) = (1, 2)$ would also have been a valid solution. Such a preference can be enforced by replacing the keyword satisfy by the objective function minimize x in the statement solve of line 4.

MiniBrass [26], also a modelling language equipped with an analysis tool, extends MiniZinc in two ways. On the one hand, it enriches the MiniZinc constraint modelling language with preference models containing soft constraints. Soft constraints are constraints that might be omitted if the problem would be unsatisfiable otherwise. MiniBrass supports a range of algebraic structures called Partial Valuation Structures (PVSes) [27] that enable the prioritization of constraints. On the other hand, MiniBrass implements a branch-and-bound search algorithm which iteratively generates MiniZinc models by adding constrains from the preference model whose solutions are considered subsequently better, according to the underlying PVS. In a sense, MiniBrass is providing the means for traversing the complete lattice of constraint systems, induced by the preference model [5, Thm. 2.9][3], and searching for an optimum solution. A more comprehensive explanation of the many algorithmic aspects involved in the implementation can be found in [26, p. 21].

While MiniBrass provides various predefined PVSes, e.g., for constraint preferences given as graph, fuzzy constraints, weighted CSPs, and many more, it also admits the definition of custom PVSes, if needed.

Definition 4 (Partial Valuation Structure – Definition 1, [27]). *A partial valuation structure $M = (X, \cdot, \varepsilon, \leq)$ is given by an underlying set X, an associative and commutative multiplication operation $\cdot : X \times X \to X$, a neutral element $\varepsilon \in X$ for $\cdot$, and a partial ordering $\leq \subseteq X \times X$ such that the multiplication $\cdot$ is*

---

[2] The interested reader might, however, have a look at the handbook https://www.minizinc.org/doc-latest/en/index.html.

[3] While [5, Thm. 2.9] is stated for c-semirings, PVSes can be converted to and created from c-semirings [5,13,26], another popular algebraic framework for soft constraints.

monotone in both arguments w.r.t. $\leq$, *i.e.*, $m_1 \cdot m_2 \leq m_1' \cdot m_2'$ *if* $m_1 \leq m_1'$ *and* $m_2 \leq m_2'$, *and* ε *is the top element w.r.t.* $\leq$.

We write $m_1 < m_2$ if $m_1 \leq m_2$ and $m_1 \neq m_2$, and $m_1 \parallel m_2$ if neither $m_1 \leq m_2$ nor $m_2 \leq m_1$. We write $|M|$ for the underlying set and $\cdot_M$, ε_M, and $\leq_M$ for the other parts of M.

Among the many PVSes already defined in MiniBrass we can find the PVS type `WeightedCsp` from [26, p. 27]. Such a PVS allows for assigning a weight to each of the soft constraints, which will act as preferences. In the resulting MiniZinc model, heavier constraints will be preferred over lighter ones.

Example 2 shows the use of PVSes for extending Example 1 by an instance of `WeightedCsp` in order to formalize a preference model.

Example 2. MiniBrass preference model:

```
1  include "defs.mbr";
2  PVS: prefer2 = new WeightedCsp("prefer2") {
3    soft-constraint xEquals2: 'x==2';
4    soft-constraint yEquals2: 'y==2' :: weights('2');
5  };
6  solve prefer2;
```

Line 1 includes the standard MiniBrass definitions (`defs.mbr`) which, among others, allows the usage of `WeightedCsp`. The identifier `prefer2` in line 2 is the name we choose for our PVS instance. Lines 3 and 4 declare two soft constraints requiring x and y to be equal to 2 but establish `yEquals2` to be heavier (i.e., has weight 2 in contrast to 1 which is the default weight for the CSP). Therefore, the complete model consists of both, the hard constraints of the MiniZinc specification shown in Example 1 and the MiniBrass preference model shown above. As x and y have to be different according to the hard constraint, it is not possible to fulfill both soft constraint simultaneously. Even though $(x, y) = (2, 1)$ fulfils the hard constraints, the only admissible optimal solution is $(x, y) = (1, 2)$ because the soft constraint `yEquals2` is heavier than `xEquals2`.

New PVSes can be constructed by combining two PVSes using either the lexicographic or the Pareto product. The lexicographic combination M `lex` N prioritizes the ordering of solutions of M and only considers N when M cannot decide between two solutions. In the Pareto combination M `pareto` N, a solution is better than another if it is better for both M and N.

4 Modeling QoS-Aware Service Selection in MiniBrass

The tool we are presenting, named QosAgg, takes as inputs the workflow description including the quantitative attributes over which the QoS is to be evaluated, and the service definitions together with their possible assignments to tasks. Its output is the MiniZinc code containing the CSP to be solved including basic declarations, enums for tasks and services, decision variables assigning one service to every task and one branch per path choice. The model generated by QosAgg corresponds to a 0/1 multi-dimensional multi-choice knapsack problem [15, 30]:

task instances are the bags, and we can put precisely one service into each bag. Next, one array per QoS attribute is created, containing the values for every service.

A key element in the translation to a CSP is, as we mentioned before, the aggregation of QoS attributes along the paths of the workflow in a way that makes possible to check the satisfaction of the desired constraints. From a theoretical point of view, bounded loops are no more than syntactic sugar, so we start by unfolding them in order to obtain the equivalent graph that can only be *null*, a *single task*, a *sequential composition*, a *parallel composition* or a *choice composition*. Then, for a graph G aggregation $q(G)$ is then defined recursively on its structure as follows:

- Let $\eta(T)$ denote the service chosen to perform the *single task* T,
- Let $\eta(G_0 + G_1 + \cdots + G_n)$ denote the specific subgraph selected by the choice,
- $q(null)$ yields the valuation which is $\text{agg}_\rightarrow()$ for all the QoS attributes,
- $q(T)$, with T a *single task*, yields the QoS contract of $\eta(T)$,
- $q(G_0 \rightarrow G_1 \rightarrow \cdots \rightarrow G_n)$ yields the valuation $\text{agg}_\rightarrow(q(G_0), q(G_1), \ldots, q(G_n))$,
- $q(G_0 \parallel G_1 \parallel \cdots \parallel G_n)$ yields the valuation $\text{agg}_\parallel(q(G_0), q(G_1), \ldots, q(G_n))$,
- $q(G_0 + G_1 + \cdots + G_n)$ yields the valuation $q(\eta(G_0 + G_1 + \cdots + G_n))$.

Essentially, q aggregates over the parallel and sequential composition using the corresponding aggregation operators. It deals with single tasks, and choices by using decision variables that let the solver make the best decision for the overall QoS. We continue by showing the modeling workflow of the running example introduced in Sect. 2.

Example 3 (A skateboard company). We start by showing in Listing 1.1 the input file for QosAgg containing the workflow definition, the provision contracts and the quantitative attributes that constitute the QoS model.

```
workflow wf {
  graph: Init -> ((Wheels? | Boards?) + Assemble)^10 -> Pack;

  provision bigStore for Init: cost = 60, time = 20, storage = 15;
  provision smallStore for Init: cost = 30, time = 10, storage = 10;

  provision badWheels for Wheels: cost = 5, time = 2, wheels = 4;
  provision okWheels for Wheels: cost = 5, time = 2, wheels = 4;
  provision expensiveWheels for Wheels: cost = 10, time = 2, wheels = 4;
  provision goodWheels for Wheels: cost = 5, time = 2, wheels = 4;

  provision singleBoard for Boards: cost = 7, time = 3, boards = 1;
  provision threeBoard for Boards: cost = 16, time = 10, boards = 3;

  provision singleAssembly for Assemble: cost = 2, time = 4, products = 1,
      wheels = -4, boards = -1;
  provision threeAssembly for Assemble: cost = 6, time = 10, products = 3,
      wheels = -12, boards = -3;

  provision noPacking for Pack: cost = 0, time = 0;
  provision woodPacking for Pack: cost = 20, time = 10;
  provision cardboardPacking for Pack: cost = 3, time = 3;

  attribute cost of var int; aggregation cost: sum;
  attribute time of var int; aggregation time: sum, max;
```

```
attribute boards of int default 0; aggregation boards: sum;
attribute wheels of int default 0; aggregation wheels: sum;
attribute products of int default 0; aggregation products: sum;
attribute storage of var int default 0;
};
```

Listing 1.1. QoS model

If we run MiniZinc to solve the CSP produced by QosAgg, it will output a statement displaying a solution to the problem including a path across the workflow together with the selected services for each task instance in the path, and the aggregated value for each QoS attribute for that selection.

Arbitrary hard constraints can be added on top of the basic CSP problem output by QosAgg in order to force MiniZinc to find more specific solutions satisfying both, the basic model, and the newly added hard constrains. For example, we can enrich our model by defining the notion of **profit** by means of fixing the retail price (in this case at 25) and considering the aggregated cost and the aggregated number of finished products along the selected path. This will make MiniZinc compute the value of the variable **profit** enabling, for example, the possibility of enforcing a lower bound for its value stating that we only accept solutions leading to a profit greater than such a bound (shown in Listing 1.2). This is done by feeding MiniZinc with both, the basic MiniZinc model obtained from QosAgg with the following handcrafted MiniZinc specification:

```
int: price = 25;
int: bound = 10;
var int: profit = price * wf_aggregated_products - wf_aggregated_cost;

constraint profit > bound;
```

Listing 1.2. MiniZinc constrain model

Analysing the resulting model will lead to any solution (i.e., a path in the workflow and an assignment of services to tasks) in which the value calculated for **profit** is greater than 10. MiniZinc can also be run with the statement **solve maximize profit**; forcing the tool to find an optimum solution in which the value of **profit** is not only greater than 10, but also the maximum possible.

Going further, we propose to aim at a richer form of constraints. Adding soft constraints to our model allows to, for example, force the solvers to search for solutions that increase profit and decrease time consumption. This can be done by writing a MiniBrass preference model resorting to two instances of the predefined PVS type **CostFunctionNetwork** and the lexicographical product for combining them as shown in Listing 1.3.

```
PVS: profit = new CostFunctionNetwork("profit") {
  soft-constraint profit: '500-profit';
};
PVS: time = new CostFunctionNetwork("time") {
  soft-constraint time: 'wf_aggregated_time';
};
solve profit lex time;
```

Listing 1.3. MiniBrass preference model

The process continues by feeding MiniBrass input the preference model shown above, and the basic MiniZinc resulting from combining: 1) the basic model output by QosAgg from the original model, enriched with 2) the additional handcrafted hard constraints of a choice.

It will then initiate the search for an optimum solution to the Soft CSP. As we mentioned before, this is done by applying a branch-and-bound searching algorithm over the complete lattice of constraint systems, induced by the PVS formalizing the preference model. The procedure implemented in MiniBrass will iteratively generate MiniZinc CSPs by adding constraints forcing any solution to be better than the one found in the previous iteration. In each iteration MiniZinc is run finding such solution. The iterative process is performed until the CSP gets unsatisfiable, at which point, an optimal solution has been found in the previous iteration.

Running MiniBrass on: a) the combination of the output of running QosAgg on the model shown in Listing 1.1 and the MiniZinc constrain model shown in Listing 1.2, and b) the MiniBrass preference model shown in Listing 1.3, yields the statement shown in Listing 1.4.

```
Profit: 13
Selection graph for wf:
    Init=bigStore → (Wheels=goodWheels | ) → (Wheels=goodWheels | ) → (
        Wheels=goodWheels | Boards=threeBoard) → Assemble=threeAssembly → (
        Wheels=goodWheels | Boards=threeBoard) → (Wheels=goodWheels | ) →
        Assemble=singleAssembly → (Wheels=goodWheels | ) → Assemble=
        singleAssembly → Assemble=singleAssembly → Pack=cardboardPacking
Aggregations for wf:
    cost: 137
    time: 73
    boards: 0
    wheels: 0
    products: 6
```

Listing 1.4. MiniZinc solution with aggregation values

The solution has a profit value of 13, workflow is displayed with the selected services for each task instance, and the aggregated value obtained for each QoS attribute is shown. The total cost of the solution is 137, the total time is 73, and the total number of skateboards produced is 6. The attributes **boards** and **wheels** are used to keep track of the number of boards and wheels produced. When the task **Assemble** is executed to produce skateboards it consumes **boards** and **wheels** and produces **products**. A final number of 0 for **boards** and **wheels** means that all the boards and wheels produced have been consumed to produce skateboards.

4.1   Adding Checkpoints to QosAgg Workflows

Up to this point, we showed how to model the problem of assigning services to tasks organized in a complex workflow, and how it can be solved based on the satisfaction of a combination of: 1) hard constraints added to the basic model, the latter obtained from the description of the workflow, the declaration of the QoS attributes and the declaration of services capable of performing each of the tasks, and 2) soft constrains declared as a preference model through the use of PVSes.

This approach yields a framework in which it is possible to reason about the overall aggregated-by-attribute QoS of workflows and the local QoS of the distinct tasks, but we lack everything in between. This void might lead to a problem when a desired property is supposed to hold after the execution of a specific part of a workflow which is not after its completion. Consider the example of attributes that do not exclusively grow (resp. shrink), but that can both grow and shrink, and we need to preserve certain invariants regarding greater and lower bounds for such attributes. A classic example is that of producers and consumers of resources.

Example 4. Imagine a workflow graph $A \rightarrow B \rightarrow C$ where tasks A and C are meant to produce some resource, and B consumes it. Let there be services a_1, a_2 for task A, b_1, b_2 for B, and c for C, with QoS attributes "cost" and "resource" (interpreted as the cost associated to the execution of the service, and the resources produced/consumed by the service) with addition as aggregation function, and the following QoS contracts:

	a_1	a_2	b_1	b_2	c
cost	1	2	1	2	1
resource	1	2	-2	-1	2

Then, if we solve optimizing aiming at the lower overall cost, we end up with the selection a_1, b_1, and c with aggregated cost 3. It is clear that this solution is not satisfying as service a_1 only produces one resource item, but b_1 consumes two. Adding a constraint to the overall aggregation of the resource attribute is not of any use because service c adds two more resource items at the end, compensating the (infeasible) "debt" caused by b.

Example 4 exposes the need of some form of constraints over the aggregated value of QoS attributes at chosen points within the workflow. Such points in the execution of a workflow are referred to as "checkpoints" and are placed directly before and after tasks. They allow us to specify *invariants* by addressing all the relevant checkpoints in a certain fragment of interest of the workflow, or to specify pre-/post-conditions for specific tasks only by addressing the checkpoints appearing before and after such a task. Figure 1 illustrates this.

Aggregation on Checkpoint. Checkpoints mark those points in the workflow where constraints are plausible to be placed. Adding constraints at checkpoints requires the capability of aggregating the values of QoS attributes up to the specific checkpoint of interest. The reader should note that the definition of the aggregation presents no further difficulty with respect to what we discussed at the beginning of the present section but with the sole difference that now the

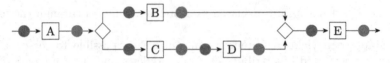

Fig. 1. Checkpoints in a workflow. ● are pre-conditions, ● post-conditions. (Color figure online)

evaluation is only performed over the maximal subgraph starting at the beginning of the workflow, and leading to the checkpoint one is interested in as an ending point.

Constraints on Checkpoints. Checkpoints allow us a smoother implementation of various constraints. Going back to our running example, we can observe that there is an actual risk of: 1) the sum of the produced wheels, boards, and finished skateboards in the storage might exceed the capacity we booked, or 2) the numbers of wheels, boards, and skateboards might be negative;

or, at least, there is no formal impediment for any of those situations to occur. Therefore, we would like to guarantee that none of those situations happens to be true at any point in the path selected as a solution. The following constraint shows how checkpoints help in enforcing this type of properties:

```
constraint forall(cp in wf_all_checkpoints)(
  wf_checkpoints_boards[cp] + wf_checkpoints_wheels[cp] +
      wf_checkpoints_products[cp] <= storage /\
  wf_checkpoints_boards[cp] >= 0 /\ wf_checkpoints_wheels[cp] >= 0 /\
      wf_checkpoints_products[cp] >= 0
);
```

In the previous constraint `wf_all_checkpoints` is the designated name for the set containing all the checkpoints of the workflow, and `wf_checkpoints_boards`, `wf_checkpoints_wheels` and `wf_checkpoints_products` are arrays containing the aggregated attribute value up to every checkpoint in `wf_all_checkpoints`.

Finally, by resorting to this type of constraints we can recall Example 4 and provide an elegant solution for the problem we used as motivation. The following constraint is what we need: "`constraint forall(cp in wf_all_checkpoints) (wf_checkpoints_resource[cp] >= 0);`".

Loops introduce a complex control flow structure that requires special treatment in order to provide a flexible way of establishing constraints allowing them to restrict all the iterations or just a single one, as shown in the following example. Let a workflow have graph $(A^3 \parallel B)^2$ and a single QoS attribute named `resource`. As tasks in a path are named according to their concrete instance once the iterations are unfolded, all of them have their own associated checkpoints so we can, for example, ensure that we start with at least five resource items in the first iteration by adding the following constrain: "`constraint wf_checkpoints_resource[wf_A_pre_1_1] >= 5;`".

Analogously, "`wf_A_pre_2_3`" would be the name for the checkpoint for the last iteration. A constraint ensuring that after executing (any instance of) B there are less than five resource items can be stated as follows: "`constraint forall(cp in wf_checkpoints_B_post)(wf_checkpoints_resource[cp] < 5);`".

The case of workflows containing choices present a different, and very important issue. Consider workflow "*Give + Take*" and again a single QoS attribute named **resource**. The services for *Give* all produce items; the services for *Take* all consume them. Again we want to ensure that no resource is used before it has been produced. Adding the constraint "`constraint forall(cp in wf_all_checkpoints)(wf_checkpoints_resource[cp] >= 0)`" solves the problem but only partially. Note that, as there is no loop, the only reasonable choice is the path executing *Give* and omitting task *Take*, and that is the right solution. However, MiniZinc yields that the problem is unsatisfiable; this is because `wf_all_checkpoints` also contains the checkpoint `wf_Take_post`, and there the resource balance is negative. Nevertheless, when choosing the path with *Give*, we can ignore that checkpoint as the execution never even comes across task *Take*.

This is a problem regarding the reachability of specific points. To solve this issue we added expressions for each task instance stating whether it is reachable, i.e., part of the selected path, or not. We use these expressions to include only those checkpoints in the predefined checkpoint sets that are part of the selected path. For a task instance to be reachable, all the choices that it is part of need to select the branches leading towards the instance.

Once again, for the code generation, we recursively descend in the workflow graph. Each time we come across a choice composition, we remember the name of its choice decision variable and the branch we descended into. When we reach a single task, the conjunction of all choice variables we came across having the value required for the branch we went into gives us the reachability expression. In the case of the task Take in motivating situation described above, this would be: "`choice1 == 2`". Therefore, the checkpoint set `wf_all_checkpoints` is generated by filtering all the checkpoints for reachability. However, individual checkpoints, like "`wf_Take_post`" in our example, require manual handling. For example, the "`constraint wf_checkpoints_resource[wf_Take_post] >= 0`" has to hold even if "`wf_Take_inst`" is not reachable. One way to solve this is to only "enable" constraints when the instance is reachable. This is done by resorting to the assertion "`wf_reachable`" with which it is possible to state the constraint: "`constraint wf_reachable[wf_Take_inst] -> wf_checkpoints_resource[wf_Take_post] >= 0;`".

4.2 Toolchain Architecture

In the figure, we depict the architecture of the toolchain we propose for solving the problem of QoS-aware service selection for tasks organized as complex workflows described at the beginning of this section.

Dark grey nodes symbolize tools and light grey ones are files; among the latter, those with solid outline are either the model, or the output statement, and those with the dashed outline are intermediate files resulting from processing the

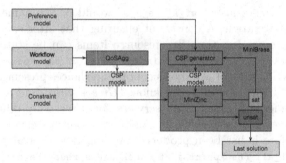

model. The model consists of: 1) the *workflow model* containing: a) the graph of tasks, b) the QoS attributes, each of them with their corresponding aggregation functions for both, parallel composition and sequential composition, and c) the services' QoS specification and possible assignment to tasks; 2) the *constraint model* consisting of the hard constraints the user wants the solution to satisfy, and 3) the *preference model* consisting of the soft constraints the user wants to guide the search for a solution.

The tools include: 1) QosAgg that takes the workflow model as input and produces a file containing the basic CSP model containing the specification of the corresponding 0/1 multi-dimensional multi-choice knapsack problem, 2) MiniBrass that takes the CSP model resulting from combining the output of QosAgg and the constraint model, and the preference model, and implements the branch-and-bound search algorithm for incrementally finding the best solution, according to the preference model, and 3) MiniZinc that runs the solver over the complete model in order to find the optimum solution.

5   Preliminary Performance Analysis

In this paper we proposed a toolchain for QoS-aware service selection for tasks organized as complex workflows. Among the different tools involved in it, we were responsible only for the development of QosAgg. On the one hand, an exclusive performance analysis of QosAgg does not lead to any significant conclusion because, as we mentioned before, it is a simple parsing process translating workflow models to Soft CSP; on the other hand, any discussion on the theoretical complexity/empirical study of the toolchain formed by MiniBrass, MiniZinc and Gurobi on arbitrary Soft CSP[4], does not provide the right insight on the actual performance of such tools in analysing the Soft CSPs obtained from QosAgg. For

---

[4] The interested reader is pointed to [5, 28] for the results associated to the theoretical complexity of the formal framework underlying MiniBrass and to [26, section 5] for an empirical evaluation. In the case of the complexity associated to the use of MiniZinc there is not much to be said about the translation to FlatZinc (i.e., its target language) because most of the computational effort resides in the execution of the solver [20]. Regarding Gurobi; a comprehensive empirical study against the SAS solvers, available at https://www.sas.com, running over the Mittelmann's benchmark can be found in [12].

this reason, we chose to perform an empirical performance study of the complete toolchain we proposed as a blackbox.

For comparability reasons, the workflow model, the constraint model and preference models are synthetically generated in a specific way to be explained below. All the experiments are carried out using MiniZinc 2.6.4 with the proprietary solver Gurobi 9.5.2 on a machine having an Apple M1 chip with eight cores and 16 GB RAM on a 64 bit macOS Monterey.

This experimental study pretends to shed some light on how the structure of the workflow drives the complexity of the analysis so we devised experiments aiming at revealing the compositional nature of the computational effort required to solve a problem. To this end we: 1) performed an empirical study of the cost associated to solving Soft CSPs obtained from workflows consisting of single tasks whose complexity varies according to: a) the number of service providers, and b) the number of quantitative attributes involved in the model, 2) studied the correlation between the cost associated to the analysis of the composition of workflows (sequential, parallel and choice) and a function of the costs associated to the analysis of the workflows involved in such a composition. In this case we varied the amount of workflows (only considering simple tasks) in the composition.

The property under analysis in all cases is the lex composition of the maximization of the value of each attribute. We start by identifying the impact of the number of attributes and providers on the computational cost of solving the optimum service assignment for workflows consisting of a single task. To this end we fixed the structure of the workflow, the hard constrains and the soft constrains in order to obtain a family of Soft CSPs whose analysis can reflect the growth in the computational effort required while a problem gets bigger, either in terms of the amount of attributes or the amount of service providers. In order to ameliorate statistical deviations, we ran the tool over 10 randomly generated instances of workflows consisting of a single task and varying the number of attributes ranging from 10 to 100 stepping by 10 and providers ranging from 1 to 2000 stepping by 100, and reported the average of the values obtained in the runs. From the experimental data we can derive the following observations: 1) the computational cost associated to QosAgg, when varying the amount of service providers, grows linearly in all the cases with[5] $R^2 \geq 0.99$, 2) the computational cost associated to MiniBrass, when varying the amount of service providers, grows polinomially (with grade 2) with $R^2 \geq 0.79$, with the exceptions of the experiments for 1 attribute, in which $R^2 = 0.7462$; the average R^2 is 0.8901, 3) the computational cost associated to QosAgg, when varying the amount of attributes, grows linearly in all the cases with $R^2 \geq 0.9$, 4) the computational cost associated to MiniBrass, when varying the amount of attributes, grows polynomially (with grade 2) with $R^2 \geq 0.74$; the average R^2 is 0.857, 5) the computational cost associated to QosAgg is at most around 30% of the total cost of analysis.

---

[5] R squared, denoted R^2, is the *coefficient of determination* that provides a measure of how well the model fits the data.

We continue by analyzing the computational cost associated to the workflow composition operators (i.e., sequential, parallel and choice composition). We generated 10 sets containing 10 workflows consisting of a single task, 100 providers and 50 QoS attributes. In order to understand how the size of the composition impacts the cost of analysis, each set is used to conduct an experiment in which we subsequently increment the size of the composition from 1 to 10 subworkflows. In both parallel and sequential composition we used max as the aggregation function. From the previous experimental data we can derive the following observations about the behaviour of the sequential and parallel composition: 1) the computational cost associated to the execution of QosAgg, when varying the amount of workflows in the composition, grows linearly in average and in all the individual cases. In the average case the fitting has $R^2 \geq 0.99$, 2) the computational cost associated to the execution of MiniBrass, when varying the amount of workflows in the composition, grows exponentially both in average and in all the individual cases. In the average case the fitting has $R^2 \geq 0.98$, and 3) the computational cost associated to the execution of MiniBrass excedes the timeout of one hour for cases of compositions consisting of 8 or more workflows (except for 3 and 2 cases for sequential and parallel composition respectively).

The results for sequential and parallel composition are similar, this is due to the fact that in both cases we are using the same aggregation function, which yields the same minizinc model. The reader should also note that the analysis time may vary a lot depending on many other factors; we can identify some obvious ones like: 1) the choice, and diversity, of aggregation functions associated to the quantitative attributes, 2) the hard and soft constraints, which can severely influence the behaviour of the analysis tools, and 3) how intricate is the structure of the workflow,

among others. In the case of the choice composition operator we can derive the following observations: 1) the computational cost associated to the execution of QosAgg, when varying the amount of workflows in the choice composition, grows linearly in average and in all the individual cases. In the average case the fitting has $R^2 \geq 0.99$, and 2) the computational cost associated to the execution of MiniBrass, when varying the amount of workflows in the choice composition, grows polinomially (with grade 2) both in average and in all the individual cases. In the average case the fitting has $R^2 \geq 0.99$.

In summary, the execution cost of QosAgg increases linearly and accounts for a relatively small portion of the overall analysis cost. On the other hand, the execution cost of MiniBrass exhibits exponential growth in the case of parallel and sequential composition, while demonstrating polynomial growth in the case of choice composition. Unsurprisingly, the cost of executing MiniBrass constitutes the majority of the total analysis cost.

6   Conclusions and Further Research

We presented a toolchain supporting optimum QoS-aware service selection for tasks organized as workflows, based on soft constrain solving. QosAgg is used to generate a skeleton MiniZinc model from workflow specifications (i.e., a description of the workflow, an enumeration of the QoS attributes together with their corresponding aggregation operator, and the list of providers for each task, including their QoS profile, expressed as values for the QoS attributes). Such a MiniZinc model contains, non-exclusively, decision variables corresponding to aggregations of the QoS attributes that can be used to enforce additional constrains over specific points of the workflow. On top of the resulting MiniZinc CSP, it is possible to add soft constrains resulting in a Soft CSP that can be solved using MiniBrass. We performed a preliminary performance analysis under the hypothesis that the computational cost of solving the Soft CSPs generated is driven, and compositionally determined, by the composition operators used to create workflows. Such study exhibited the impact of the exponential nature of solving the Soft CSPs by MiniBrass on the overall performance of the toolchain.

QosAgg creates decision variables for all possible path and service selections. These might be too many for MiniZinc to handle for more extensive use cases; in that case, it might be necessary to make MiniZinc evaluate only one specific path choice at a time and repeat that for all the possible paths in an iterative process in order to obtain scalability. Moreover, we focused on offline optimization only (i.e., all information had to be provided from the beginning). In reality, one might only have estimations of the values as QoS contracts whose real run-time value might affect future decisions leading to a dynamic notion of optimum relative to the online behavior of the selected providers. There is on going research about how to integrate offline and online decision-making [7].

Finally, there are many situations our workflows cannot model directly and need to be sorted out manually that are left for further research. To name a few: there are no built-in conditional path choices that depend on aggregated values. Support for compensation actions [10] would also be helpful, e.g., for the case where services can fail. Services at the moment are assumed to have constant QoS attributes across all executions. Support for probabilistic decisions would make it much easier to model decisions that we cannot influence, e.g., because the user of the composite service makes them, etc.

References

1. Arbab, F., Baier, C., Rutten, J., Sirjani, M.: Modeling component connectors in reo by constraint automata: (extended abstract). Electron. Notes Theor. Comput. Sci. **97**, 25–46 (2004). https://doi.org/10.1016/j.entcs.2004.04.028
2. Arbab, F., Santini, F.: Preference and similarity-based behavioral discovery of services. In: ter Beek, M.H., Lohmann, N. (eds.) WS-FM 2012. LNCS, vol. 7843, pp. 118–133. Springer, Heidelberg (2013). https://doi.org/10.1007/978-3-642-38230-7_8. ISBN 978-3-642-38230-7
3. Arbab, F., Santini, F., Bistarelli, S., Pirolandi, D.: Towards a similarity-based web service discovery through soft constraint satisfaction problems. In: Proceedings of the 2nd International Workshop on Semantic Search over the Web, ICPS Proceedings, New York, NY, USA. Association for Computing Machinery (2012). https://doi.org/10.1145/2494068.2494070. ISBN 978-1-4503-2301-7

4. Baryannis, G.: Service composition. In: Papazoglou, M.P., Pohl, K., Parkin, M., Metzger, A. (eds.) Service Research Challenges and Solutions for the Future Internet. LNCS, vol. 6500, pp. 55–84. Springer, Heidelberg (2010). https://doi.org/10.1007/978-3-642-17599-2_3. ISBN 978-3-642-17599-2

5. Bistarelli, S., Montanari, U., Rossi, F.: Semiring-based constraint satisfaction and optimization. J. ACM **44**(2), 201–236 (1997). https://doi.org/10.1145/256303.256306. ISSN 0004-5411

6. Bouguettaya, A., Sheng, Q.Z., Daniel, F. (eds.): Web Services Foundations. Springer, New York (2014). https://doi.org/10.1007/978-1-4614-7518-7. ISBN 978-1-4614-7517-0

7. De Filippo, A., Lombardi, M., Milano, M.: Integrated offline and online decision making under uncertainty. J. Artif. Int. Res. **70**, 77–117 (2021). https://doi.org/10.1613/jair.1.12333. ISSN 1076-9757

8. Deng, S., Huang, L., Wu, H., Wu, Z.: Constraints-driven service composition in mobile cloud computing. In: 2016 IEEE International Conference on Web Services (ICWS), pp. 228–235 (2016). https://doi.org/10.1109/ICWS.2016.37

9. Dokter, K., Gadducci, F., Santini, F.: Soft constraint automata with memory. In: de Boer, F., Bonsangue, M., Rutten, J. (eds.) It's All About Coordination. LNCS, vol. 10865, pp. 70–85. Springer, Cham (2018). https://doi.org/10.1007/978-3-319-90089-6_6. ISBN 978-3-319-90089-6

10. El Hadad, J., Manouvrier, M., Rukoz, M.: Tqos: transactional and qos-aware selection algorithm for automatic web service composition. IEEE Trans. Serv. Comput. **3**(1), 73–85 (2010). https://doi.org/10.1109/TSC.2010.5

11. Freuder, E.C., Mackworth, A.K.: Constraint satisfaction: an emerging paradigm. In: Handbook of Constraint Programming, vol. 2, 1 edn. (2006). ISBN 978-008-04-6380-3

12. Helm, W.E., Justkowiak, J.-E.: Extension of Mittelmann's benchmarks: comparing the solvers of SAS and Gurobi. In: Fink, A., Fügenschuh, A., Geiger, M.J. (eds.) Operations Research Proceedings 2016. ORP, pp. 607–613. Springer, Cham (2018). https://doi.org/10.1007/978-3-319-55702-1_80

13. Hosobe, H.: Constraint hierarchies as semiring-based csps. In: 2009 21st IEEE International Conference on Tools with Artificial Intelligence, pp. 176–183. IEEE (2009). https://doi.org/10.1109/ICTAI.2009.43

14. Lecue, F., Mehandjiev, N.: Towards scalability of quality driven semantic web service composition. In: 2009 IEEE International Conference on Web Services, pp. 469–476. IEEE (2009). https://doi.org/10.1109/ICWS.2009.88. ISBN 978-0-7695-3709-2

15. Martello, S., Toth, P.: Algorithms for knapsack problems. In: Martello, S., Laporte, G., Minoux, M., Ribeiro, C. (eds.) Surveys in Combinatorial Optimization, number 132 in North-Holland Mathematics Studies, North-Holland, pp. 213–257 (1987). https://doi.org/10.1016/S0304-0208(08)73237-7

16. Menascé, D.A.: Qos issues in web services. IEEE Internet Comput. **6**(6), 72–75 (2002). https://doi.org/10.1109/MIC.2002.1067740. ISSN 1941-0131

17. Meseguer, P., Rossi, F., Schiex, T.: Soft constraints. In: Handbook of Constraint Programming, vol. 9, 1 edn., pp. 281–328 (2006). ISBN 978-008-04-6380-3

18. Michlmayr, A., Rosenberg, F., Leitner, P., Dustdar, S.: End-to-end support for qos-aware service selection, invocation and mediation in vresco. Technical report, Vienna University of Technology (2009). https://dsg.tuwien.ac.at/Staff/sd/papers/TUV-1841-2009-03.pdf

19. Moghaddam, M., Davis, J.G.: Service selection in web service composition: a comparative review of existing approaches. In: Bouguettaya, A., Sheng, Q., Daniel, F. (eds.) Web Services Foundations, pp. 321–346. Springer, New York (2014). https://doi.org/10.1007/978-1-4614-7518-7_13

20. Nethercote, N., Stuckey, P.J., Becket, R., Brand, S., Duck, G.J., Tack, G.: MiniZinc: towards a standard CP modelling language. In: Bessière, C. (ed.) CP 2007. LNCS, vol. 4741, pp. 529–543. Springer, Heidelberg (2007). https://doi.org/10.1007/978-3-540-74970-7_38. ISBN 978-3-540-74970-7

21. Papazoglou, M.P., Traverso, P., Dustdar, S., Leymann, F.: Service-oriented computing: state of the art and research challenges. Computer **40**(11), 38–45 (2007). https://doi.org/10.1109/MC.2007.400. ISSN 1558–0814

22. Rosenberg, F., Celikovic, P., Michlmayr, A., Leitner, P., Dustdar, S.: An end-to-end approach for qos-aware service composition. In: 2009 IEEE International Enterprise Distributed Object Computing Conference, pp. 151–160. IEEE (2009). https://doi.org/10.1109/EDOC.2009.14. ISBN 978-0-7695-3785-6

23. Rossi, F., van Beek, P., Walsh, T. (eds.): Handbook of Constraint Programming, 1 edn. Elsevier Science Inc., Amsterdam (2006). ISBN 978-008-04-6380-3

24. Sakellariou, R., Yarmolenko, V.: On the flexibility of ws-agreement for job submission. In: Proceedings of the 3rd International Workshop on Middleware for Grid Computing, ICPS Proceedings. Association for Computing Machinery (2005). https://doi.org/10.1145/1101499.1101511. ISBN 978-1-59593-269-3

25. Sargolzaei, M., Santini, F., Arbab, F., Afsarmanesh, H.: A tool for behaviour-based discovery of approximately matching web services. In: Hierons, R.M., Merayo, M.G., Bravetti, M. (eds.) SEFM 2013. LNCS, vol. 8137, pp. 152–166. Springer, Heidelberg (2013). https://doi.org/10.1007/978-3-642-40561-7_11. ISBN 978-3-642-40561-7

26. Schiendorfer, A., Knapp, A., Anders, G., Reif, W.: MiniBrass: soft constraints for MiniZinc. Constraints **23**(4), 403–450 (2018). https://doi.org/10.1007/s10601-018-9289-2

27. Schiendorfer, A., Knapp, A., Steghöfer, J.-P., Anders, G., Siefert, F., Reif, W.: Partial valuation structures for qualitative soft constraints. In: De Nicola, R., Hennicker, R. (eds.) Software, Services, and Systems. LNCS, vol. 8950, pp. 115–133. Springer, Cham (2015). https://doi.org/10.1007/978-3-319-15545-6_10. ISBN 978-3-319-15545-6

28. Schiex, T., Fargier, H., Verfaillie, G.: Valued constraint satisfaction problems: hard and easy problems. In: Proceedings of the Fourteenth International Joint Conference on Artificial Intelligence, IJCAI 1995, Montréal, Québec, Canada, 20–25 August 1995, vol. 2, pp. 631–639. Morgan Kaufmann (1995)

29. Wei, L., Junzhou, L., Bo, L., Xiao, Z., Jiuxin, C.: Multi-agent based QoS-aware service composition. In: 2010 IEEE International Conference on Systems, Man and Cybernetics, pp. 3125–3132. IEEE (2010). https://doi.org/10.1109/ICSMC.2010.5641725

30. Tao, Yu., Zhang, Y., Lin, K.-J.: Efficient algorithms for web services selection with end-to-end qos constraints. ACM Trans. Web **1**(1), 6-es (2007). https://doi.org/10.1145/1232722.1232728. ISSN 1559–1131

31. Zemni, M.A., Benbernou, S., Carro, M.: A soft constraint-based approach to QoS-aware service selection. In: Maglio, P.P., Weske, M., Yang, J., Fantinato, M. (eds.) ICSOC 2010. LNCS, vol. 6470, pp. 596–602. Springer, Heidelberg (2010). https://doi.org/10.1007/978-3-642-17358-5_44. ISBN 978-3-642-17358-5

32. Zheng, X., Luo, J.Z., Song, A.B.: Ant colony system based algorithm for qos-aware web service selection. In: Kowalczyk, R. (ed.) Grid Service Engineering and Management "The 4th International Conference on Grid Service Engineering and Management" GSEM 2007, number 117 in Lecture Notes in Informatics, Bonn, Germany, pp. 39–50. Gesellschaft für Informatik e. V. (2007). https://dl.gi.de/server/api/core/bitstreams/4cefa9ab-94e1-4d82-b2ea-4d8ea1041838/content. ISBN 978-3-88579-211-6

Runtime Composition of Systems of Interacting Cyber-Physical Components

Benjamin Lion[1]($\boxtimes$), Farhad Arbab[1,2], and Carolyn Talcott[3]

[1] CWI, Amsterdam, The Netherlands
{lion,arbab}@cwi.nl
[2] Leiden University, Leiden, The Netherlands
[3] SRI International, Menlo Park, CA, USA

Abstract. The description of concurrent systems as a network of interacting processes helps to reduce the complexity of the specification. The same principle applies for the description of cyber-physical systems as a network of interacting components. We introduce a transition system based specification of cyber-physical components whose semantics is compositional with respect to a family of algebraic products. We give sufficient conditions for execution of a product of cyber-physical components to be correctly implemented by a lazy runtime expansion of the product construction. Our transition system algebra is implemented in the Maude rewriting logic system. As an example, we show that, under a coordination protocol, a set of autonomous energy-aware robots can self-sort themselves on a shared physical grid.

1 Introduction

Cyber-physical systems are highly interactive. Self driving cars are instances of cyber-physical systems with a significant amount of interaction between cyber and physical aspects. The controller in the car periodically samples its environment through its cameras and other sensors, and performs actions to drive the car. Dually, the environment responds to the action of the car by applying the corresponding power on the wheel, consuming energy, and eventually moving the car on the ground. The specification of a problem involving parts with cyber-physical aspects is complex and requires a specification of each individual part, plus how the parts interact. For instance, consider a car rental agency, for which autonomous cars are parked in a line. Having cars parked too far from the agency wastes time for the renters. The agency may therefore want to sort the cars at the end of the day, so that the reserved cars are first in line for the next day. As one can imagine, such a problem involves several parts in interaction. We give hereafter a specification of a simplified version of this problem, that involves sorting robots on a 2 by n grid.

Interaction in Cyber-Physical Systems. We simplify the example of self driving car on a rental parking with a set of robots moving on a field. Consider a set

© Springer Nature Switzerland AG 2023
A. Madeira and M. A. Martins (Eds.): WADT 2022, LNCS 13710, pp. 141–162, 2023.
https://doi.org/10.1007/978-3-031-43345-0_7

of 5 robots, roaming on a grid of size 2 by 5, as displayed in Fig. 1. Robots are identified with a unique identifier, and are initially positioned as shown in the left configuration of Fig. 1. Each robot is equipped with a battery from which it draws some energy for its move. A robot can move on an adjacent cell as long as the cell is free, i.e., no other robot is located on the cell. A robot may have a sensor that tells whether the next cell is free, and may send or receive messages from other robots. However, the system of robots is inherently concurrent, as each robot runs at its own speed, draws current from its battery, may sample the environment at arbitrary times, and take decisions according to its own strategy. In the system depicted in Fig. 1, can the robots sort themselves in ascending order while maintaining the energy level of their batteries above zero? To answer this question requires analysis of the interactions among both cyber and physical parts of the system.

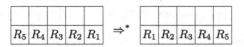

Fig. 1. Initial configuration of the unsorted robots (left), and final configuration of the sorted robots (right).

Specification. The sorting problem highlights the need for a component-based approach to design cyber-physical systems. Both cyber aspects (logic of each robot) and physical parts (grid and batteries of robots) have a decisive contribution for having the robots eventually sorted. Yet, the resulting cyber-physical system is modular: the same set of robots may run on a different grid, with different batteries; or the same grid may welcome different types of robots, with other kinds of sensors.

In [16], we define an algebraic model in which components are first class entities and denote sequences of observables, called Timed-Event Sequences (TES), from both cyber and physical aspects of systems. Interaction between components is defined exogenously using algebraic operators on components. The model of components is declarative: a component denotes a set of sequences of observations, and abstracts from the processes that generate such sequences. A product of two components declares what set of sequences of each component is conserved to comprise the resulting product component, and our algebraic framework supports an open-ended set of product operators parameterized on user-defined composability relations.

In this paper, we give a state-based specification for components to operationally define their behavior. A procedure is then required to generate the behavior of their composition such that the result faithfully respects the interaction constraints among components.

Compositional Runtime. The procedure that composes state-based components is either done statically, or dynamically at runtime. In the first case, the resulting composition may be optimized to improve its execution, while the second case allows for modularity and runtime modifications.

Traditionally, a composition is flattened [17] by syntactically enumerating all combinations of states and transitions. The flattened result contains all valid behaviors and therefore faithfully respects the interaction constraints. As state space may quickly get large, flattening the composition may be undesirable.

Instead, we seek a runtime composition operator that jointly executes stepwise each component. The proof obligation for the correctness of such runtime procedure is that the resulting behavior correctly respects the interaction constraints reflected in the product operator over components. For instance, given that component behavior is non-blocking, the runtime should not generate a finite sequence of composite observables for which there is no continuation (nonblockingness [10]). We characterize a set of components for which our step-wise composition is correct: components should be deadlock free and pairwise compatible. As a result, given compatible components, correctness of the step-wise product reduces to showing that after each step, the system of components remains deadlock free. We use our result to analyze in Maude a system of robots that sort themselves.

Contributions. The contributions of this paper are:

- a large family of operators to model interaction of state-based descriptions of cyber-physical components;
- a proof of semantic correctness for a range of user-defined products of TES transition systems;
- a sufficient condition for applying a decomposition operator in incremental steps at runtime;
- an application of our model on an example of self-sorting robots.

The state based model in our formalism allows for a uniform description of arbitrary composition and arbitrary nesting of cyber-physical aspects of components. Such diversity of operators is desirable to model the diversity of interaction among cyber-physical components.

2 Related Work

Process Algebra. The algebra of components described in this paper is an extension of [16]. Algebra of communicating processes [9] (ACP) achieves similar objectives by decoupling processes from their interaction. For instance, the encapsulation operator in process algebra is a unary operator that restricts which actions occurs, i.e., $\delta_H(t \parallel s)$ prevents t and s from performing actions in H. Moreover, composition of actions is expressed using communication functions, i.e., $\gamma(a, b) = c$ means that actions a and b, if performed together, form the new action c. Different types of coordination over communicating processes are studied in [5]. In [3], the authors present an extension of ACP to include time-sensitive processes. Our work accommodates the counterparts of the δ_H and γ operators from ACP and provides many more operators needed for direct expression of interaction of cyber-physical components.

Discrete Event Systems. In [13], the author lists the current challenges in modelling cyber-physical systems in such a way. The author points to the problem of modular control, where even though two modules run without problems in isolation, the same two modules may block when they are used in conjunction.

In [18], the authors present procedures to synthesize supervisors that control a set of interacting processes and, in the case of failure, report a diagnosis. Cyber-physical systems have also been studied from an actor-model perspective, where actors interact through events [11,19]. In our work, we add to the event structure a timing constraint, and expose conditions to take the product of discrete event systems at runtime.

Components. In [2], the authors give a co-inductive definition of components, to which [16] is an extension. In [4], the authors propose a state based specification as constraint automata. A transition in a constraint automaton is labelled by a guarded command, whose satisfaction depends on the context of its product (other constraint automata). Except from [12], constraint automata do not have time as part of their semantics (i.e., only specify time insensitive components), and only describe observables on ports. In that respect, our model extends constraint automata by generalizing the set of possible observables, and adding the time of the observables as part of the transition.

Timed Systems. In [8], the authors use heterogeneous timed asynchronous relational nets (HT-ARNs) to model timed sensitive components, and a specification as timed IO-automata. The authors show some conditions (progress-enabledness and r-closure) for the product of two HT-ARNs to preserve progress-enabledness. We may have recovered a similar result, but with some modifications. Our product is more expressive: κ needs not be only synchronization of shared events, but can have more intricate coordination [16] (e.g., exclusion of two events). We do not necessitate our process to be r-closed, and in general, we do not want to explicitly write the silent observations.

The conjunction operator in Timed Automata defines a Timed Automaton whose transitions are either synchronous transition labelled by shared actions (or shared delay), or a transition with an independent action. The conjunction operator, however, is limited and cannot directly express the wide range of relations and compositions that occur within cyber-physical systems. The definition of a parametrized class of operators on TES transition systems makes the interaction constraints explicit in our model and enables modular design of state-based cyber-physical systems.

3   Components in Interaction

In [16], we give a unified semantic model to capture cyber and physical aspects of processes as components and characterize their various types of interactions as user-defined products in an algebraic framework. Moreover, we show some general conditions for products on components to be associative, commutative, and idempotent. In this section, we recall the basic definitions of a component and product from [16], and introduce in Section 2.2 some instances of product that suit our example in this paper.

Notations. Given $\sigma : \mathbb{N} \rightarrow \Sigma$, let $\sigma[n] \in \Sigma^n$ be the finite prefix of size n of σ and let $\sim_n$ be an equivalence relation on $(\mathbb{N} \rightarrow \Sigma) \times (\mathbb{N} \rightarrow \Sigma)$ such that $\sigma \sim_n \tau$ if and only if $\sigma[n] = \tau[n]$. Let $FG(L)$ be the set of *left factors* of a set $L \subseteq \Sigma^\omega$, defined as $FG(L) = \{\sigma[n] \mid n \in \mathbb{N}, \ \sigma \in L\}$. We use σ' to denote the derivative of the stream σ, such that $\sigma'(i) = \sigma(i+1)$ for all $i \in \mathbb{N}$. We write $\sigma^{(n)}$ for the n-th derivative of σ, i.e., the stream such that $\sigma^{(n)}(i) = \sigma(n+i)$ for all $i \in \mathbb{N}$. For a pair (σ, τ) of TESs, we use $(\sigma, \tau)'$ to denote the new pair of TESs for which the observation(s) with the smallest time stamp has been dropped, i.e., $(\sigma, \tau)' = (\sigma^{(x)}, \tau^{(y)})$ with x (resp. y) is 1 if $\mathrm{pr}_2(\sigma)(0) \leq \mathrm{pr}_2(\tau)(0)$ (resp. $\mathrm{pr}_2(\tau)(0) \leq \mathrm{pr}_2(\sigma)(0)$) and 0 otherwise.

Let $\mathbb{E}$ be the domain of events. A timed-event stream $\sigma \in TES(E)$ over a set of events $E \subseteq \mathbb{E}$ is an infinite sequence of *observations*, where an observation $\sigma(i) = (O, t)$ consists of a pair of a subset of events in $O \subseteq E$, called *observable*, and a positive real number $t \in \mathbb{R}_+$ as time stamp. A timed-event stream (TES) has the additional properties that consecutive time stamps are increasing and non-Zeno, i.e., for any TES σ and any time $t \in \mathbb{R}$, there exists an element $\sigma(i) = (O_i, t_i)$ in the sequence such that $t < t_i$. For $\sigma \in TES(E)$ and $t \in \mathbb{R}_+$, we use $\sigma(t)$ to denote the observable O in σ if there exists $i \in \mathbb{N}$ with $\sigma(i) = (O, t)$, and $\emptyset$ otherwise. We write $dom(\sigma)$ for the set of all $t \in \mathbb{R}_+$ such that there exists $i \in \mathbb{N}$ with $\sigma(i) = (O_i, t)$ with $O_i \subseteq E$. Note that, for $t \in \mathbb{R}_+$ where $\sigma(t) = \emptyset$, the meaning of $\sigma(t)$ is ambiguous as it may mean either $t \notin dom(\sigma)$, or there exists an $i \in \mathbb{N}$ such that $\sigma(i) = (\emptyset, t)$. The ambiguity is resolved by checking if $t \in dom(\sigma)$. The operation $\cup$ forms the interleaved union of observables occurring in a pair of TESs, i.e., for two TESs σ and τ, we define $\sigma \cup \tau$ to be the TES such that $dom(\sigma \cup \tau) = dom(\sigma) \cup dom(\tau)$ and $(\sigma \cup \tau)(t) = \sigma(t) \cup \tau(t)$ for all $t \in dom(\sigma) \cup dom(\tau)$.

We recall the greatest post fixed point of a monotone operator, that we later use as a definition scheme and as a proof principle. Let X be any set and let $\mathcal{P}(X) = \{V \mid V \subseteq X\}$ be the set of all its subsets. If $\Psi : \mathcal{P}(X) \rightarrow \mathcal{P}(X)$ is a monotone operator, that is, $R \subseteq S$ implies $\Psi(R) \subseteq \Psi(S)$ for all $R \subseteq X$ and $S \subseteq X$, then Ψ has a greatest fixed point $P = \Psi(P)$ satisfying:

$$P = \bigcup \{R \mid R \subseteq \Psi(R)\}$$

This equality can be used as a proof principle: in order to prove that $R \subseteq P$, for any $R \subseteq X$, it suffices to show that R is a post-fixed point of Ψ, that is, $R \subseteq \Psi(R)$.

3.1   Components

A component uniformly models both cyber and physical aspects through a sequence of observables.

Definition 1 (Component). *A component $C = (E, L)$ is a pair of an interface E, and a behavior $L \subseteq TES(E)$.* △

A complex system typically consists of multiple components that interact with each other. For that purpose, we capture in an interaction signature the type of the interaction between a pair of components, and we define a family of binary products acting on components, each parametrized with an interaction signature. Formally, an interaction signature $\Sigma = (R, \oplus)$ is a pair of a composability relation $R(E_1, E_2) \subseteq TES(E_1) \times TES(E_2)$ and a composition function $\oplus : TES(\mathbb{E}) \times TES(\mathbb{E}) \to TES(\mathbb{E})$ for arbitrary sets of events $E_1, E_2 \subseteq \mathbb{E}$. As a result, the product of two components, under a given interaction signature, returns a new component whose behavior reflects that the two operand components' joint behavior is constrained according to the interaction signature.

Intuitively, the newly formed component describes, by its behavior, the evolution of the joint system under the constraint that the interactions in the system satisfy the composability relation. Formally, the product operation returns another component, whose set of events is the union of sets of events of its operands, and its behavior is obtained by composing all pairs of TESs in the behavior of its operands deemed composable by the composability relation.

Definition 2 (Product). *Let $\Sigma = (R, \oplus)$ be an interaction signature, and $C_i = (E_i, L_i)$, $i \in \{1, 2\}$, two components. The product of C_1 and C_2, under Σ, denoted as $C_1 \times_\Sigma C_2$, is the component (E, L) where $E = E_1 \cup E_2$ and L is defined by*

$$L = \{\sigma_1 \oplus \sigma_2 \mid \sigma_1 \in L_1, \ \sigma_2 \in L_2, \ (\sigma_1, \sigma_2) \in R(E_1, E_2)\}$$

While the behaviors of a component are streams, it is natural to consider termination of a component. We express a terminating behavior of component $C = (E, L)$ as an element $\sigma \in L$ such that there exists $n \in \mathbb{N}$ with $\sigma^{(n)} \in TES(\emptyset)$. In other words, a terminating behavior σ is such that, starting from the n-th observation, all next observations are empty.

Given a component C, we define C^* to be the component that may terminate after every sequence of observables. Formally, C^* is the component whose behavior is the prefix closure of C, i.e., the component $C^* = (E, L^*)$, where

$$L^* = L \cup \{\tau \mid \exists n \in \mathbb{N}.\exists \sigma \in L. \ \tau \sim_n \sigma, \ \tau^{(n)} \in TES(\emptyset)\}$$

In [16], we give a co-inductive definition for some R and $\oplus$ given a composability relation on observations, and a composition function on observations.

Let $\kappa(E_1, E_2) \subseteq (\mathcal{P}(E_1) \times \mathbb{R}_+) \times (\mathcal{P}(E_2) \times \mathbb{R}_+)$ be a composability relation on observations, and, for any $\mathcal{R} \subseteq TES(E_1) \times TES(E_2)$, let $\Phi_\kappa(E_1, E_2)(\mathcal{R}) \subseteq TES(E_1) \times TES(E_2)$ be such that:

$$\Phi_\kappa(E_1, E_2)(\mathcal{R}) = \{(\tau_1, \tau_2) \mid (\tau_1(0), \tau_2(0)) \in \kappa(E_1, E_2) \wedge (\tau_1, \tau_2)' \in \mathcal{R}\}$$

The *lifting* of κ on *TES*s, written $[\kappa]$, is the parametrized relation obtained by taking the greatest post fixed point of the function $\Phi_\kappa(E_1, E_2)$ for arbitrary pairs $E_1, E_2 \subseteq \mathbb{E}$, i.e., the relation $[\kappa](E_1, E_2) = \bigcup_{\mathcal{R} \subseteq TES(E_1) \times TES(E_2)} \{\mathcal{R} \mid \mathcal{R} \subseteq \Phi_\kappa(E_1, E_2)(\mathcal{R})\}$.

Two observations are synchronous if the two following conditions hold:

1. every observable that shares an event with the other component interface must occur simultaneously with one of its related observables; and
2. only an observable that does not share events with the other component interface can happen before another observable, i.e., at a strictly lower time.

Definition 3 (Synchronous observations). *We define κ^{sync} as the synchronous composability relation on observations and $((O_1, t_1), (O_2, t_2)) \in \kappa^{sync}(E_1, E_2)$ if and only if every shared event always occurs at the same time, i.e., $t_1 < t_2$ implies $O_1 \cap E_2 = \emptyset$, and $t_2 < t_1$ implies $O_2 \cap E_1 = \emptyset$, and $t_2 = t_1$ implies $O_1 \cap E_2 = O_2 \cap E_1$;*

Let $\bowtie$ be the product defined as $\bowtie = \times_{([\kappa^{sync}], \cup)}$. Intuitively, $\bowtie$ synchronizes all observations that contain events shared by the interface of two components. As a result of [16], $\bowtie$ is associative and commutative. Section 3.2 introduces a motivating example in which robots, roaming on a shared physical medium, must coordinate to sort themselves. We define algebraically the system consisting of 5 robots and a grid, to which we then add some coordinating protocol components. For more details on each component, see [14].

3.2   Self-Sorting Robots

We consider the battery, robot, and grid components introduced in [14] in the following interaction:

$$Sys(n, T_1, \ldots, T_n) = \otimes_{i \in \{1, \ldots, n\}} (R(i, T_i) \times_{\Sigma_{R_i B_i}} B_i) \times_{\Sigma_{RG}} G_\mu(\{1, \ldots, n\}, n, 2)$$

where n is the number of robots $R(i, T_i)$, each interacting with a private battery B_i under the interaction signatures $\Sigma_{R_i B_i}$, and in product with a grid G under the interaction signature Σ_{RG}. We use $\otimes$ for the product with the free interaction signature (i.e., every pair of TESs is composable), and the notation $\otimes_{i \in \{1, \ldots, n\}} \{C_i\}$ for $C_1 \otimes \ldots \otimes C_n$ as $\otimes$ is commutative and associative.

We fix $n = 5$ and the same period T for each robot. We write E for the set of events of the composite system $Sys(5, T)$, and R_i for robot $R(i, T)$ with identifier i. Figure 1 in the introduction shows five robot instances, each of which has a unique and distinct natural number assigned, positioned at an initial location on a grid. The goal of the robots in this example is to move around on the grid such that they end up in a final state where they line-up in the sorted order according to their assigned numbers.

We consider trace properties $P \subseteq TES(E)$ and say that C satisfies P if and only if $L \subseteq P$, i.e., all the behavior of C is included in the property P. For the system $Sys(5, T)$, we consider the following property: *eventually, the position of each robot* R_i is $(i,0)_{R_i}$, i.e., every robot successfully reaches its place. This property is a trace property, which we call P_{sorted} and consists of every behavior $\sigma \in TES(E)$ such that there exists an $n \in \mathbb{N}$ with $\sigma(n) = (O_n, t_n)$ and $(i,0)_{R_i} \in O_n$ for all robots R_i. In Sect. 3.3, we explore ways to enforce the property P_{sorted} on the system of robots, and in Sect. 5 verify its validity given an operational specification for each robot given in Sect. 4.

3.3   Properties of Components and Coordination

Robots may beforehand decide on some strategies to swap and move on the grid such that their composition satisfies the property P_{sorted}. For instance, consider the following strategy for each robot R_i:

- *swapping*: if the last read (x, y) of its location is such that $x < n$, then moves North, then West, then South.
- *pursuing*: otherwise, move East.

Remember that the grid prevents two robots from moving to the same cell, which is therefore removed from the observable behavior. We emphasize that some sequences of moves for each robot may deadlock, and therefore are not part of the component behavior of the system of robots, but may occur operationally by constructing a behavior step-by-step (see Sect. 4.2). Consider Fig. 2, for which each robot follows its internal strategy. Because of non-determinism introduced by the timing of each observations, one may consider the following sequence of observations: first, R_1 moves North, then West; in the meantime, R_2 moves West, followed by R_3, R_4, and R_5. By a similar sequence of moves, the set of robots ends in the configuration on the right of Fig. 2. In this position and for each robot, the next move dictated by its internal strategy is disallowed, which corresponds to a *deadlock*. While behaviors do not contain finite sequences of observations, which makes the scenario of Fig. 2 not expressible as a TES, such scenario may occur in practice. We give in next Section some analysis to prevent such behavior to happen.

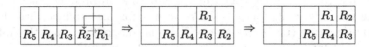

Fig. 2. Initial state of the unsorted robot (left) leading to a possible deadlock (right) if each robot follows its strategy.

Alternatively, the collection of robots may be coordinated by an external protocol that guides their moves. Besides considering the robot and the grid components, we add a third kind of component that acts as a coordinator. In other words, we make the protocol used by the robots to interact explicit and external to them and the grid; i.e., we assume exogenous coordination. Exogenous coordination allows robots to decide a priori on some strategies to swap and move on the grid, in which case their external coordinator component merely unconditionally facilitates their interactions. Alternatively, the external coordinator component may implement a protocol that guides the moves of a set of clueless robots into their destined final locations. The most intuitive of such coordinators is the property itself as a component. Indeed, let $C_{sorted} = (E, L)$ be such that $E = \bigcup_{i \in I} E_{R_i}$ with $I = \{1, 2, 3, 4, 5\}$ and $L = P_{sorted}$. Then, and as shown in [16], the coordinated component

$$Sys(5, T) \bowtie C_{sorted}$$

trivially satisfies the property P_{sorted}. While easily specified, such coordination component is non-deterministic and not easily implementable. We provide an example of a deterministic coordinators.

As discussed, we want to implement the property P_{sorted} as a collection of small coordinators that swap the position of unsorted robots. Intuitively, this protocol mimics the behavior of bubble sort, but for physical devices. Given two robot identifiers R_1 and R_2, we introduce the swap component $S(R_1, R_2)$ that coordinates the two robots R_1 and R_2 to swap their positions. Its interface $E_S(R_1, R_2)$ contains the following events:

- $start(S(R_1, R_2))$ and $end(S(R_1, R_2))$ that respectively notify the beginning and the end of an interaction with R_1 and R_2. Those events are observed when the swap protocol is starting or ending an interaction with either R_1 or with R_2.
- $(x, y)_{R_1}$ and $(x, y)_{R_2}$ that occur when the protocol reads, respectively, the position of robot R_1 and robot R_2,
- d_{R_1} and d_{R_2} for all $d \in \{N, W, E, S\}$ that occur when the robots R_1 and R_2 move;
- $lock(S(R_1, R_2))$ and $unlock(S(R_1, R_2))$ that occur, respectively, when another protocol begins and ends an interaction with either R_1 and R_2.

The behavior of a swapping protocol $S(R_1, R_2)$ is such that it starts its protocol sequence by an observable $start(S(R_1, R_2))$, then it moves R_1 North, then R_2 East, then R_1 West and South. The protocol starts the sequence only if it reads a position for R_1 and R_2 such that R_1 is on the cell next to R_2 on the x-axis. Once the sequence of moves is complete, the protocol outputs the observable $end(S(R_1, R_2))$. If the protocol is not swapping two robots, or is not locked, then robots can freely read their positions.

Swapping protocols interact with each others by locking other protocols that share the same robot identifiers. Therefore, if $S(R_1, R_2)$ starts its protocol sequence, then $S(R_2, R_i)$ synchronizes with a locked event $lock(S(R_2, R_i))$, for $2 < i$. Then, R_2 cannot swap with other robots unless $S(R_1, R_2)$ completes its sequence, in which case $end(S(R_1, R_2))$ synchronizes with $unlock(S(R_2, R_i))$ for $2 < i$. We extend the underlying composability relation κ on observations such that, for $i < j$, simultaneous observations (O_1, t) and (O_2, t) are composable, i.e., $((O_1, t), (O_2, t)) \in \kappa$, if:

$$start(S(R_i, R_j)) \in O_1 \implies \exists k.k < i.lock(S(R_k, R_i)) \in O_2 \vee$$
$$\exists k.j < k.lock(S(R_j, R_k)) \in O_2$$

and

$$end(S(R_i, R_j)) \in O_1 \implies \exists k < i.unlock(S(R_k, R_i)) \in O_2 \vee$$
$$\exists j < k.unlock(S(R_j, R_k)) \in O_2$$

For each pair of robots R_i, R_j such that $i < j$, we introduce a swapping protocol $S(R_i, R_j)$. As a result, the coordinated system is given by the following:

$$Sys(5, T) \bowtie_{i<j} S(R_i, R_j)$$

Note that the definition of $\bowtie$ imposes that, if one protocol starts its sequence, then all protocols that share some robot identifiers synchronize with a lock event. Similar behavior occurs at the end of the sequence. See Example 2 for an operational specification of the robot, grid, and swap component.

4   An Operational Specification of Components

In Sect. 3.1, we give a declarative specification of components, and consider infinite behaviors only. We give, in Sect. 4.1, an operational specification of components using TES transition systems. We relate the parametrized product of TES transition systems with the parametrized product on their corresponding components, and show its correctness. The composition of two TES transition systems may lead to transitions that are not composable, and ultimately to a deadlock, i.e., a state with no outgoing transitions.

4.1   TES Transition Systems

The behavior of a component as in Definition 1 is a set of TESs. We give an operational definition of such set using a labelled transition system.

Definition 4 (TES transition system). *A TES transition system is a triple* $(Q, E, \rightarrow)$ *where Q is a set of state identifiers, E is a set of events, and $\rightarrow \subseteq (Q \times \mathbb{N}) \times (\mathcal{P}(E) \times \mathbb{R}_+) \times (Q \times \mathbb{N})$ is a labelled transition relation, where labels on transitions are observations and a state is a pair of a state identifier and a counter value, such that* $[q, c] \xrightarrow{(O,t)} [q', c']$ *implies that* $c' \geq c$.

We use the notation $\theta([q, c])$ to refer to the counter value c labeling the state.

Example 1 (Strictly progressing TES transition system). We call a TES transition systems *strictly progressing* if, for all transitions $[q, c] \xrightarrow{(O,t)} [q', c']$, we have that $c' > c$. An example of a TES transition system that is strictly progressing is one for which the counter label increases by 1 for every transition, i.e., $[q, c] \xrightarrow{(O,t)} [q', c+1]$.

Remark 1. The counter value labeling a state of a TES transition system is related to the number of transitions a TES transition system has taken. The counter value is therefore not related to the time of the observation labeling the transition. However, it is possible for some transitions in the TES transition system to keep the same counter value in the post state. As shown later, we use the counter value to model fairness in the product of two TES transition systems.

We present two different ways to give a semantics to a TES transition system: inductive and co-inductive. Both definitions give the same behavior, as shown in Theorem 1, and we use interchangeably each definition to simplify the proofs of, e.g., Theorem 2.

Semantics 1 (Runs). A run of a TES transition system is an infinite sequence of consecutive transitions, such that the sequence of observations labeling the transitions form a TES, and the counter in the state is always eventually strictly increasing. Formally, the set of runs $\mathcal{L}^{\text{inf}}(T, s_0)$ of a TES transition system $T = (Q, E, \rightarrow)$ initially in state s_0 is:

$$\mathcal{L}^{\text{inf}}(T, s_0) = \{\tau \in TES(E) \mid \exists \chi \in (Q \times \mathbb{N})^{\omega}.\chi(0) = s_0 \wedge \forall i.\chi(i) \xrightarrow{\tau(i)} \chi(i+1) \wedge$$
$$\exists j > 0.\ \theta(\chi(i+j)) > \theta(\chi(i))\}$$

Note that the domain of quantification for $\mathcal{L}^{\text{inf}}(T, s_0)$ ranges over TESs, therefore the time labeling observations is, by definition, strictly increasing and non-Zeno. The component semantics of a TES transition system $T = (Q, E, \rightarrow)$ initially in state q is the component $C = (E, \mathcal{L}^{\text{inf}}(T, q))$.

Semantics 2 (Greatest Post Fixed Point). Alternatively, the semantics of a TES transition system is the greatest post fixed point of a function over sets of TESs paired with a state. For a TES transition system $T = (Q, E, \rightarrow)$, let $\mathcal{R} \subseteq TES(E) \times (Q \times \mathbb{N})$. We introduce $\phi_T : \mathcal{P}(TES(E) \times (Q \times \mathbb{N})) \rightarrow \mathcal{P}(TES(E) \times (Q \times \mathbb{N}))$ as the function:

$$\phi_T(\mathcal{R}) = \{(\tau, s) \mid \exists n.\exists p \in (Q \times \mathbb{N}),\ s \xrightarrow{\tau[n]} p \wedge \theta(p) > \theta(s) \wedge (\tau^{(n)}, p) \in \mathcal{R}\}$$

where $\tau[n]$ is the prefix of size n of the TES τ.

We can show that ϕ_T is monotone, and therefore ϕ_T has a greatest post fixed point $\Omega_T = \bigcup\{\mathcal{R} \mid \mathcal{R} \subseteq \phi_T(\mathcal{R})\}$. We write $\Omega_T(q) = \{\tau \mid (\tau, s) \in \Omega_T\}$ for any $s \in Q \times \mathbb{N}$. Note that the two semantics coincide.

Theorem 1 (Equivalence). *For all $s \in Q \times \mathbb{N}$, $\mathcal{L}^{\text{inf}}(T, s) = \{\tau \mid (\tau, s) \in \Omega_T\}$.*

The semantics of a TES transition system is defined as the component whose behavior contains all runs of the TES transition system. Operationally, however, the (infinite) step-wise generation of such a sequence does not always return a valid prefix of a run. We introduce finite sequences of observables of a TES transition system, and define a deadlock of a TES transition system as a reachable state without an outgoing transition.

Let $T = (Q, E, \rightarrow)$ be a TES transition system. We write $q \xrightarrow{u} p$ for the sequence of transitions $q \xrightarrow{u(0)} q_1 \xrightarrow{u(1)} q_2 \ldots \xrightarrow{u(n-1)} p$, where $u = \langle u(0), \ldots, u(n-1) \rangle \in (\mathcal{P}(E) \times \mathbb{R}_+)^n$. We write $|u|$ for the size of the sequence u. We use $\mathcal{L}^{\text{fin}}(T, q)$ to denote the set of finite sequences of observables labeling a finite path in T starting from state q, such that

$$\mathcal{L}^{\text{fin}}(T, s) = \{u \mid \exists p. s \xrightarrow{u} p \wedge \forall i < |u| - 1. u(i) = (O_i, t_i) \wedge t_i < t_{i+1}\}$$

Let $FG(L)$ be the set of left factors of a set $L \subseteq \Sigma^\omega$, defined as $FG(L) = \{\sigma[n] \mid n \in \mathbb{N}, \sigma \in L\}$. We write $\sigma(n)$ for the n-th derivative of σ, i.e., the stream such that $\sigma(n)(i) = \sigma(n+i)$ for all $i \in \mathbb{N}$.

Remark 2 (Deadlock). Observe that $FG(\mathcal{L}^{\text{inf}}(T, q)) \subseteq \mathcal{L}^{\text{fin}}(T, q)$ which, in the case of strict inclusion, captures the fact that some states may have no outgoing transitions and therefore deadlock.

Remark 3 (Abstraction). There may be two different TES transition systems T_1 and T_2 such that $\mathcal{L}^{\text{inf}}(T_1) = \mathcal{L}^{\text{inf}}(T_2)$, i.e., a set of TESs is not uniquely characterized by a TES transition system. In that sense, the TES representation of behaviors is more abstract than TES transition systems.

We use the transition rule $q \xrightarrow{(O,t)} q'$ where the counter is not written to denote the set of transitions

$$[q, c] \xrightarrow{(O,t)} [q', c']$$

for $c' \geq c$ with $c, c' \in \mathbb{N}$.

Example 2. The behavior of a robot introduced earlier is a TES transition system $T_R = (\{q_0\}, E_R, \rightarrow)$ where $q_0 \xrightarrow{(\{e\}, t)} q_0$ for arbitrary t in $\mathbb{R}_+$ and $e \in E_R$. Similarly, the behavior of a grid is a TES transition system $T_G(I, n, m) = (Q_G, E_G(I, n, m), \rightarrow)$ where:

- $Q_G \subseteq (I \rightarrow ([0; n] \times [0; m]))$,
- $f \xrightarrow{(O,t)} f'$ for arbitrary t in $\mathbb{R}_+$, such that
  - $d_R \in O$ implies $f'(R)$ is updated according to the direction d if the resulting position is within the bounds of the grid;
  - $(x, y)_R \in O$ implies $f(R) = (x, y)_R$ and $f'(R) = f(R)$;
  - $f'(R) = f(R)$, otherwise.

The behavior of a swap protocol $S(R_i, R_j)$ with $i < j$ is a TES transition system $T_S(R_1, R_2) = (Q, E, \rightarrow)$ where, for $t_1, t_2, t_3 \in \mathbb{R}_+$ with $t_1 < t_2 < t_3$:

- $Q = \{q_1, q_2, q_3, q_4, q_5, q_6\}$;
- $E = E_{R_i} \cup E_{R_j} \cup \{lock(R_i, R_j), unlock(R_i, R_j), start(R_i, R_j), end(R_i, R_j)\}$
- $q_1 \xrightarrow{(\{lock(R_i, R_j)\}, t_1)} q_2$;
- $q_2 \xrightarrow{(\{unlock(R_i, R_j)\}, t_1)} q_1$;

$-\ q_1 \xrightarrow{(\{start(R_i,R_j),(x,y)_{R_i},(x+1,y)_{R_j}\},t_1)} q_3;$

$-\ q_3 \xrightarrow{(\{N_{R_j}\},t_1)} q_4 \xrightarrow{(\{W_{R_j},E_{R_i}\},t_2)} q_5 \xrightarrow{(\{S_{R_j}\},t_3)} q_6;$

$-\ q_6 \xrightarrow{(\{end(R_i,R_j)\},t_1)} q_1;$

We use the letters E, W, S, and N, for an observation of a robot moving in the directions East, West, South, and North, respectively. ∎

The product of two components is parametrized by a composability relation κ on observations and syntactically constructs the product of two TES transition systems.

Definition 5 (Product). *The product of two TES transition systems $T_1 = (Q_1, E_1, \rightarrow_1)$ and $T_2 = (Q_2, E_2, \rightarrow_2)$ under the constraint κ is the TES transition system $T_1 \times_\kappa T_2 = (Q_1 \times Q_2, E_1 \cup E_2, \rightarrow)$ such that:*

$$\frac{[q_i, c_i] \xrightarrow{(O_i,t_i)}_i [q_i', c_i'] \quad i \in \{1,2\} \quad ((O_1,t_1),(\emptyset,t_1)) \in \kappa(E_1, E_2) \quad t_1 < t_2}{[(q_1,q_2), \min(c_1,c_2)] \xrightarrow{(O_1,t_1)} [(q_1',q_2), \min(c_1',c_2)]}$$

$$\frac{[q_i, c_i] \xrightarrow{(O_i,t_i)}_i [q_i', c_i'] \quad i \in \{1,2\} \quad ((\emptyset,t_2),(O_2,t_2)) \in \kappa(E_1, E_2) \quad t_2 < t_1}{[(q_1,q_2), \min(c_1,c_2)] \xrightarrow{(O_2,t_2)} [(q_1',q_2), \min(c_1,c_2')]}$$

$$\frac{[q_i, c_i] \xrightarrow{(O_i,t_i)}_i [q_i', c_i'] \quad i \in \{1,2\} \quad ((O_1,t_1),(O_2,t_2)) \in \kappa(E_1, E_2) \quad t_2 = t_1}{[(q_1,q_2), \min(c_1,c_2)] \xrightarrow{(O_1\cup O_2,t_1)} [(q_1',q_2'), \min(c_1',c_2')]}$$

Remark 4. The notion of an observation is an abstraction that groups an atomic set of events within an ϵ neighborhood of a time t (see [16]). The statement that two observations happen *at the same time* therefore becomes meaningful, and describes two sets of events that occur atomically within an ϵ neighborhood of the same time.

Observe that the product is defined on pairs of transitions, which implies that if T_1 or T_2 has a state without outgoing transition, then the product has no outgoing transitions from that state. The reciprocal is, however, not true in general. We write $C_{T_1 \times_\kappa T_2}((s_1, s_2))$ for the component $C_{T_1 \times_\kappa T_2}([(q_1,q_2), \min(c_1,c_2)])$ where $s_1 = [q_1, c_1]$ and $s_2 = [q_2, c_2]$.

Theorem 2 states that the product of TES transition systems denotes (given a state) the set of TESs that corresponds to the product of the corresponding components (in their respective states). Then, the product that we define on TES transition systems does not add nor remove behaviors with respect to the product on their respective components.

Example 3. Consider two strictly progressing (as in Example 1) TES transition systems $T_1 = (Q_1, E_1, \rightarrow_1)$ and $T_2 = (Q_2, E_2, \rightarrow_2)$. Then, consider a transition in the product $T_1 \times_\kappa T_2$ such that

$$[(q_1, q_2), c] \xrightarrow{(O_1,t_1)} [(q_1', q_2), c]$$

we can deduce that T_1 made a step while the counter c labelling the state didn't change. Therefore, T_2 in state q_2 has a counter labelling its state that is higher than the counter labelling the state in q_1. Alternatively, if

$$[(q_1, q_2), c] \xrightarrow{(O_1, t_1)} [(q_1', q_2), c+1]$$

then the counter at q_2 may become lower than the counter at which T_1 performs the next transition, which means that eventually T_2 has to take a transition.

The composability relation κ in the product of two TES transition systems (see Definition 5) accepts an independent step from T_1 (resp. T_2) if the observation labeling the step relates to the simultaneous silent observation from T_2 (resp. T_1). Given two composable TESs σ and τ respectively in the component behavior of T_1 and T_2, the composability relation $[\kappa]$ must relate heads of such TESs co-inductively. As we do not enforce silent observations to be effective from the product rules (1) and (2), we consider composability relations such that:

- if $((O_1, t_1), (\emptyset, t_1)) \in \kappa(E_1, E_2)$ then $((O_1, t_1), (O_2, t_2)) \in \kappa(E_1, E_2)$ for any $O_2 \subseteq \mathcal{P}(E_2)$ and $t_2 > t_1$; and
- if $((\emptyset, t_2), (O_2, t_2)) \in \kappa(E_1, E_2)$ then $((O_1, t_1), (O_2, t_2)) \in \kappa(E_1, E_2)$ for any $O_1 \subseteq \mathcal{P}(E_1)$ and $t_1 > t_2$

The two rules above encode that an observation from T_1 is independent to T_2 (i.e., $((O_1, t_1), (\emptyset, t_1)) \in \kappa(E_1, E_2)$ if and only if T_1 and T_2 can make observations at difference times (i.e., $((O_1, t_1), (O_2, t_2)) \in \kappa(E_1, E_2)$ for arbitrary (O_2, t_2) from T_2 with $t_2 > t_1$.

Theorem 2 (Correctness). *For two TES transition systems T_1 and T_2, and for κ satisfying the constraint above:*

$$C_{T_1 \times_\kappa T_2}(s) = C_{T_1}(s_1) \times_{([\kappa], [\cup])} C_{T_2}(s_2)$$

with $s_1 = [q_1, c_1] \in (Q_1 \times \mathbb{N})$, $s_2 = [q_2, c_2] \in (Q_2 \times \mathbb{N})$, and $s = [(q_1, q_2), \min(c_1, c_2)]$.

Remark 5 (Fairness). Fairness, in our model, is the property that, in a product of two TESs $T_1 \times_\kappa T_2$, then always, eventually, T_1 and T_2 each makes progress. The definition of the product of two TES transition systems defines the counter value of the composite state as the minimal counter value from the two compound states. The semantic condition that considers runs with counter values that are always eventually increasing is sufficient for having T_1 and T_2 to always eventually take a step, as shown in Theorem 2.

Remark 6. Note that the generality of Theorem 2 comes from the parametrized composability relation κ. Thus, for instance, the synchronous product of I/O automata can be expressed by a suitable composability relation κ that synchronizes the occurrence of shared inputs and outputs for parallel composition or conjunction (see [7]).

We give in Example 4 the TES transition systems resulting from the product of the TES transition systems of two robots and a grid. Example 4 defines operationally the components in Sect. 2.2, i.e., their behavior is generated by a TES transition system.

Example 4. Let T_{R_1}, T_{R_2} be two TES transition systems for robots R_1 and R_2, and let $T_G(\{1\}, n, m)$ be a grid with robot R_1 alone and $T_G(\{1, 2\}, n, m)$ be a grid with robots R_1 and R_2. We use κ^{sync} as defined in Definition 3.

The product of T_{R_1}, T_{R_2}, and $T_G(\{1, 2\}, n, m)$ under κ^{sync} is the TES transition system $T_{R_1} \times_{\kappa^{sync}} T_{R_2} \times_{\kappa^{sync}} T_G(\{1, 2\}, n, m)$ such that it synchronizes observations of the two robots with the grid, but does not synchronize events of the two robots directly, since the two sets of events are disjoint. ∎

As a consequence of Theorem 1, letting κ^{sync} be the composability relation used in the product $\bowtie$ and writing $T = T_{R_1} \times_{\kappa^{sync}} T_{R_2} \times_{\kappa^{sync}} T_G$, $C_T(q_1, q_2, q_3)$ is equal to the component $C_{T_{R_1}}(q_1) \bowtie C_{T_{R_2}}(q_2) \bowtie C_{T_G}(q_3)$.

Definition 6. *Let T be a TES transition system, and let $C_T(q) = (E, \mathcal{L}^{inf}(T, q))$ be a component whose behavior is defined by T. Then, C is deadlock free if and only if $FG(\mathcal{L}^{inf}(T, q)) = \mathcal{L}^{fin}(T, q) \neq \emptyset$. As a consequence, we also say that (T, q) is deadlock free when $C_T(q)$ is deadlock free.*

A class of deadlock free components is that of components that accept arbitrary insertions of $\emptyset$ observables in between two observations. We say that such component is *prefix-closed*, as every sequence of finite observations can be continued by an infinite sequence of empty observables, i.e., C is such that $C = C^*$ (as defined after Definition 5). We say that a TES transition system T is prefix-closed in state s if and only if $C_T(s) = C_T^*(s)$. For instance, if T is such that, for any state s and for any $t \in \mathbb{R}_+$ there is a transition $s \xrightarrow{(\emptyset, t)} s$, then T is prefix-closed.

Lemma 1. *If T_1 and T_2 are prefix-closed in s_1 and s_2 respectively, then $T_1 \times_{\kappa^{sync}} T_2((s_1, s_2))$ is prefix-closed.*

We search for the condition under which deadlock freedom is preserved under a product. Section 3.3 gives a condition for the product of two deadlock free components to be deadlock free.

4.2 Compatibility of TES Transition Systems

Informally, the condition of κ-compatibility of two TES transition systems T_1 and T_2, respectively in initial state s_{01} and s_{02}, describes the existence of a relation $\mathcal{R}$ on pairs of states of T_1 and T_2 such that:

- $(s_{01}, s_{02}) \in \mathcal{R}$, and
- for every state $(s_1, s_2) \in \mathcal{R}$, there exists an outgoing transition from T_1 (reciprocally T_2) that composes under κ with an outgoing transition of T_2 (respectively T_1) and the resulting pair of states is in the relation $\mathcal{R}$.

Formally, a TES transition system $T_1 = (Q_1, E_1, \rightarrow_1)$ from state s_{01} is κ-compatible with a TES transition system $T_2 = (Q_2, E_2, \rightarrow_2)$ from state s_{02}, and we say (T_1, s_{01}) is κ-compatible with (T_2, s_{02}) if there exists a relation $\mathcal{R} \subseteq (Q_1 \times \mathbb{N}) \times (Q_2 \times \mathbb{N})$ such that $(s_{01}, s_{02}) \in \mathcal{R}$ and for any $(s_1, s_2) \in \mathcal{R}$,

- there exist $s_1 \xrightarrow{(O_1, t_1)}_1 s_1'$ and $s_2 \xrightarrow{(O_2, t_2)}_2 s_2'$ such that $((O_1, t_1), (O_2, t_2)) \in \kappa(E_1, E_2)$; and
- for all $s_1 \xrightarrow{(O_1, t_1)}_1 s_1'$ and $s_2 \xrightarrow{(O_2, t_2)}_2 s_2'$ if $((O_1, t_1), (O_2, t_2)) \in \kappa(E_1, E_2)$ then $(u_1, u_2) \in \mathcal{R}$, where $u_i = s_i$ if $t_i = \min\{t_1, t_2\}$, and $u_i = s_i'$ otherwise for $i \in \{1, 2\}$.

In other words, if (T_1, s_1) is κ-compatible with (T_2, s_2), then there exists a composable pair of transitions in T_1 and T_2 from each pair of states in $\mathcal{R}$ (first item of the definition), and all pairs of transitions in T_1 composable with a transition in T_2 from a state in $\mathcal{R}$ end in a pair of states related by $\mathcal{R}$. If (T_2, s_2) is κ-compatible to (T_1, s_1) as well, then we say that (T_1, s_1) and (T_2, s_2) are κ-compatible.

Theorem 3 (Deadlock free). *Let (T_1, s_1) and (T_2, s_2) be κ-compatible. Let $C_{T_1}(s_1)$ and $C_{T_2}(s_2)$ be deadlock free, as defined in Definition 6. Then, $C_{T_1}(s_1) \times_{([\kappa], [\cup])} C_{T_2}(s_2)$ is deadlock free.*

In general however, κ-compatibility is not preserved over products, as demonstrated by Example 5. For the case of coordinated cyber-physical systems, components are usually not prefix-closed as there might be some timing constraints or some mandatory actions to perform in a bounded time frame.

Example 5. Suppose three TES transition systems $T_i = (\{q_i\}, \{a, b, c, d\}, \rightarrow_i)$, with $i \in \{1, 2, 3\}$, defined as follows for all $n \in \mathbb{N}$:

- $q_1 \xrightarrow{(\{a,b\}, n)}_1 q_1$ and $q_1 \xrightarrow{(\{a,c\}, n)}_1 q_1$;
- $q_2 \xrightarrow{(\{a,c\}, n)}_2 q_2$ and $q_2 \xrightarrow{(\{a,d\}, n)}_2 q_2$;
- $q_3 \xrightarrow{(\{a,d\}, n)}_3 q_3$ and $q_3 \xrightarrow{(\{a,b\}, n)}_3 q_3$.

The TES transition systems $T_1(q_1)$, $T_2(q_2)$, and $T_3(q_3)$ are pairwise κ^{sync}-compatible because each pair-wise product has an outgoing transition with an infinite run. However, $T_1(q_1)$ is not κ^{sync}-compatible with $T_2(q_2) \times_{\kappa^{sync}} T_3(q_3)$ because no transition can synchronize between all three TES transition systems. ∎

Lemma 2. *Let $\times_\kappa$ be commutative and associative, and for arbitrary $E_1, E_2 \in \mathbb{E}$, and $t \in \mathbb{R}_+$, let $((\emptyset, t), (\emptyset, t)) \in \kappa(E_1, E_2)$. Moreover, let S be a set of TES transition systems, such that for $T \in S$ and every state $[q, n]$ in T, we have $[q, n] \xrightarrow{(\emptyset, t)} [q, n]$. For $S = S_1 \uplus S_2$ a partition of S, $\times_\kappa \{T\}_{T \in S_1}$ and $\times_\kappa \{T\}_{T \in S_2}$ are κ-compatible and the component $C_{\times_\kappa \{T\}_{T \in S}}$ is deadlock free.*

The consequence of two TES transition systems T_1 and T_2 being κ-compatible on (s_1, s_2) and deadlock free, is that they can be run *step-by-step* from (s_1, s_2)

and ensure that doing so would not generate a sequence of observations that is not a prefix of an infinite run. However, there is still an obligation for the *step-by-step* execution to produce a run that is in the behavior of the product, i.e., to perform a step-by-step product at runtime. Indeed, the resulting sequence of states must always increase the counter value, which means that the selection of a step must be *fair* (as introduced in Remark 5). We show in Example 6 an example for which an infinite sequence of transitions in the product (e.g., produced by a step-by-step implementation of the product) would not yield a run, due to fairness violation.

Example 6. Let $T_1 = (\{q_1\}, \{a\}, \rightarrow_1)$ and $T_2 = (\{q_2\}, \{b\}, \rightarrow_2)$ be two TES transition systems such that: $[q_1, c] \xrightarrow{(\{a\}, t)}_1 [q_1, c+1]$ and $[q_2, c] \xrightarrow{(\{b\}, t)}_2 [q_2, c+1]$ for all $t \in \mathbb{R}_+$ and all $c \in \mathbb{N}$. Let κ be such that $((\{a\}, t), (\emptyset, t)) \in \kappa(\{a\}, \{b\})$ and $((\emptyset, t), (\{b\}, t)) \in \kappa(\{a\}, \{b\})$. Then, the product $T_1 \times_\kappa T_2$ has the composite transitions $[(q_1, q_2), c] \xrightarrow{(\{a\}, t)} [(q_1, q_2), c]$ and $[(q_1, q_2), c] \xrightarrow{(\{b\}, t)} [(q_1, q_2'), c]$ for all $c \in \mathbb{N}$ and $t \in \mathbb{R}_+$.

The product, therefore has runs of the kind $[(q_1, q_2), c] \xrightarrow{(\{a\}, t_i)} [(q_1', q_2), c]$ where for all $i \in \mathbb{N}$, $c_i + 1 = c_{i+1}$ and $t_i < t_{i+1}$ (increasing) and there exists $j \in \mathbb{N}$ with $i < t_j$ (non-Zeno). Thus, this run does only transitions from T_1 and none from T_2: there is a step for which the counter c does not increase anymore. One reason is that rule (1) of the product is always chosen. Instead, by imposing that we always eventually take rule (3), we ensure that the step-by-step product is fair.

We consider a class of TES transition systems for which a *step-by-step* implementation of their product is fair, i.e., always eventually the counter of the composite state increases. More particularly, we consider TES transition systems that always eventually require synchronization. Therefore, the product always eventually performs rule (3), and the runs are consequently fair. Such property is a composite property, that can be obtained compositionally by imposing a trace property on a TES transition system, such as: for every trace, there is always eventually a state for which all outgoing transitions must synchronize with an observation from the other TES transition system.

Remark 7. In the actor model, fairness is usually defined as an individual property: always eventually an action that is enabled (such as reading a message in a queue) will be performed. This notion of fairness differs from the one we introduced for TES transition systems. In our model, fairness formalizes a collective property, namely that each component always eventually progresses to yield an observation.

Definition 7 (k-synchronizing). *Two TES transition systems T_1 and T_2 are k-synchronizing under κ if every sequences of k transitions in the product $T_1 \times_\kappa T_2$ contains at least one transition constructed by rule (3) of the product in Definition 5.*

Lemma 3. *Let T_1 and T_2 be two k-synchronizing TES transition systems. Then, a step-by-step execution of the product $T_1 \times_\kappa T_2$ is fair, namely, every finite sequence of transitions is a prefix of an infinite run in the product behavior, i.e., $FG(\mathcal{L}^{inf}(T_1 \times_\kappa T_2, q)) = \mathcal{L}^{fin}(T_1 \times_\kappa T_2, q)$.*

Remark 8. The step-by-step implementation of the product is sound if TES transition systems always eventually synchronize on a transition. Definition 7 and Lemma 3 show that if two TES transition systems are k-synchronizing, then their product can be formed lazily, step-by-step, at runtime.

5   Application: Self-Sorting Robots

We implemented in Maude a framework to simulate concurrent executions of TES transition systems, where time stamps are restricted to natural numbers. Using the description given in Example 2 for the grid and for robots, we add to their composition several protocols that aim at preventing deadlock. The source for the implementation is accessible at [1] to reproduce the results of this section.

Components in Maude. The implementation of TES transition systems in Maude focuses on a subset that has some properties. First, TES transition systems in Maude have time stamps that range over the set of positive natural numbers $\mathbb{N}$. We do not implement components with real time.

Second, TES transition systems run at a fixed sampling rate. Let T be the sampling period. This property encodes that, between two transitions in the TES transition system, a fixed time duration of T has passed. A TES transition system may allow for arbitrary delay of its transitions by a fixed multiple k of delay T. In which case, we say that the TES transition system is *delay insensitive*. Formally, for every $q \xrightarrow{(O,n)} p$ of a delay insensitive TES transition system with period T, we have $n = k \cdot T$ for some $k \in \mathbb{N}$. We therefore write $q \xrightarrow{O} p$ to denote the set of transitions $q \xrightarrow{(O,k\cdot T)} p$ for all $n \in \mathbb{N}$.

In Maude, the state of a TES transition system component is represented by a term and the state of a composed system is a multiset of component states. Transitions of the step-wise product are defined in terms of such system states. For instance, the swap protocol between robots $R(3)$ and $R(1)$ is the defined in Maude as:

```
[swap(R(3),R(1)): Protocol | k("s") |-> ds(q(0)); false; mt]
```

where `swap(R(3),R(1))` is the name of the component; `Protocol` is its class; `k("s")` maps to the initial state of the protocol `q(0)`; `"false"` denotes the status of the protocol; and `"mt"` is the set of transitions that the protocol may take.

Runtime Composition. The product of TES transition systems is constructed at runtime, step by step. We use κ^{sync} for the product of TES transition systems.

Given a list of initialized TES transition system, the runtime computes the set of all possible composite transitions, from which transitions that violate the

---

Algorithm 1. RUNTIME COMPOSITION

Require:
- n initialized TES transition systems $S = \{T_1(q_1), \ldots, T_n(q_n)\}$
1: **procedure** RUNTIMECOMPOSITION
2:      **for** $T_i(q_i) \in S$ **do** add $\{q_i \xrightarrow{O_i}_i p_i \mid p_i \in Q_i\}$ to Tr
3:      **while** $trs_i, trs_j \in Tr$ **do**
4:          **for** $q_i \xrightarrow{O_i} p_i \in trs_i$ and $q_j \xrightarrow{O_j} p_j \in trs_j$ **do**
5:            **if** $((O_i, 1), (O_j, 2)) \in \kappa^{sync}(E_i, E_j)$ **then**
6:              add $(q_i, q_j) \xrightarrow{O_i} (p_i, q_j)$ to trs_{ij}
7:            **if** $((O_i, 2), (O_j, 1)) \in \kappa^{sync}(E_i, E_j)$ **then**
8:              add $(q_i, q_j) \xrightarrow{O_j} (q_i, p_j)$ to trs_{ij}
9:            **if** $((O_i, 1), (O_j, 1)) \in \kappa^{sync}(E_i, E_j)$ **then**
10:             add $(q_i, q_j) \xrightarrow{O_i \cup O_j} (p_i, p_j)$ to trs_{ij}
11:          $Tr := (Tr \setminus \{trs_i, trs_i\}) \cup \{trs_{ij}\}$
12:      **let** $trs \in Tr$
13:      **let** $(q_1, \ldots, q_n) \xrightarrow{O} (r_1, \ldots, r_n) \in trs$
14:      **for** $i \leq n$ **do** $T_i(q_i) \Rightarrow T_i(r_i)$

---

composability relation κ^{sync} are filtered out, and one transition that is composable is non-deterministically chosen.

Algorithm 1 shows the procedure RUNTIMECOMPOSITION that corresponds to a one step product of the input TES transition systems. Note that such procedure applied recursively on its results would generate a behavior that is in behavior of the product of the TES transition systems.

Results. Initially, the system consists of three *robots*, with identifiers $R(0)$, $R(1)$, and $R(2)$, each coordinated by two protocols $swap(R(i), R(j))$ with $i, j \in \{0, 1, 2\}$ and $j < i$. The trolls move on a grid and trolls $R(0)$, $R(1)$, and $R(2)$ are respectively initialized at position $(2; 0)$, $(1; 0)$, and $(0; 0)$.[1] The property P_{sorted} is a reachability property on the state of the grid, that states that *eventually, all robots are in the sorted position*. In Maude, given a system of 3 robots, we express such reachability property with the following search command:

```
search [1] init =>*
    [sys::Sys  [ field : Field | k((0;0)) |-> d(R(0)),
                k((1;0)) |-> d(R(1)),
                k((2;0)) |-> d(R(2)) ; true ; mt]] .
```

The initial configuration of the grid is such that robot 0 is on location $(2; 0)$, robot 1 on $(1; 0)$, and robot 2 on $(0; 0)$. Since the grid is of size 3 by 2, robots need to coordinate to reach the desired sorted configuration. The search commands search for a final state where the robots are sorted.

---

[1] We refer to [6] for a more detailed description of the Maude framework.

Table 1 features three variations on the sorting problem. The first system is composed of robots whose moves are free on the grid. The second adds one battery for each component, whose energy level decreases for each robot move. The third system adds a swap protocol for every pair of two robots. The last system adds a protocol and batteries to compose with the robots.

We record, for each of those systems, whether the sorted configuration is reachable (P_{sorted}), and if all three robots can run out of energy (P_{bat}).

Table 1. Evaluation of different systems for the P_{sorted} and P_{bat} behavioral properties, where st. stands for states, rw for rewrites. Note that the P_{bat} property is not evaluated when the system does not contain battery components.

System	P_{sorted}	P_{bat}
$\underset{0 \leq i \leq 2}{\bowtie} R_i \bowtie G$	12.10^3 st., 25s, 31.10^6 rw	
$\underset{0 \leq i \leq 2}{\bowtie} (R_i \bowtie B_i) \bowtie G$	12.10^3 st., 25s, 31.10^6 rw	true
$\underset{0 \leq i \leq 2}{\bowtie} R_i \bowtie G \underset{0 \leq i < j \leq 2}{\bowtie} S(R_i, R_j)$	8250 st., 44s, 80.10^6 rw	
$\underset{0 \leq i \leq 2}{\bowtie} (R_i \bowtie B_i) \bowtie G \underset{0 \leq i < j \leq 2}{\bowtie} S(R_i, R_j)$	8250 st., 71s, 83.10^6 rw	false

Observe that the reachability query returns a solution for both system: the one with and without protocols. However, the time to reach the first solution increases as the number of transition increases (adding the protocol components). We leave as future work some optimizations to improve on our results.

6   Conclusion

We introduce a transition system based specification of cyber-physical systems whose semantics is compositional with respect to a family of algebraic products. We give sufficient conditions for execution of a product to be correctly implemented by a lazy expansion of the product construction. We proved, using an implementation of our framework in Maude, a set of autonomous robots that move on a grid, coordinated by a local swapping protocol, satisfy the emergent property of ending in sorted position.

This work is a first step towards a finite characterization of component behaviors. We give in [15] a specification of TES transition systems as rewriting agents, and explore other case studies for showing safety properties of cyber-physical systems. As a future work, the extension of the framework with real time can open reasoning about optimal frequencies at which robots can interact to fulfill a coordination pattern.

Acknowledgement. Talcott was partially supported by the U. S. Office of Naval Research under award numbers N00014-15-1-2202 and N00014-20-1-2644, and NRL grant N0017317-1-G002. Arbab was partially supported by the U. S. Office of Naval

Research under award number N00014-20-1-2644. We thank the reviewers for their critical comments and their helpful suggestions.

References

1. https://scm.cwi.nl/CSY/cp-agent
2. Arbab, F., Rutten, J.J.M.M.: A coinductive calculus of component connectors. In: Wirsing, M., Pattinson, D., Hennicker, R. (eds.) WADT 2002. LNCS, vol. 2755, pp. 34–55. Springer, Heidelberg (2003). https://doi.org/10.1007/978-3-540-40020-2_2. ISBN 978-3-540-20537-1
3. Baeten, J.C.M., Middelburg, C.A.: Real time process algebra with time-dependent conditions. J. Log. Algebraic Methods Program. **48**(12), 1–38 (2001). https://doi.org/10.1016/S1567-8326(01)00004-2
4. Baier, C., et al.: Modeling component connectors in Reo by constraint automata. Sci. Comput. Program. **61**(2), 75–113 (2006). https://doi.org/10.1016/j.scico.2005.10.008. ISSN 0167–6423
5. Bergstra, J.A., Klop, J.W.: Process algebra for synchronous communication. Inf. Control **60**(1), 109–137 (1984). https://doi.org/10.1016/S0019-9958(84)80025-X. ISSN 0019–9958
6. Clavel, M., et al.: All About Maude - A High-Performance Logical Framework. LNCS, vol. 4350. Springer, Heidelberg (2007). https://doi.org/10.1007/978-3-540-71999-1
7. David, A., et al.: Timed I/O automata: a complete specification theory for real-time systems. In: Johansson, K.H., Yi, W. (eds.) Proceedings of the 13th ACM International Conference on Hybrid Systems: Computation and Control, HSCC 2010, Stockholm, Sweden, 12–15 April 2010, pp. 91–100. ACM (2010). https://doi.org/10.1145/1755952.1755967
8. José Luiz Fiadeiro and Antónia Lopes: Heterogeneous and asynchronous networks of timed systems. Theor. Comput. Sci. **663**, 1–33 (2017). https://doi.org/10.1016/j.tcs.2016.12.014
9. Fokkink, W.J.: Introduction to Process Algebra. Texts in Theoretical Computer Science. An EATCS Series. Springer, Heidelberg (2000). https://doi.org/10.1007/978-3-662-04293-9. ISBN 978-3-540- 66579-3
10. van Hulst, A.C., Reniers, M.A., Fokkink, W.J.: Maximally permissive controlled system synthesis for non-determinism and modal logic. Disc. Event Dyn. Syst. **27**(1), 109–142 (2016). https://doi.org/10.1007/s10626-016-0231-8
11. Kappé, T., et al.: Soft component automata: composition, compilation, logic, and verification. Sci. Comput. Program. **183**, 102300 (2019). https://doi.org/10.1016/j.scico.2019.08.001
12. Kokash, N., Jaghoori, M.M., Arbab, F.: From timed reo networks to networks of timed automata. Electron. Notes Theor. Comput. Sci. **295**, 11–29 (2013). https://doi.org/10.1016/j.entcs.2013.04.004. ISSN 1571–0661
13. Lafortune, S.: Discrete event systems: modeling, observation, and control. In: Annual Review of Control, Robotics, and Autonomous Systems, vol. 2, no. 1, pp. 141–159 (2019). https://doi.org/10.1146/annurev-control-053018-023659
14. Lion, B., Arbab, F., Talcott, C.: Runtime composition of systems of interacting cyber-physical components (2022)

15. Lion, B., Arbab, F., Talcott, C.L.: A rewriting framework for interacting cyber-physical agents. In: Margaria, T., Steffen, B (eds.) Leveraging Applications of Formal Methods, Verification and Validation. Adaptation and Learning - 11th International Symposium, ISoLA 2022, Rhodes, Greece, 22–30 October 2022, Proceedings, Part III. Lecture Notes in Computer Science, vol. 13703, pp. 356–375. Springer, Heidelberg (2022). https://doi.org/10.1007/978-3-031-19759-8_22

16. Lion, B., Arbab, F., Talcott, C.L.: A semantic model for interacting cyber-physical systems. In: Lange, J., et al. (eds.) Proceedings 14th Interaction and Concurrency Experience, ICE 2021, Online, 18 June 2021, vol. 347, pp. 77–95. EPTCS (2021). https://doi.org/10.4204/EPTCS.347.5

17. Mohajerani, S., Malik, R., Fabian, M.: A framework for compositional nonblocking verification of extended finite-state machines. Disc. Event Dyn. Syst. **26**(1), 33–84 (2016). https://doi.org/10.1007/s10626-y015-0217-y

18. Sampath, M., Lafortune, S., Teneketzis, D.: Active diagnosis of discrete-event systems. IEEE Trans. Autom. Control **43**(7), 908–929 (1998). https://doi.org/10.1109/9.701089

19. Talcott, C.: Cyber-physical systems and events. In: Wirsing, M., Banâtre, J.-P., Hölzl, M., Rauschmayer, A. (eds.) Software-Intensive Systems and New Computing Paradigms. LNCS, vol. 5380, pp. 101–115. Springer, Heidelberg (2008). https://doi.org/10.1007/978-3-540-89437-7_6

SpeX: A Rewriting-Based Formal Specification Environment

Ionuţ Ţuţu$^{(\boxtimes)}$

Simion Stoilow Institute of Mathematics of the Romanian Academy,
Bucharest, Romania
ittutu@gmail.com, ionut.tutu@imar.ro

Abstract. This is a gentle introduction to SpeX, a rewriting-based logical environment and executable framework implemented in Maude that facilitates the experimental development of formal specification languages and tools. The environment is language agnostic, so it is not geared towards any particular syntax, semantics, or supporting technology; instead, it provides a rich collection of libraries that assist the continuous integration of parsers and information processors. We outline the general architecture of SpeX, discuss its operational semantics, and illustrate the steps necessary in order to integrate new languages.

Keywords: Logical environment · Formal specification · Experimental development · Conditional rewriting · Maude implementation

1 Introduction

The development of new formal specification languages is often a necessary yet challenging, even arduous, task. Declarative logical frameworks, such as LF [7], MMT [11], and RL [9], facilitate this process by means of highly expressive meta-languages and tools through which a wide array of logical systems and calculi can be represented and reasoned about. This representational approach makes it easy to provide generic tool support for newly developed formalisms, but it requires both language developers and end users to be familiar with the logical framework of choice. On the other hand, systems such as the $\mathbb{K}$ framework [12] (which deals primarily with the design and analysis of programming languages) and Hets [10] (the Heterogeneous Tool Set, which provides an integrating framework of multiple logical systems, together with proof tools and logic translations) feature a clear separation between the meta-language utilized by system developers and the specification language and tools offered to end users.

In this work, we explore a similar route to that of $\mathbb{K}$ and Hets in order to develop a rewriting-based environment, called SpeX, for working with formal specifications. This includes, for example, tool support for parsing and for

This work was supported by a grant of the Romanian Ministry of Education and Research, CCCDI – UEFISCDI, project number PN-III-P2-2.1-PED-2019-0955, within PNCDI III.

A. Madeira and M. A. Martins (Eds.): WADT 2022, LNCS 13710, pp. 163–178, 2023.
https://doi.org/10.1007/978-3-031-43345-0_8

analysing specifications, as well as automatically generated interpreters. However, unlike $\mathbb{K}$, the environment we propose targets specification languages and is inherently heterogeneous; and unlike Hets, for which specifications are built over logical systems formalized as institutions [5] by means of a fixed set of structuring constructs [13], SpeX admits a much weaker notion of 'language', enabling us to capture, for instance, comorphisms of structured institutions [15] where the structuring mechanisms can change as well along language translations.

Despite these small advancements, the basic functionality of SpeX is modest compared to any of the tools and frameworks mentioned above. Its main asset is the environment's potential to be easily extended in order to accommodate new specification languages or features, many of which may be experimental. That is, the purpose of SpeX is distinctly academic, aiming to help bridge the gap between the theory and practice of formal specification and verification by providing researchers in the area with an environment that encourages prototyping and testing ideas and techniques even from early stages of development. To that end, we introduce a suite of software libraries, all implemented in Maude [2], that support the integration of new formal specification languages.

From an architectural standpoint, SpeX consists of a small supervisory kernel that manages input/output operations and, most importantly, hosts a number of information processors – one for each specification language that is integrated into the environment. Some processors are concrete, pertaining to a given logical system (say, equational or first-order logic), while others are generic, allowing various combinations of specification-building operators to be defined on top of base logical systems that meet certain requirements. Therefore, for any instance of SpeX, the capabilities of the environment are dictated by the processors and corresponding languages it hosts. At most one of those processors can actively take part in a user interaction at a given time, and the active processor may change as a result of that interaction, hence SpeX may react differently (even to the same input) depending on which processor is currently selected.

To illustrate the general approach and the steps needed in order to extend the environment, we consider two kinds of languages. The first one is a simple, understated language used for numerical calculations; this enables us to swiftly go through some of the details of implementing parsers and processors without having to invest much time in defining and understanding the actual language. The second one is a new, far more complex language based on hidden algebra [6] that allows for the specification of hierarchical compositions of behavioural objects [3]; we use this example to show that the SpeX primitives employed in language integration are sufficiently powerful and flexible to support the development of full-blown modern algebraic-specification formalisms.

The paper is structured as follows: in Sect. 2, we discuss the architecture of SpeX and introduce the main Maude libraries on which the environment is based; Sect. 3 is devoted to the execution of SpeX, which is approached from a different angle, as a distributed system comprising interacting streams, a core interpreter, and processors; in Sect. 4, we discuss the tool's object-based implementation via term rewriting; Sect. 5 shows the process through which new languages can be integrated into the environment; and, lastly, in Sect. 6, we briefly demonstrate more advanced parsing and processing capabilities.

2   System Overview

Figure 1 gives a cursory look at the architecture of SpeX. The environment is defined by a collection of interwoven Maude libraries. Some of them are *common libraries* (abbreviated CL in the diagrammatic representation), which provide extensive support for working with basic data types such as lists, sets, associative arrays, as well as numbers, strings, identifiers, syntax trees, configurations, and so on. Common libraries are often used as a base when integrating language processors. All major components of SpeX rely on them.

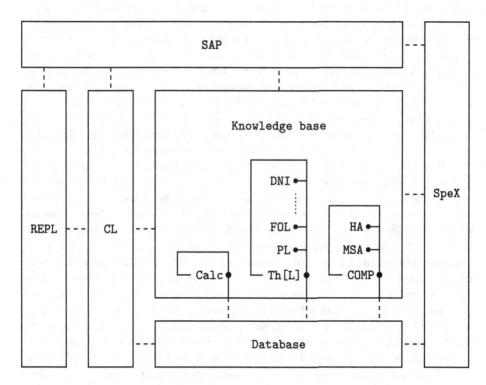

Fig. 1. A bird's-eye view of SpeX

Next, there is REPL, a library that defines the command-line top level of the SpeX interpreter by means of *read-eval-print loops* (reminiscent of the classic interactive environments used in implementations of Lisp). Each input stream – linked, e.g., to the standard input inherited from a Unix shell or to a file – is seamlessly handled through such a loop: during each iteration, a text fragment is automatically read and tokenized into identifiers; the resulting sequence is sent to the interpreter to be evaluated; once completed, the evaluation yields another sequence of identifiers, which is written to the standard output stream.

The main feature of REPL is that it sets apart the evaluation step – which is language and input dependent – from the management of input/output streams and the reading and printing of identifiers. The former requires a foreign component to perform the evaluation, whereas the latter is ready-made and fully implemented within read-eval-print loops. Hence, interpreters using the REPL library, such as SpeX, need only focus on the evaluation part.

The library SAP provides support for grammar-based *syntactic analysis and printing*, thus extending the reading and printing capabilities of REPL from identifiers to syntax trees. By *syntactic analysis*, or *parsing*, we mean the process of inferring the structure of a plain text according to the rules of some pre-defined formal grammar (defined by language developers). This may also include tests to ensure that the input conforms to certain language-specific constraints – e.g., that all non-logical symbols used in a sentence are properly declared beforehand. Parsing yields three kinds of outcomes: it may be successful, producing a syntax tree that can be further dealt with by the interpreter; it may deem the input incomplete, calling for more text to be read before drawing a conclusion; or it may fail, in which case it provides an appropriate error message indicating why the text cannot be parsed. The *printing* facilities of SAP provide the means to flatten a syntax tree back to a sequence of identifiers/symbols. This may also be used as a form of pretty-printing according to the formatting guidelines of a given grammar, which depends on the language under consideration.

All language processors integrated into the SpeX environment have access to a shared *database* (depicted in the lower part of the diagrammatic representation in Fig. 1) where they can publish data that may be of use to other processors. This aspect is particularly advantageous in the context of heterogeneous specification frameworks, as it allows specification modules to be reused across languages. Similarly to parsing and processing, the nature of the shared data is language dependent; for example, it may include collections of named specification modules that could be retrieved afterwards by processors and imported in other specifications that may be written in a different language. SpeX stores a user-defined database record for every language it supports, and continuously updates that record upon each input-processing step. In practice, the SpeX database is hierarchical: each of its records is identified by a language name and stores language-specific shared data, which, as hinted above, is typically given by a database-like structure as well, mapping specification names to modules. As a general rule, processors can make use of any shared data (of any supported language), but the updates are limited to their own database records.

The *knowledge base* is the dominant and largest architectural component of SpeX. It acts as an ever-expanding repository of language-specific text processors. Some of those processors, such as `Calc`, which we discuss in Sect. 5 of this paper, are monolithic; they are adapted to a specific flat (i.e., unstructured) language and are independent of any other processor integrated into the environment. This is the simplest kind of language processor that one can define in SpeX. Others are parameterized. For example, in Fig. 1, we indicate by `Th[L]` a family of processors that deal with theory presentations over an arbitrary base language L: say, a textbook language such as propositional logic (denoted `PL`) or first-order logic (`FOL`); or more advanced, experimental languages such as the modal logic of dynamic networks of interactions (`DNI`), which was recently proposed in [17] for modelling system reconfigurations; each of these base languages is handled by a separate SpeX processor, distinct from `Th[L]`. Furthermore, one can also develop heterogeneous processors. That is the case of `COMP`, which accommodates hierarchical compositions of behavioural objects [3] and integrates both many-sorted (`MSA`) and hidden (`HA`) algebraic specification modules.

Lastly, the SpeX supervisor, depicted in the right-hand side of the diagram in Fig. 1, brings together the functionalities of all other architectural components (particularly those of the knowledge base), manages the execution of language processors, and provides a simple command-line interface for interacting with the environment. In essence, through plain lines of text, which may be typed directly at the command line or loaded from a file, users can select a language (e.g., `Calc` or `Th[PL]`), then process any subsequent input (unless they switch to a different language at some point) according to the definition of that language.

3   Object Interactions

From an operational perspective, SpeX can be seen as a distributed system consisting of several different kinds of entities: read-eval-print loops (one for each input source), a homonymous core interpreter, text processors (one for each language integrated into the environment) and, potentially, sub-processors (in case of parametric or heterogeneous languages, for example). In typical object-oriented fashion, we model such entities as *objects* and we use *messages* to formalize the medium through which entities exchange information.

The sequence diagram in Fig. 2 traces some of the most important object interactions that occur during an execution of the tool. The protagonists, listed at the top of the diagram, are: `O`, a read-eval-print loop; `SpeX`, the core interpreter; and `$[L]`, the text processor that is meant to handle input for a selected language L. They operate in parallel; each has its own lifeline scattered with coloured activation bars used to show that the object is engaged in a specific activity. The process flow is suggested through arrows drawn between activation bars and labelled with messages. We use solid arrows for standard (synchronous) messages and dashed arrows for those messages that should be considered replies.

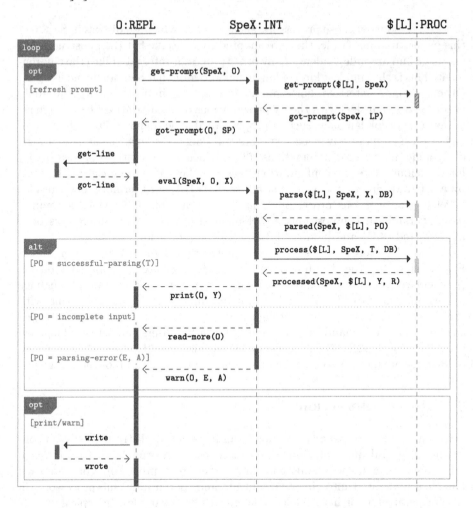

Fig. 2. Interactions between the main entities of the SpeX environment

The object O wraps both input and output streams. Unless the user terminates the REPL – by issuing the quit or eof command – the outer loop in the sequence diagram is carried out for each line of the input stream, as long as there are tokens available. Within the loop, if the input stream matches the command line, the first optional fragment is used to compile a prompt to be displayed to the user before an attempt to read a new line. That prompt may be of the form SpeX >, Calc >, Th[PL] >, etc., depending on which language is selected.

Next, through `get/got-line` messages, the REPL obtains a new raw text line from an external object – the input stream. It pre-processes that line into a sequence X of tokens, which is then sent to the interpreter to be evaluated. The evaluation takes place in one or two steps, depending on whether or not the input is valid/well formed with respect to the language L. Therefore, first, X needs to be parsed. The procedure is determined both by the definition of L and by the current state of the SpeX database, DB. In return, we get a parsing outcome, denoted PO, for which we consider three possible cases:

1. PO = `successful-parsing(T)`, indicating that the text is syntactically correct with respect to the definition of L and producing a corresponding syntax tree T. In this case, the second evaluation step is to send the syntax tree T back to `$[L]` in order to be processed, generating a result Y that is meant to be printed and an updated database record R for the language L.
2. PO = `incomplete input`, indicating that the interpreter cannot make a decision based on the input available thus far; more text needs to be read.
3. PO = `parsing-error(E, A)`, indicating that the text cannot be parsed. In this case, we get an error message E together with a series of additional error arguments A that may be helpful for troubleshooting purposes.

When the parsing outcome is definite – i.e., successful or erroneous – the final optional fragment in the sequence diagram is used for writing a suitable text message to the output stream (another external object). That message is either a textual representation of the result Y obtained when processing the syntax tree T, or an error report based on the message E and the error arguments A.

4   A Rewriting-Based Infrastructure

SpeX is implemented in Maude [2] (see also [1]), a high-performance specification and programming language based on equational logic and conditional rewriting with extensive support for object-based development and for meta-level applications. This means, in a nutshell, that the execution of SpeX is captured using a term-rewriting system of 'configurations' by which we model states of the environment at various points in time. More formally, the configurations we employ in this context are multisets of (states of) objects and messages.

In keeping with standard Maude notation, we build configurations from objects and messages through plain juxtaposition. We denote objects by terms of the form `< O : C | Atts >`, where O is an object identifier, C is a class identifier, and `Atts` is a multiset of object attributes – used to capture various aspects of an object's state. In a similar manner, messages are denoted by terms of the form `m(O, Args)`, where m is a message constructor, O is an object identifier – the intended receiver of the message – and `Args` is a list of arguments defining the contents of the message. Occasionally, the first element in `Args` is used to identify the sender of the message; this is particularly useful for messages that are expected to be followed by some kind of reply.

The interactions outlined in Sect. 3 are defined by rewrite rules that specify how configurations should change upon the delivery of messages. These rules are typically of the form < 0 : C | Atts > m(0, Args) ⇒ Cfg, where Cfg is a configuration fragment that captures the end result of delivering an m-message to (an instance of) the object 0. Many times, the fragment Cfg consists of an updated instance of the object 0 together with new messages that 0 sends to other objects. As an example, consider the following rewrite rule, which models the follow-up of a successful parsing operation:

```
rl < SpeX : INT | parsing 0 input, Atts >
   parsed(SpeX, NPL, successful-parsing(T))
⇒ < SpeX : INT | processing 0 input, Atts >
   process(head(NPL), tail(NPL), SpeX, T, db(Atts)) .
```

In the listing above, 0, Atts, NPL, and T are all universally quantified variables. 0 stands for the current REPL; we use it in the object attributes **parsing 0 input** and **processing 0 input** to mark different stages during the execution of the SpeX interpreter. The variable Atts designates any additional attributes of the interpreter, such as the current state of its database, given by db(Atts); most of those attributes are of little significance in this transition but need to be preserved for further interactions. Next, NPL stands for a non-empty list of processor identifiers; this is a slight departure from the diagram given in Fig. 2 (where we use a single identifier instead of a list), yet necessary in order to accommodate more complex execution scenarios that may involve sub-processors. Finally, T matches the syntax tree that ensues when parsing a well-formed input.

The rules defining the execution of SpeX – or of any other similarly purposed rewrite-based interpreter – can easily become much more complex than this. To be practically useful, the tool may need, for instance, to manage input and output streams, to display results and error messages appropriately (independently of how those results or messages are generated), or to handle language-specific commands in addition to the ordinary declarative input. Repeated and perhaps divergent implementations of this sort of routine mechanisms (which are actually language independent) may be detrimental to the experimental development of new specification formalisms. Therefore, what SpeX proposes is an infrastructure where the language-independent part of the interpreter/environment is ready for immediate use, allowing researchers and developers to focus on language-specific aspects. This separation of concerns is also apparent in the sequence diagram depicted in Fig. 2. The red and blue activation bars indicate language-independent activities that belong to the core section of the SpeX infrastructure. The red activation bars correspond to objects that are external to Maude's ordinary rewriting of configurations, while the blue activation bars denote activities that are already fully implemented – through rewrite rules like the one listed above. Developers of specification languages need to implement only those activities for $[L] that are represented by yellow activation bars; and even then, in some cases (e.g., when compiling the command prompt), the SpeX libraries offer default implementations or templates.

5   Language Integration

To illustrate the integration of new formalisms, we consider a simple declarative language used by a hypothetical numerical calculator – admittedly, not a conventional specification language, yet sufficiently close to its modern algebraic relatives and simple enough to allow us to discuss the idiosyncrasies of extending the SpeX knowledge base without delving too much into language-specific issues.

The calculator language, which we name `Calc`, consists of a single kind of declaration: 'let' statements of the form `id := exp` meant to associate a numerical expression `exp` with an identifier `id` that could then be used in other expressions or commands. Expressions are built from rational numbers and from values of identifiers, denoted `[id]`, through repeated applications of the basic operators of arithmetic. Their semantics is given by unique 'evaluation' homomorphisms (defined inductively on the structure of expressions) to an algebra of rational numbers. For inspection purposes, in addition to declarations, we also consider evaluation commands, written `eval id`, which are meant to compute the value of an identifier according to the expression that is assigned to it.

Figure 3 depicts a typical work session in SpeX. On the left, we have the contents of a file named `triangular.calc`, which provides a definition of triangular numbers using the language `Calc`. On the right, there is the log of a user's command-line interaction with SpeX and the `Calc` processor. We use colours to highlight different types of text: blue for language-independent commands that are handled directly by the SpeX interpreter; yellow to indicate declarations and commands that are specific to `Calc`; and red for the command-line prompt. The first command, `load triangular.calc`, is used to read the definition of triangular numbers from a file. Within that file, `lang Calc` is used to select the language `Calc`. From that point on, each subsequent line of `triangular.calc` is handled by the `Calc` processor, which, in return, prints a suitable confirmation message (e.g., `Defining id Tn`). Back at the command line, the prompt is automatically changed to reflect the selection of `Calc`. The `eval` command is used to compute the fourth triangular number, returning 10.

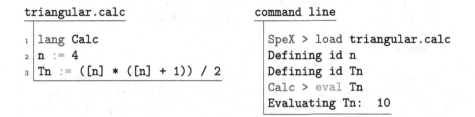

Fig. 3. Defining and evaluating triangular numbers in `Calc`

Integrating languages such as `Calc` is usually done in three phases: (*i*) develop an algebraic representation of the data structures and operations that are proper to the language; (*ii*) provide specialized support for syntactic analysis and print-ing; and (*iii*) implement a dedicated object-based processor using rewrite rules.

The first phase is undoubtedly the most important, because that is where the abstract syntax of the language is introduced (in contrast to concrete syntax, which is dealt with in the second phase), along with elements related to the semantics of the language and to the formal methods it supports: for `Calc`, there is only one such method, namely the evaluation of numerical expressions.

Algebraic Representation

At run time, SpeX is defined by one large rewrite theory encompassing all libraries discussed so far and the details of all languages recorded in the knowl-edge base. To compartmentalize that information, we employ language identi-fiers: singleton data types (as used, e.g., in the development of Hets [10]) that 'label' the data structures and operations of a language. For example, for `Calc` we write:

```
fmod CALC/LID is
  sort Calc .
  op Calc : → Calc [ctor] .
endfm
```

We declare a separate functional module for the abstract syntax of the expres-sions used in `Calc`. In the listing below, `RAT` and `QID` are the predefined Maude modules of rational numbers (having the sort `Rat`) and of quoted identifiers (`Qid`). The atomic expressions, given by `num` and `val`, have an additional argu-ment that allows us to determine with ease that they belong to the language `Calc`.

```
fmod CALC/EXP is
  protecting CALC/LID + RAT + QID .
  sort Exp{Calc} .
  op num : Calc Rat → Exp{Calc} [ctor] .
  op val : Calc Qid → Exp{Calc} [ctor] .
  op _+_ : Exp{Calc} Exp{Calc} → Exp{Calc} [ctor] .
  ...
endfm
```

The representations of `Calc` declarations, for which we use the sort `Decl{Calc}`, of the memory of the calculator, `Memory{Calc}`, formalized as a dictionary mapping identifiers to expressions, and of the commands associated with the language `Calc` are defined in a similar manner. The full implementation of these data types is available in the source-code repository [16] of SpeX.

As mentioned at the beginning of this section, the semantics of `Calc` is based on the following well-known universal property of the free algebra defining the abstract syntax of the language: every mapping of identifiers to values – in par-ticular, any finite mapping such as those determined by the states of the memory of the calculator – can be uniquely extended to a homomorphism between the algebra of numerical expressions and an algebra of rational numbers. We capture those homomorphisms through an operation **eval** parameterized by memory states and defined by structural induction.

```
fmod CALC/EVAL is
  protecting CALC/MEMORY .
  op eval : Exp{Calc} Memory{Calc} → Rat .
  eq eval(num(L, V), M) = V .
  eq eval(val(L, N), M) = eval(M[N], M \ N) .
  eq eval(E1 + E2, M) = eval(E1, M) + eval(E2, M) .
  ...
endfm
```

In the listing above, L is a variable that denotes the current language, `Calc`; V and N denote rational values and identifiers, respectively; M is a memory state; we write M[N] to indicate the numerical expression stored in that state for the identifier N, provided that M contains such a record, and M \ N to indicate the memory state obtained from M by discarding the record that corresponds to N; lastly, E1 and E2 are other variables of sort `Exp{Calc}`.

Syntactic Analysis and Printing

This phase makes ample use of the library SAP, which serves as a foundation for implementing parsers and printers in a modular manner by means of combinatory techniques similar to those advanced in [8,14]. We begin by defining the concrete syntax of `Calc`. For that purpose, we use the Maude module **GRAMMAR**, which is part of SAP and allows us to introduce formal grammars in a BNF-like notation.

```
fmod CALC/LANGUAGE is
  protecting CALC/LID + GRAMMAR .
  op grammar : Calc → Grammar .
  eq grammar(Calc)
   = grammar 'Calc/Syntax is
      'Decl ::= "_:=_" : 'Id 'Exp [prec(35)]
      'Id   ::= token "id"
      'Exp  ::= just 'Num
             |  "[_]" : 'Id
             |  "_+_" : 'Exp 'Exp [assoc prec(33)]
             |  ...
      'Num  ::= <number>
      'Cmd  ::= "eval_" : 'Id
     endgr .
endfm
```

To implement the parser, we use the SAP module **SYNTACTIC-ANALYSIS** – actually, an instance of it, since that module is parameterized; see [16] for details. The analysis technique we consider is context sensitive: it captures context through a notion of *syntactic-analysis state*, which is language dependent and may change while the input is parsed. For `Calc`, the syntactic-analysis states are simply sets consisting of those identifiers whose declarations have previously been parsed. So, in the running scenario presented in Fig. 3, the analysis state is initially empty; it consists of the identifier n after processing the second line of `triangular.calc`; and is given by both n and Tn when the file is fully loaded.

The main parsing operation is implemented as follows:

```
op parse_input_in_ : Calc QidList AnalysisState{Calc} → ...
eq parse L input (X) in SAS
 = parse L declaration (X) in SAS
   or-else parse L command (X) in SAS .
```

Here, L is once more a variable of sort `Calc` (standing for the current language); X denotes a list of quoted identifiers (the text to be parsed); and SAS is a syntactic-analysis state. The right-hand side of the equation combines two other more basic parsers – for declarations and for commands – using the SAP operator `or-else`. This means that the second parser is executed only if the first one fails. Each of those two parsers is implemented according to the following pattern:

```
eq parse L declaration (X) in SAS
 = scan L input (X : 'Decl)
   then analyse L declaration in SAS .
```

The right-hand side of this equation is almost entirely defined by SAP operators. On the first line, `scan L input (X : 'Decl)` corresponds to a shallow parser that checks whether X can be derived from `'Decl` using the production rules of the `Calc` grammar. If it succeeds, the parser drafts a syntax tree for X. On the second line, that tree is then traversed – and, for more complex languages, edited if necessary – to ensure that it meets certain additional constraints; in our case, to check that all identifiers used in an expression belong to SAS.

Therefore, the only substantial task for language developers at this stage is to define the tree traversal `analyse_declaration`. This is typically done by induction on the structure of syntax trees. For example, following the successful execution of the shallow parser mentioned above, we get a syntax tree of the form `{'_:=_[N, E] : 'Decl}`, where `'_:=_` corresponds to its root, N and E are the subtrees of the root, and `'Decl` is a tree annotation (the trees we consider here are slightly more complex than the usual Maude meta-representation of terms). The listing below shows how one may specify the analysis of declarations:

```
eq analyse L declaration {'_:=_[N, E] : 'Decl}
 = try { '_:=_ [
     solve L id (N),
     analyse L expression (E)
   ] : 'Decl } ,
```

where `solve_id` and `analyse_expression` are additional analysis actions specific to `Calc`, and `try` is another predefined SAP operator. The right-hand side of the equation can be read as follows: attempt to solve the first subtree (i.e., to check that the token used is a valid identifier); if that succeeds, continue to analyse the second subtree as an expression. If both actions succeed, then compile a new syntax tree with the same root and annotation as the original one, and with subtrees defined by `solve_id` and `analyse_expression`; otherwise, we get a parsing error that is handled automatically by SAP and REPL – the role of the latter is to identify where exactly in the input stream did the error occur.

The printing part is straightforward. For `Calc` expressions, we can write:

```
op print : Exp{Calc} → QidList .
eq print(E) = print Calc term show-exp(E) .
```

where `show-exp` is a function that converts `Calc` expressions to syntax trees (which, in Maude's terminology, are annotated terms), and the actual printing – i.e., flattening of a syntax tree into a list of tokens – is managed by SAP.

The Language Processor

Every processor integrated into SpeX is defined by a Maude module that imports (an instance of) either `SPEX-PROCESSOR` or `BASIC-SPEX-PROCESSOR`. These system modules provide the basic building blocks – language-specific object and class identifiers, attributes, messages, etc. – used for implementing processors. The end result can usually be obtained by writing a small number of rewrite rules. Those rules address aspects such as the starting up or the shutting down of a processor, prompt handling, parsing, processing, and the execution of commands. The first three of these have default implementations in `BASIC-SPEX-PROCESSOR`, which is the base module we are using for the `Calc` language.

The rule listed below integrates the syntactic analysis of `Calc` declarations and commands into the parsing infrastructure of SpeX: to parse an input X, we simply run the `Calc` parser presented in the previous section in the analysis state given by all identifiers recorded in the memory of the calculator.

```
rl < $[L] : PROC | running, Atts >
     parse($[L], SpeX, X, DB)
 ⇒ < $[L] : PROC | running, Atts >
     parsed(SpeX, $[L], parse L input X
                         in AnalysisState[L]{ids(DB[L])}) .
```

Next, the processing of a declaration amounts to recording it into the `Calc` memory – for which we use the predefined operation `insert` – and in presenting an appropriate confirmation message to the user. For the latter, we merely check whether the declaration is fresh or an update of a previously declared identifier.

```
crl < $[L] : PROC | running, Atts >
      process($[L], SpeX, T, DB)
  ⇒ < $[L] : PROC | running, Atts >
      processed(SpeX, $[L],
```

```
        if defined(DB[L][N])
        then Advisory: log('redefining 'id) N
        else log('Defining 'id) N fi,
        insert(N, E, DB[L]))
    if (N := E) := read-decl(L, T) .
```

The rule used for computing the value of a recorded identifier – obtained by evaluating the expression assigned to it – can be written in much the same way. The only major difference is that, instead of process($[L], SpeX, T, DB), we need to react to a message of the form do($[L], Cmd[L]{eval N}, DB), where N is the identifier whose value we aim to compute. The result may be undefined because redefining identifiers is prone to introduce circular references; see the full implementation of Calc in [16, Lang/Calc] for details omitted here.

```
    crl < $[L] : PROC | executing SpeX command, Atts >
        do($[L], Cmd[L]{eval N}, DB)
    ⇒ < $[L] : PROC | running, Atts >
        processed(SpeX, $[L], log('Evaluating) N '\n
          if ?V :: Rat
          then print(num(L, ?V))
          else 'undefined fi)
    if ?V := eval(DB[L][N], DB[L] \ N) .
```

All in all, the integration of Calc requires a few dozen equations, most of which (nearly two thirds) are used for syntactic analysis, and only three rewrite rules.

6   Beyond Calculators

The method presented in Sect. 5 works equally well for much more complex languages like, say, the language of full first-order theory presentations, which is also integrated into SpeX. In most cases, complexity arises in the form of sheer volume of features: multiple types of declarations, variables, logical connectives (especially quantifiers), various commands, etc. All contribute to an increasingly large knowledge base. However, the main development phases are the same.

One of the most advanced languages currently integrated into SpeX is COMP [4], a specification language that embodies the behavioural-abstraction paradigm and supports the formal development of component-based systems in a modular, hierarchical fashion. The main specification units of COMP, called object modules, consist of hidden-algebra [6] declarations of data types and states, including ordinary operations, observations, actions, projections (in case of components), and corresponding axioms. Structured specifications are obtained through special composition operators introduced in [3] that enable the hierarchical construction of larger and more intricate objects from simpler components.

The listing below gives an example of a more sophisticated kind of input for COMP that can be handled using the SpeX libraries discussed in this paper. The behavioural specification describes the functioning of a watch. It is obtained through the synchronized composition (see [3] for details) of three other object modules (counters) that specify the hour, minute, and second indicators. The only axiom shown here defines how the ticking of the watch (modelled using an action) affects the hour indicator.

```
bobj WATCH is
  syncing (UP-TO-24-COUNTER as HOUR)
      and (UP-TO-60-COUNTER as MINUTE)
      and (UP-TO-60-COUNTER as SECOND) .
  var X : State . vars H, M, S : Nat .
  act tick_ : State → State .
  ax HOUR/Display(tick X) = inc HOUR/Display(X)
      if MINUTE/value(X) = 59 and SECOND/value(X) = 59 .
  ...
endbo

open WATCH
  let ax ... [label: Lemma-1] .
  check tick inc-min (H:Nat : M:Nat : S:Nat)
      ~ inc-min tick (H:Nat : M:Nat : S:Nat) .
close
```

The open...close environment that follows the specification, and which is similar in style to the proof scores written in the OBJ family of languages, includes commands that support the formal verification method of COMP. In this case, we use them to introduce lemmas and to check a behavioural property, namely the non-interference of a mechanism added for adjusting the minute indicator (inc-min) with the internal ticking of the watch. Further details on the syntax, semantics, and verification method of COMP are available at [4].

7   Conclusions

In this paper, we have presented an executable logical environment, called SpeX, that fosters the development of new specification languages, or features thereof, through an infrastructure based on term rewriting where languages and tools can be integrated and interconnected with ease, in an experimental manner. We have discussed the basic building blocks of SpeX, its operational semantics, and some of the primitives that support the integration of specification languages.

For language developers, the main benefit of using SpeX lies in its rapid-prototyping capabilities: language features, for example, can usually be added using only a handful of equations. This stems from the combination of a rich collection of libraries with a simple, expressive, and executable implementation language such as Maude – there is also a downside here though, since language integrators need to be familiar with both Maude and the SpeX libraries.

For end users, on the other hand, the utility of any instance of the SpeX environment resides in the language processors it hosts. Currently, besides DNI [17] and COMP [4] – two successful demonstrations of experimental language development using SpeX – the knowledge base includes definitions of standard base languages corresponding to propositional, equational, and first-order logic, among others, as well as basic structuring mechanisms that rely on imports. Work is under way to implement generic specifications (over arbitrary base languages) and to provide parametric support for theorem proving.

Acknowledgements. I am grateful to Răzvan Diaconescu for several fruitful discussions on the design of SpeX and for our joint work on COMP. Many thanks also go to the anonymous referees for their helpful feedback, which has led to an improved presentation on integrating languages into the SpeX environment.

References

1. Clavel, M., et al.: Maude Manual (Version 3.2.1) (2022)
2. Clavel, M., et al.: All About Maude - A High-Performance Logical Framework. LNCS, vol. 4350. Springer, Heidelberg (2007). https://doi.org/10.1007/978-3-540-71999-1
3. Diaconescu, R.: Behavioural specification for hierarchical object composition. Theor. Comput. Sci. **343**(3), 305–331 (2005)
4. Diaconescu, R., Țuțu, I.: The COMP system (2022). http://www.imar.ro/~diacon/COMPproject/COMP.html
5. Goguen, J.A., Burstall, R.M.: Institutions: abstract model theory for specification and programming. J. ACM **39**(1), 95–146 (1992)
6. Goguen, J.A., Malcolm, G.: A hidden agenda. Theor. Comput. Sci. **245**(1), 55–101 (2000)
7. Harper, R., Honsell, F., Plotkin, G.D.: A framework for defining logics. J. ACM **40**(1), 143–184 (1993)
8. Hutton, G.: Higher-order functions for parsing. J. Funct. Program. **2**(3), 323–343 (1992)
9. Martí-Oliet, N., Meseguer, J.: Rewriting logic as a logical and semantic framework. In: WRLA 1996. Electronic Notes in Theoretical Computer Science, vol. 4, pp. 190–225. Elsevier (1996)
10. Mossakowski, T., Maeder, C., Lüttich, K.: The heterogeneous tool set (Hets). In: CADE-21. CEUR Workshop Proceedings, vol. 259 (2007)
11. Rabe, F., Kohlhase, M.: A scalable module system. Inf. Comput. **230**, 1–54 (2013)
12. Roşu, G.: Matching logic. Logical Methods Comput. Sci. **13**(4) (2017)
13. Sannella, D., Tarlecki, A.: Specifications in an arbitrary institution. Inf. Comput. **76**(2/3), 165–210 (1988)
14. Swierstra, S.D.: Combinator parsers: from toys to tools. Electron. Notes Theor. Comput. Sci. **41**(1), 38–59 (2001)
15. Țuțu, I.: Comorphisms of structured institutions. Inf. Process. Lett. **113**(22–24), 894–900 (2013)
16. Țuțu, I.: SpeX source-code repository. GitLab (2022). https://gitlab.com/ittutu/spex/
17. Țuțu, I., Chiriță, C.E., Fiadeiro, J.L.: Dynamic reconfiguration via typed modalities. In: Huisman, M., Păsăreanu, C., Zhan, N. (eds.) FM 2021. LNCS, vol. 13047, pp. 599–615. Springer, Cham (2021). https://doi.org/10.1007/978-3-030-90870-6_32

Author Index

A. Madeira and M. A. Martins (Eds.): WADT 2022, LNCS 13710, p. 179, 2023.
https://doi.org/10.1007/978-3-031-43345-0

Printed in the United States
by Baker & Taylor Publisher Services